# HOW TO
# MAKE MONEY
# GROWING TREES

# HOW TO
# MAKE MONEY
# GROWING TREES

JAMES M. VARDAMAN

**WILEY**

**A WILEY-INTERSCIENCE PUBLICATION**

John Wiley & Sons

New York  Chichester  Brisbane  Toronto  Singapore

*Library of Congress Cataloging-in-Publication Data*

Vardaman, James M.
    How to make money growing trees/James M. Vardaman.
       p.   cm.
    "A Wiley-Interscience publication."
    Bibliography: p.
    ISBN 0-471-60919-6
    1. Lumber trade--Management. 2. Forest products industry-
-Management. 3. Forest management. 4. Forests and forestry-
-Economic aspects. 5. Tree farms--Economic aspects.   I. Title.
HD9750.5.V3 1989
6344.9'8'068--dc19                                        88-23488
                                                            CIP

Printed in the United States of America

10 9

# Preface

After *Tree Farm Business Management* was first published in 1965, the steady growth of knowledge in biology and new developments in economics made a revision necessary in 1978. Then the pace of change accelerated. The forestry sector of the economy went through a sharp depression brought on by the highest interest rates most of us ever saw, return on assets became of supreme importance in timberland investments, hitherto-sacred and very beneficial tax laws were wiped out, and new developments in the biology and technology of growing trees came so fast that even foresters struggled to keep up. Consequently, by this year the book needed not so much a revision as a complete rewriting, which involved eliminating whole chapters, and adding new ones and appendixes. By the time I stopped writing, the old title was no longer descriptive and needed to be changed.

But perhaps the biggest change of all was that, after reaching the age of 67 and practicing forestry for more than 45 years, I finally realized that the smartest and most successful timberland investor is the small private landowner, the person who owns 40 to 4000 acres.

While I was going to forestry school, I thought the sun rose and set on the U.S. Forest Service and wasn't smart enough to understand what irresistible bureaucratic and political pressures it had to contend with. Later I convinced myself that the big timber companies practiced the ultimate in forest management. Their operations were so huge, and they seemed especially skillful because they took place under the discipline of private enterprise. I wasn't smart enough to realize that they are concentrated in a tiny segment of the economy and can be devastated whenever a severe depression comes along. Early in my career, I believed all the publications and speeches that characterized the small private landowners as one of forestry's biggest problems. My beliefs seemed to be confirmed by some of the stupid things that I saw some of them do, but I wasn't smart enough to realize that I was looking at the exceptions and not the rule. It took the very hard times of the early 1980s to make me appreciate the true wisdom, skill, and success of these owners.

Why are these small private landowners so successful? Mostly because they have the greatest staying power of all owners. Their main assets are in, and their primary incomes arise from, all other parts of the economy, and they are almost free of debt. Also, they are independent and skeptical, spend their own money, and bring to bear on their timberland investments all the expertise they acquire in their main occupations. I will go into these matters at length in the book, but you should be warned that I am an unabashed admirer of small private landowners.

These owners are primarily interested in making money. They usually love several aspects of owning timberland, but they measure their success by return on investment. This is why I changed the emphasis in the book and then changed the title to the more descriptive *How To Make Money Growing Trees.*

In 45 years I have had many opportunities to make mistakes and have taken advantage of all of them. Since a key part of making money is avoiding losses, I thought that the least I could do was to write a book that would help others learn from my mistakes. It would be even better if I could also give them the most up-to-date information about the financial aspects of forestry. Therefore, I have set down on paper all I have learned since I started my firm in 1951. For the past 20 years, we have concentrated on selling timber, the most important operation of all. No one else can match our experience; for at least the last ten years, we have been the major seller of open-market timber in every part of the South. The lessons we have learned are certain to help others with similar problems.

But the growth of forestry knowledge is continual, and economic conditions change a little bit every day. Although I have covered the fundamentals of the business of tree growing in this book, those who are interested in the subject should keep up to date by every available means. One is a free quarterly newsletter published by my firm since 1974; because its circulation exceeds 100,000, it is the most widely read publication on the business of tree growing. Although buying this book doesn't entitle you to a lifetime subscription, we will be glad to send it to you as long as we publish it. To get on our mailing list, write me at James M. Vardaman & Co., Inc., P.O. Drawer 22766, Jackson, MS 39225.

JAMES M. VARDAMAN

*Jackson, Mississippi*
*August 1988*

# Contents

# 1

# The Nature of the Business

Growing trees to make money, the purposeful production of timber to sell on the open market, is a new business, not much more than 40 years old. Although investors and speculators have been buying, selling, cutting, and using trees since colonial days, it was not clear that we could grow them as a crop until soon after World War II. By that time paper companies had invested enormous sums in pulp mills, and fearing that timber supplies might not always be adequate to support them, their managers began planting trees on a large scale. Soon all the signs of industrial forestry, clearcuts, sites prepared with huge machines, and plantations of all ages, were common sights in the timber-producing sections of the country.

These were the signs that investors were looking for, the evidence of an active timber market, the clues that there was pressure on the forest resource. Obviously someone was spending vast amounts to produce trees. If a long driving trip through any part of the country revealed large areas of heavy timber, a thinking investor realized that timber supplies there must be much greater than demand and that profits were to be made in timber-manufacturing mills rather than in timber-producing lands. Once demand was equal to supply or threatened to surpass it, however, growing trees for market became a promising investment.

After giving the go sign to investors, these industrial forests became huge, free, essential, research laboratories for them. Although forestry had been practiced in Europe for hundreds of years, the emphasis there had been on biology, and some of the techniques developed would not work for investors. Much had to be learned about plantation forestry; for only one example, the recommended planting rate in the beginning was more than 2700 seedlings per acre, and it took years for foresters to realize that such dense stocking is very costly to install and takes too long to produce trees of merchantable sizes. Fortunately, results of all these experiments were not buried in the scientific literature, but were spread across the land so thoroughly that they would not be ignored.

By the 1980s these developments had won the confidence of institutional investors, the professionals who manage pension funds and insurance companies. But most timberland is owned by private individuals or entities in blocks of only 100 acres or so, and it is time for them to appreciate the true nature of the business. There are about 4,500,000 of them, and their combined capital resources and investment expertise are far greater than those of big timber companies and institutional investors put together. For them timberland investment means certain things and makes certain demands.

Timberland investment means profit and protection against inflation. A forest will grow even if you do nothing; so far as I know, it is the only asset that visibly gets larger and more valuable even when neglected. Under good management, annual returns should be from 6 to 8% over the long run from biological growth alone without any price changes, and since timber is a commodity, timberland offers protection against inflation.

Timberland investment means adventure. Every tract is unique, one of a kind, like nothing else in the world, and since every owner is also unique, he and his investment have a chance to produce results that surpass all others. Furthermore, no one can predict one second of the future or anticipate the good or bad that it contains, and uncertainty always produces adventure. On the other hand, since the land and its productive power will always be there, I think that the uncertain future always holds more pluses than minuses.

Timberland investment is fun. Can you explore the mysteries of life with your son on a leisurely walk through a factory? Can your daughter pick flowers in a bank? Do you choose an apartment house for a picnic? Can you get away from it all in a stock or a bond? What other investment offers the appeal of a walk through the woods during the crisp days of autumn? Some say that one of my clients has more money than sense, and he did pay two prices for his timberland. But when he talks about it, his eyes light up, and you cannot shut him up, and when his wife and his mother-in-law talk about it, the same thing applies to them. How can anyone say that he made a bad investment?

It is contentment. Hunger for land, even one small city lot, some place on which to build a castle in which he is king, is one of man's universal characteristics. A timberland investor standing in the middle of his 40 acres is lord of all he surveys. Of course, he cannot see very far, but he owns all that he can see. Some of the poorest persons own timberland, and their forest management is thought to be terrible, but they will fight very hard to preserve their ownership. Owning land satisfies a craving deep inside them, and who is to say that their lands are not well used?

Timberland investment is complexity. Biology and its forestry branch, law, geology, accounting, business management, salesmanship, economics, and politics are intertwined in the business of growing timber for profit, and the investor dares not ignore any of these fields. Fortunately, he need not master all of them; there are plenty of specialists available in each, and he must learn only how to use them.

Finally, it is faith, patience, and frugality. Timberland owners must have the faith to plant crops that will be harvested by their children or grandchildren, and unless they watch their pennies, the inheritance that they hope to pass on to their heirs will slip into the hands of others. God makes trees slowly. Growing one from a seed to pulpwood size requires 15 years, and longer periods are necessary for maximum financial returns. Frugality must be a day-to-day thing, for a wasted dollar now will be a large sum after compounding at interest for 20 years.

But success with timberland makes demands on the investor, and the most important of these is staying power. Nobody expressed this better than Arthur Temple, for 40 years the guiding spirit of the Temple interests that include eight paper mills, many mills for other products, and 1,750,000 acres of timberlands. In an interview published in our newsletter, he said,

I bought the land because I knew the area, the type of timber, and the site index, and I knew that sooner or later they would bring me out. It would really be a question of whether I made a lot of money or a little money as long as I had staying power. That's the only thing people have to worry about; they shouldn't get into this business unless they have staying power. It's not much of a racket for people who want to get rich quickly, but it will make you rich if you can stay. The biggest owner of real estate in Mexico City once told me, "Arthur, real estate is for people who are already rich." I asked, "Why?" He replied, "Because they have staying power." He's certainly right about timberland. In it you have to be prepared for an eight- to ten-year period when prices are low.

Another comment on staying power came from Leland R. Speed, the founder of Eastover Group, several real estate companies whose assets total $227,000,000. Here are excerpts from a 1987 interview with him:

JMV:  Does the illiquid nature of timberland bother you?

LRS:  You sure have to consider liquidity. When it's cold, nothing is colder than dirt. You can sell a dog shopping center or a dog apartment house when you can't move dirt at any price. But timberland is a little different because it's not totally dirt. In most cases, it's producing something every year.

The million of small landowners have great staying power because their timberlands are only small fractions of their total assets. If necessary, they can go years without selling anything while they wait for a good market.

Close to staying power in importance is independence. Getting the maximum price at every sale is essential, and as you will see later, no buyer has ever been able over the long run to pay top dollar each time. Therefore, long-term cutting contracts with one buyer or forest-management programs that allow one buyer first refusal on sales are sure to reduce all-important income. If such arrangements seem to be the best that you can do, you may be better off to sell your tract to a better manager and put your money in something else.

A timberland investor is essentially a manager of investment capital. Some capitalists measure their assets in number of shares or square feet of rental space or units of production capacity; he measures his in acres, trees, minerals, or inches of rainfall. Although his assets may differ from theirs in form, his function is the same: he must manage what he has so that it produces a return commensurate with the amount invested and the risk he assumes.

The way he looks at things was demonstrated in a 1979 interview with R. Baxter Brown, a securities broker and investment advisor who, since the early 1950s, has successfully competed on a local scale with the giants of the industry. Here are excerpts from the interview:

JMV:  Timberlands produce cash incomes only at intervals of ten or so years, but they require small cash outlays each year for taxes and maintenance. Do these features bother you?

RBB:  No. You have to recognize that timberlands are not for every investor. If you must have an annual cash flow, you should be in stocks or bonds or something similar. On the other hand, for many, many investors, a zero or negative cash flow is no real problem.

JMV: There have been efforts to create annual cash flows either from government subsidies or through long-term leases by timber companies. If these efforts were successful, would they increase your interest?

RBB: I couldn't say for sure until I know the details, but I doubt it. First of all, I like the ability to postpone income and the chance to sell all my timber at market peaks. Second, I like the tax treatment timber sales receive. If annual payments of some kind don't receive the same tax treatment, they would change the situation for the worse and actually reduce my interest.

JMV: You can sell stocks or bonds in a few minutes and close the sale a few days later, but even in the best market area, you probably couldn't get a good bid on timberland in less than 30 days, and it may take another 30 to 60 days to close the sale. Is this lack of liquidity a big obstacle?

RBB: I said before that timberlands aren't for every investor. I wouldn't go into them except with the part of my capital that I could commit long-term, and I would certainly expect profits large enough to make it worthwile to sacrific some liquidity. Sooner or later you may develop a market place that will add liquidity and solve another big problem.

JMV: What other big problem?

RBB: That of appraising my investment. I wouldn't want to sell it, but I would certainly want to know what it was worth at frequent intervals. This is my way of measuring my performance as an asset manager. I guess I could get a professional appraisal from someone like you, but I'd much rather do it myself by "reading the tape."

The timberland investor manages by making decisions. In the beginning, he chooses advisers in forestry, accounting, and law, and with their help analyzes the business before him. First, he takes a detailed and complete inventory; he must know as much as possible about his assets and their capabilities. Next, he explores all possibilities open to him, giving due weight to each factor and deciding which assumptions and predictions are reasonable and which programs fit into his master plan. Then, he decides which programs to adopt and how to execute them. Finally, he brings them up for review at periodic intervals and decides whether to continue, expand, reduce, or eliminate them, or to dispose of the assets entirely. He sits in the seat of power; he decides, and others carry out his orders. Few timberland investors are technically qualified or physically competent to do the fieldwork, and fewer still have the time or inclination to do so. Their fortes are management and supervision. Nevertheless, to keep the enterprise as a whole moving in the right direction, they must know what their specialists do and understand the problems that face them. The purpose of this book is to advance this understanding, and we shall examine these matters in later chapters.

Although I have tried to make each chapter complete in itself, this is impossible when dealing with complex, related matters, so you must consider the book as a whole and refer from one chapter to another when necessary. I thought about helping you with cross-references, but the footnotes became so numerous and irritating that I decided to leave you to your own devices. Throughout the book, you may find unfamiliar technical terms. I have not defined them as they occur, since this would break continuity because both definition and discussion are sometimes necessary. You will find these terms in the Glossary, where I have also included terms that, although not mentioned in this book, are common in the business. I worried about the order of chapters and ultimately decided that there is no logical order since the situation of each reader differs slightly from that of all others. You will find that every important aspect is covered somewhere. Finally, I have expressed the same thing in different ways in different places; for example, I have used 2-in. diameter breast high (DBH) classes in one place and 1-in. DBH classes in another. This is my way of emphasizing that the business is extremely varied and that there are usually several ways to do the same thing.

Now let us discuss the most fascinating business I know of.

# 2

# Available Forestry Services

The woods are full of foresters available to assist you, and the number of choices may be confusing. These persons vary widely in competence and experience, areas we cannot explore, but it is helpful to know what they do, why they do it, and who pays them. Some are free, and some cost money; I will start with those who seem to be free.

## FORESTERS EMPLOYED BY STATES

For many years, state governments have been concerned about the consequences of poor forest management within their boundaries and have adopted programs to improve the situation. Many such programs are initiated by appropriations of the national legislature offering federal money to states on a cost-sharing basis for use to advance forestry. States are usually quick to take advantage of this opportunity. As the value of each program is demonstrated, states bear more and more of the cost; the federal share decreases until it is insignificant.

State forestry departments almost everywhere are responsible for fire control and use 80% to 90% of their budgets for this purpose. Forest management without fire control is impossible. You should support every move to increase the effectiveness of these programs. Money for fire control comes from many sources—federal and state appropriations, direct taxes on timberland, and contributions by individuals or corporations. In special situations, fire control is primarily handled by industrial associations. Taxes or contributions based on timberland ownership are fair, since beneficiaries pay in proportion to protection received, and needed increases in these assessments often meet with little resistance.

State fire-control equipment is idle much of the year and is usually available at modest rates per hour or day for plowing firebreaks on private land during the off season. In an effort to make maximum use of personnel, some states have also allowed fire-control crews, during idle hours, to plant trees or to perform timber stand improvement (TSI) work on a contract basis for private landowners. Such work during the fire season has not been entirely successful; it is almost impossible to coordinate firefighting with anything else, since fires do not start on schedule. Fire control is the major responsibility of state forestry departments, and trying to combine it with other activities is like depending on the city fire department to sweep the streets in its spare time.

Forest-management practices are best sold to landowners by demonstrations on the ground. Nearly every state provides some means for this. State forestry departments are usually organized with a forester for each county, parish, or district, and these persons are allowed to spend a small part of their time assisting private landowners with services and advice. They attempt to arouse interest in good forestry and turn the landowner over to private foresters once work of a substantial nature is required. The primary job of most area foresters is fire control, however, and educational or promotional activities must not interfere with it. As forestry grew in importance, functions of state forestry departments expanded. State forests, school lands, state parks, and other state lands came under their management, and foresters involved in the actual work of forest management appeared at state and district headquarters. These now perform many services offered by private foresters; charges, if any, are set by state headquarters.

When these programs began many years ago, timberland owners, knowing little about forestry, appeared unwilling to pay for advice and services. Therefore, most services were free but limited in some way, either in number of days worked or in number of acres marked for cutting (i.e., designating trees to be cut by marking each one with paint spots at eye level and below stump height). Soon there was dissatisfaction with the relative inefficacy of free work, and now the situation varies from state to state, with some state organizations competing with private foresters. Most offer free advice; some offer nothing but free services, some charge for all services; some charge for some services and offer others free.

States are usually the main source of tree seedlings, since utilization of idle land is in the public interest and large-scale operations are necessary to reduce costs of raising seedlings. To provide an incentive to landowners, some states offer free seedlings in limited quantities and sell additional quantities at cost. The federal government encouraged seedling production in the beginning by agreeing to bear half of any operating losses, but its contributions are now very small in most cases.

Many states have become interested in markets for timber products, especially where there are surpluses, and have added foresters specializing in wood utilization to the state staff. These persons promote the establishment of additional manufacturing plants, assist existing plants with technical manufacturing problems, and encourage the use of wood by working with architects and builders. Such programs have just begun, and their effectiveness is yet to be determined. They benefit the tree grower indirectly by increasing markets for trees.

The state extension forester and his staff usually operate from the state agricultural university, and they do not perform on-the-ground services. Their function is primarily education, and their concern is the wide dissemination of the latest forestry information. They can help you only in a general way. They are paid by the state, but part of their salaries comes from federal subsidies.

Your state forestry department will be happy to describe its programs if you call its headquarters or the area forester near you.

## FORESTERS EMPLOYED BY THE FEDERAL GOVERNMENT

You will have little direct contact with a federal forester who can help you in actual management of your tract. As you have just seen, the federal government influences private forest management by indirect activities in fire control, nursery operation, and extension and management work. Federal funds are also available for cooperative work with states and individuals for detection and control of forest insects and diseases. Foresters employed by the federal government supervise these programs to make sure that money is used as Congress directed.

You might have direct contact with the federal government through subsidies for forest-management practices disbursed through the Agricultural Stabilization and Conservation Service (ASCS). This money is allocated by an ASCS committee in each county; those wanting funds must apply for them to the county committee. The amount of money available for various practices varies widely by county from year to year; you can find out how much you can get by calling the local office.

Although federal subsidy money appears to be free and can be a great help, you should weigh certain factors before asking for it. First, the amount of money you can get may be so limited and the procedures for getting it so burdensome that the request is not worthwhile. Second, you cannot get ASCS money unless the work done on the ground meets ASCS specifications, and you might wind up spending more out-of-pocket money trying to qualify for "free" money than you would if you planned and paid for the work yourself. For example, the ASCS-approved plan for establishing trees on a given area might call for planting pine seedlings at $60 per acre; if the ASCS subsidy was 50%, your out-of-pocket expense would be $30 per acre. If the area could be regenerated by broadcasting treated pine seed at $15 per acre, you would save money by avoiding the ASCS program.

This is merely an example; such planting rates and costs and the ASCS policy may not apply in your area. All foresters in the ASCS program realize the difficulty of tailoring a nationwide program to fit perfectly each individual situation, and they strive to eliminate waste and poor forest-management practices. Nevertheless, until they succeed, you should examine the local ASCS program carefully before entering it.

For many years, the federal government has been the leading or only agency in forestry research; timberland investment today owes much of its success to this research. It is carried on in offices and field laboratories at U.S. Forest Experiment Stations in every timbered section and covers every aspect of forest management. Although the emphasis is on biology, increasing attention is directed toward financial matters. Published research reports are available at little or no cost and can be valuable to you. They may be obtained from U.S. Forest Experiment Stations; any forester can give you the proper addresses. Under certain conditions, a station will put you on the mailing list for all publications issued; you might find this helpful if you have the time and ability to absorb such volumes of information.

An exception to the rule of indirect contact is the case of the Yazoo-Little Tallachatchie Flood Prevention Project in northern Mississippi, which was administered by the U.S. Soil Conservation Service and terminated in 1985. Hundreds of millions of pine seedlings were planted under direct supervision of foresters of the U.S. Forest Service, who worked closely with landowners of the area. Effort was concentrated at first on tree planting and TSI work for the primary purpose of controlling erosion, but as trees reached merchantable size, more attention was directed to management. The forestry program of the Tennessee Valley Authority began in a similar fashion, but has evolved mainly into forestry research and promotion. The use you might make of such programs depends entirely on the local situation.

Many U.S. foresters you will see are engaged in management of national forests. They are busy with major responsibilities in managing these large areas and are not permitted to assist private landowners. They can still be helpful, however, for they encounter and solve many of the same problems you have. They sell timber on the open market and pay to have various forest-management activities carried out. They usually have recent stereoscopic aerial photographs of their lands; these also may cover your land if it is nearby. They are familiar with everything that goes on inside the forest boundary and will be glad to keep you informed of developments that might affect your land. They travel roads through the forest constantly and may pass through your land once a week. You should go out of your way to meet the district ranger stationed near you.

## FORESTERS EMPLOYED BY INDUSTRY

Forest-products manufacturers have always helped private landowners because they depend on them for most of their raw material. In the early 1940s, many companies hired "conservation foresters" to work with landowners on a free basis to improve woods practices and promote forestry. These men often marked timber, advised on forest management, distributed free seedlings, planted trees, and performed TSI work at little or no cost.

In the mid-1970s these efforts evolved into what are generally called *landowner-assistance programs*, although each company selects a unique name for its program. Typical programs start with a written agreement that the company will carry out many forest-management activities either free or at cost and that the landowner will pay ad valorem taxes, maintain boundary lines, and give the company "first refusal of all forest products sold from the land." Agreements can usually be canceled on short notice. The seemingly innocent words enclosed in quotation marks above effectively eliminate competitive bidding on timber sold from the tract. By reading Chapter 3, you will discover what a powerful adverse effect this provision usually has on the landowner's ability to get top prices.

Industrial foresters work hard in forestry associations, thank goodness. Association work is time-consuming and often thankless, but the accomplishments are valuable. Individual landowners benefit greatly, but cannot spend time on it. State associations fight for appropriations for state forestry departments, oppose legislation harmful to timberland investors, offer rewards for conviction of woods burners, promote the use of all wood products, study ad valorem taxes on timberlands and other common problems, and, in general, serve as organized voices of forestry. Industry associations have similar programs, but cover a wider area and concentrate on problems of the particular industry. For example, lumber industry associations advertise frequently in national magazines to promote the use of lumber; this expands the markets for lumber companies, which then buy more timber from you. All associations fight to retain beneficial tax treatment of timber income. Industrial foresters participate in these activities because their employers benefit directly and substantially. The fortunate thing about it is that they help you reach helpful goals that you probably could not reach without them.

## MISCELLANEOUS FREE SERVICES

Much of the United States is organized into soil conservation districts, legal subdivisions that receive technical assistance from the U.S. Soil Conservation Service and other agencies; these districts are concerned with wise land use, which sometimes includes forestry. For no cost, local employees will prepare a farm-management plan that includes a soil map of your tract. You can determine which services are offered in your area by calling the local office of the U.S. Soil Conservation Service.

All land-grant colleges conduct valuable research through agricultural experiment stations, some of which applies to forestry. Your state may have a forestry school where more information is available. Schools conduct forestry research concentrated on state problems, and many professors do part-time consulting work on a fee basis. Research results are usually published, and many projects can be inspected under certain conditions. Any forester in your area can help you reach the proper persons.

## FREE SERVICES VERSUS FEE SERVICES

The familiar axiom "Free advice is worth what you pay for it" applies to forestry. The big trouble is that the persons described above work directly for somebody else and indirectly for you. This leads to several complications.

First, their employers find it difficult to judge the quality of their woods work. The woods work services are usually offered in addition to the main effort of the company or agency, and attention must be concentrated elsewhere. The landowner served is seldom qualified to judge how good or bad the work is and rarely has any direct contact with the employers. These foresters also have many other responsibilities and can hardly be expected to be experts in everything. For example, a state forester may spend 80% of his time on fire control, 10% on administration, and 10% on management services to landowners. He may be mediocre in management, but so outstanding in fire control that he is properly classified as a valuable employee. Consequently, no one really knows his ability as a forest manager, and although no employer will knowingly allow poor performance, each finds it hard to specialize in everything.

Second, their experience may not cover many areas of vital importance to you. With the exception of some industrial foresters, the people described above are primarily experts in biology and know little about the business aspects of timberland investment. For example, few are familiar with the details of ad valorem taxes, one of the largest management expenses. Biology produces trees, but business management produces profits.

Third, their loyalty must be divided because they are paid by somebody else, and this division sometimes puts a conscientious man in an uncomfortable position. Consider the case of a paper-company forester marking a landowner's stand for a pulpwood thinning. He must please both the landowner and the pulpwood buyer, who is a dealer for his employer. Trees of many sizes can be processed into pulpwood, and some larger trees, which are more profitable for pulpwood producers, may also be suitable for poles and sawtimber, which are more profitable for landowners. How many of these should he mark? Conflicting interests of the two principals make any decision subject to criticism. Especially during the first thinning of a natural stand, many large, open-grown trees, primarily suited for pulpwood, should be cut ruthlessly; by doing so, however, he may be unjustly charged with favoring the buyer, whereas his treatment is exactly what the seller needs. Many persons working in this field are competent and experienced, and all are conscientiously trying to do a big and necessary job. The difficulty is that the nature of their employment places them on both sides of the trade.

Finally, these persons are not integral parts of or directly responsible for the transactions they participate in. They have little personal knowledge of timber prices; if these are important in the operation, they have to ask someone else for them. They are not available to handle the sticky problems that can arise from the smallest woods operation. When a tree is marked across the line on another's land, when the buyer cuts an unmarked tree or fells one on a fence, when logging damage is unnecessarily severe, or when the logger injures a third party, the landowner is left to handle irritating and maybe costly problems that are outside his experience or expertise.

Persons who charge fees for forestry advice and services do not have these limitations. They are responsible to the man who pays them, and the relationship is clearcut and more comfortable for all concerned. Although being in private practice does not guarantee greater competence or better ethics, it does subject them to competition every day. If their services are not valuable, they will soon be bankrupt, and this is as it should be. Since there are no arbitrary limits on services that can be performed, their experience tends to be wider and more closely related to the problems of the landowner. There is no division of loyalty, and often their work is checked by both the landowner and some of the free foresters described above. Several kinds of foresters provide fee services. In the next sections we discuss consulting foresters and nonprofessionals.

## CONSULTING FORESTERS

The most important professional to you is the consulting forester. His special talents, knowledge, and experience eventually bring him into contact with every timberland investor when decisions of consequence are involved. Because of his great importance, you should use particular care in selecting him.

**Selection of the Consulting Forester.** The title "consulting forester" is used by persons whose talents, experience, and character vary widely. A list of those practicing in each state can be obtained from the state forestry department. Many are members of the Society of American Foresters; most are licensed or registered by one or more states; some belong to the Association of Consulting Foresters. Although these registering agencies and professional associations strive for higher standards, none has effective police powers, and none guarantees the same level of competence you expect from someone with the title of doctor, lawyer, or certified public accountant. This should not worry you; no governmental body or professional association can guarantee more than a minimum of competence, and you need far more than the minimum. Most consulting foresters are graduates of a four-year forestry school, but some excellent ones are not. Many practice in the highest professional tradition and can make timberland profitable for you. What qualifications must a good one have, and how can you investigate him?

First, a consulting forester must be competent. You can determine his competence by talking to persons who deal with him in his daily business. Talk to his clients and to several persons who have had long business experience with him. His banker and his wife will usually speak kindly of him, and so will members of his church or civic club, but their opinions attest more to his popularity or other personal attributes than to his competence in forestry. Talk especially to several timber buyers of the area; they know very well how good or bad he is.

Second, he must be above reproach in his business dealings. His methods of handling the timber and money of his clients must be clear, careful, and straightforward and must compare favorably with operations of the trust department of a bank. In particular, payment for timber should always be made directly from buyer to seller and should pass through accounts of the consulting forester only in those rare cases when he is acting under a court decree or other legal arrangement. His clients of several years' standing can tell you about this.

Third, he must be independent. Under no circumstances should he be engaged in buying any forest product whatsoever. Some self-styled consulting foresters are primarily timber dealers; this means that they tell you what your timber is worth and then buy it from you. For the same reason that a lawyer cannot be on both sides of a lawsuit, a consulting forester cannot be on both sides of a timber trade. The same advice applies to those who seek to manage your tract merely for the privilege of buying timber that comes from it. This is a poor solution to the problem of forest management and should be discarded as soon as possible. You cannot get something for nothing, and good business requires a man to count his own money.

Fourth, he must be engaged in his practice on a full-time basis. The kind of service and advice you need can come only from a person who gains his experience and knowledge by constant and diligent application. You must have someone who understands your problems thoroughly and who is solving similar ones every business day. They are too important to be solved on a part-time basis.

Fifth, he must be thoroughly familiar with the important aspects of your local situation. He must also be aware of all the complexities of this business and know when to recommend other professional advisers. Using information presented elsewhere in this book, question him about several problems peculiar to your land. You will be able to tell in no time how well he knows his business.

Sixth, he must be articulate. He deals with terms, measures, and tools that are highly technical, and the details of his operations may be unfamiliar to many investors. These technicalities are not beyond the realm of human understanding, however, and you cannot make wise decisions unless you fully understand the problems. If the forester cannot explain them to your satisfaction, he probably does not understand them himself.

**Services of Consulting Foresters.** Consulting foresters perform every service needed by landowners and can be profitably used on the smallest tracts. Most are general practitioners, but highly trained specialists are as common in this professional field as in any other. You must realize this, for most owners need a general practitioner, not a specialist.

The general practitioner is usually very competent at estimating timber volumes. He takes inventories for the investor, calculates growth, and sets up a forest-management plan exactly tailored to the needs of his client. He marks timber for cutting, estimates its volume, sells it, and supervises its harvest. He may also take timber inventories for manufacturing concerns that desire to buy timber from land not under his management. He knows well the personality, character, and qualifications of everyone in the timber business near him.

He also plants trees, performs TSI work, and establishes boundary lines (although he is probably not a surveyor). He often appraises damage done to timberland by pipelines, powerlines, highways, fires, trespass, mineral operations, and so forth, and he usually makes an excellent witness in a lawsuit where technical forestry information has an important bearing on the case. He appraises estates for inheritance-tax purposes, especially where values are likely to be examined in detail by the Internal Revenue Service. He is especially good at resource surveys for forest-products industries seeking new locations. Existing timber volumes can be obtained from published reports, but the important questions are who owns the timber, can it be bought, and what are the prices and conditions. These data are revealed by his daily business. His independent appraisals are almost essential for landowners seeking loans. Only rarely does he have anything to do with fire suppression. Nevertheless, he is experienced in fire control (he must have such experience to practice forestry) and often prepares fire-control plans for all properties under his management. He may have heavy equipment to plow fire lines and do controlled burning, but most general practitioners do not.

In certain cases (usually involving properties larger than 10,000 acres), he is responsible for the entire operation of the property. He assesses the land, pays taxes, collects rentals on leases of cultivable land, supervises recreational use, and handles all other administrative details, in addition to the main forestry operations. He supervises the property to prevent trespass and continually advises the owner about forest-management practices that should be undertaken.

Occasionally he sells land for his client when his technical competence is necessary to present the property adequately. He sometimes buys land for his clients but rarely for himself; purchases for his own account may put him in competition with his clients.

He has many clients, sometimes hundreds, both large and small, and no client pays him more than a small fraction of his annual income. This is a healthy situation for all concerned. It assures his complete independence and enables him to give truly unbiased advice. He values each client, but can be uncompromising when matters of principle or technical competence are involved.

Specialists are what you might call "foresters' foresters." They may be experts in aerial-photograph interpretation, forest soils, tree diseases, genetics, statistical theory, game management, or many other fields. The general practitioner may need them at times and will inform you of this need when it arises. Specialists are rarely needed by most investors and should not be called in without guidance from a general practitioner familiar with the tract.

**Customary Fee Arrangements.**  The fee basis among consulting foresters is as varied as among other professionals, so I can give you only a general idea of what to expect. He will welcome inquiries on this subject, since both parties should get this settled early.

The consulting forester makes inventories, growth studies, and forest-management plans at a quoted price per acre. He handles all details of a timber sale on a commission basis, although the agreement with him will probably provide some compensation for his cost if the timber is not sold. This is essential because preparing the sale involves a large amount of woods work for him, whereas his client will still have his timber if he decides for some reason to reject all bids. His experience with timber sales and knowledge of the market enable him to predict with some accuracy what the sale price will be, so this provision seldom is used. The more a consulting forester works on a property, the more familiar he becomes with it, and the smaller his costs are, so he may lower his commission rates as the number of sales increases. In some cases, either he or his client prefers that he work on timber sales on a per-diem basis; this is a matter of choice. He plants trees and performs TSI work on a contractual basis and maintains boundary lines at a fixed charge per mile. He does most appraisal work and testifies in court when necessary at a stated fee per day or hour plus expenses. He sells land on the same basis as he sells timber, but since it is hard to sell land without a recent, reliable inventory, he may require one before undertaking the sale effort. For office conferences and advice, his charges are based on the amount of time used.

When the consulting forester is responsible for the entire management of a property, each case is a special situation. Management agreements usually provide for a monthly or quarterly retainer with additional fees based on the amount of timber produced or other work done. Although there is usually a written memorandum covering these situations, most foresters and landowners have found that a long-term forest-management contract is a waste of time. Such contracts must contain adequate escape clauses for both parties, for neither wants to continue an unsatisfactory relationship. Every consulting forester knows that the most binding agreement is one that has grown by custom through years of mutually happy dealings, and such agreements have no fixed life. They may be terminated by either party on little notice, and they preserve the independence that is so essential for investors.

The fees of the consulting forester are generally deductible for you, but some must be capitalized, and some reduce the size of capital gains. For instance, fees for supervising planting operations must be capitalized, and commissions on timber sales reduce the size of the sale. Your tax adviser can settle doubts about tax treatment of the consultant's fees.

Consulting foresters are relatively new in this country, and they are enthusiastic about their profession and love to talk about it to persons with a genuine interest. Even before you hire one, you can discuss your problems with him without fear of trespassing on his time. He will let you know gently long before you reach this point, and you will find that he is anxious to help you.

**Advantages and Disadvantages.** The consulting forester has one disadvantage: he costs money. He must be worth it, however, because although competition eliminates nonessentials (and every part of the timber business is fiercely competitive), the number of consulting foresters increases every year.

He has one big advantage: he is on your side. Growing trees for profit is a technical and long-range business, and you need the best possible assistance in order to succeed. If you make a mistake in accounting, you can find and correct it in a matter of hours. If you make a mistake in forest management, it may take you several years to realize it and 20 years to correct it. A consulting forester who has the qualifications described above offers you a valuable opportunity. Any forest management costs money. The best is reasonable, and the cheapest often ruinous.


## NONPROFESSIONAL FEE SERVICES

In general, nonprofessionals have little formal education or training in forestry; they have learned by doing. Nevertheless, they may be very good at their specialties and can be valuable to you.

A special class of contractors has grown up around the ASCS program of federal subsidies, and they are usually known by the ASCS term *vendor.* They plant trees and perform TSI work on a contract basis and know all the details of doing this under the ASCS program. They are often farmers who keep busy at this during winter months. They use farm labor of the area and can handle jobs of considerable size. They quickly absorb information learned from foresters who inspect their work, and they take great pride in good performance. They live in the area and benefit from observation of the work they have done over the years. You can locate these contractors through the local office of the ASCS and investigate their individual qualifications by talking to foresters who have used them. Big timber companies and the U.S. Forest Service use contractors who provide the same services. They tend to be bigger than the ones described above and may be better qualified and organized. You can contact them through the managers who use them. There are some important legal aspects to your relationship with contractors, and you must investigate this.

Before the rise of consulting foresters, many holdings were managed by persons I call "timbermen," for want of a better term, and some of them still practice, although the number is dwindling. Many have spent their entire lives in the woods—scaling logs, estimating and buying timber, logging, surveying lines, and performing all other tasks connected with timberland operations. They are often competent, reliable, honest, eminently practical men. They may not be familiar with the business management part of timberland invest-ment, but they are unbeatable in the woods. These men are hard to find, and I can only suggest that you inquire for them among foresters in your area.


## HOW CAN YOU USE THIS TALENT?

Such an array of services may be bewildering, and I cannot tell each of you individually how to use them. Nevertheless, certain guidelines are clear from what I have said before, and certain other points become plain from long experience in the field.

First, the most important single thing you can get from any forester or agency is good advice, and I emphasize "good." Advice comes in a flood from all those described above, and all of it is offered in a sincere effort to help you. On the other hand, it should be clear that quality varies widely. I suggest that you choose a man of wide and long experience and unquestioned reputation among professionals in the field and that you stick with him even when he tells you things that are unpleasant. He must be able, as near as possible, to see things from your exact standpoint. This would seem to exclude everyone except consulting foresters, but this is not invariably so. Some of the finest advisers are not in consulting work at all, or practice on a nonprofessional basis, or may be entirely outside the field of forestry. I believe that a good adviser is ten times more important than all other elements put together. This is true whether you own 40 or 40,000 acres.

Second, you must pick capable persons to execute programs set up in conference with the adviser. Both functions may be combined in the same person and often are, but you might be able to economize by using several persons. There are several possible solutions to your problem, and they depend mainly on size of ownership.

If you own 160 acres, by most standards a small tract, you still own an asset that is probably worth between $40,000 and $160,000, and this is more than pocket change to most investors. Such an asset requires good management. For advice, you might turn to a consulting forester near the tract; during a year, you will probably use no more than a few hours of his time. Several others may have a part in actual operations. Your inventory might be taken by a consulting forester or local timberman. Data on soils might be obtained from the Soil

Conservation Service or a soil scientist in private practice. Boundary lines might be established by a timberman or county surveyor. Tree planting and TSI work might be done by a contractor with or without ASCS subsidy. Inspections to prevent trespass or to watch for important changes in the timber stand might be conducted by you personally, one of your neighbors, a consulting forester, or a timberman. Timber sales must be handled by a qualified expert. This program leaves out most free services because few of them can help you in the actual work. Research reports issued by various agencies described above will advance your general knowledge of forestry, and you might find helpful the newsletter published by my firm. You should compare notes with any foresters you contact; this form of business intelligence work might unearth information useful to you or your adviser.

More foresters and politicans worry about and study you than all other timberland investors combined, and they have tried many schemes to improve the quality of your forest practices. They have often decided that such investments cannot be profitable for you because your ownership is too small for good management, and they have used this to justify government subsidies and programs with the subtle controls that accompany them. I believe that they are absolutely, totally wrong, that the investment can be very profitable for you, and that, because of your great staying power mentioned earlier, you may be more efficient than other classes of investors. All you have to do is face economic facts with the expert help available.

If you own 1600 acres, your problem is similar, except that you probably sell timber every year instead of every five or ten years. I suggest the same scheme of management. The quality of your adviser and the amount of time you spend on the property become more important because the asset is much larger.

If you own 16,000 to 160,000 acres, you have a substantial business that involves weekly or even daily operations. Properties of this size have special management problems not easily solved even today. You need advice of the highest caliber and services in considerable amounts. Many such owners have groped for the solution to the management problem by hiring a forester shortly after his graduation, with no qualifications other than a good education and some woods work during his college summers. If this is better than no solution, it is still a poor one. The young and inexperienced forester is overwhelmed by the complexity of his task. His head is crammed with information, but he knows little about how to apply what he learned in school and learns every day on the job. His education was short on business, law, and accounting, and the forest-management principles that seemed so simple and logical at school are suddenly difficult to apply. At the same time, he costs money. His annual salary, transportation, equipment, and related costs amount to $30,000 at a minimum, and this is $1.50 per acre on a tract as large as 20,000 acres. A more subtle and important problem arises because you hired him. His mind is working for you, and you tend to do what he recommends because you are paying him. Instead of guiding, however, he needs to be guided; he may be headed for a brilliant future, but he needs help from an experienced hand in the beginning. After several years of paying for an arrangement of this kind, the investor realizes that he has made a bad mistake that cannot be corrected for years.

Necessary services such as timber-marking, TSI work, planting, and boundary maintenance constitute a major part of the work, but although the volume of it is large, it varies from year to year and with the season of the year. Full-time employees may be fully utilized at some times and almost idle at others, and there is always the temptation to use them, merely because they are already on the payroll, for projects that are not essential. In addition, their travel time to work may be excessive if the land is scattered, and there are few chances at such economies as might arise when adjoining landowners maintain the same boundary line. These housekeeping chores represent important management costs and can be most cheaply performed when ownership is consolidated or when independent contractors perform them for many landowners in the same area. Such contractors achieve the benefits of consolidation without the necessity for land transfers, and they might be a good solution to the problem.

As always, the most important part of the problem is the need for advice. In the lower part of the size range, outside advice is almost essential; the caliber needed makes it prohibitively expensive to hire an adviser on a full-time basis. You probably do not need advice more than two or three times each quarter, but it must be excellent when you get it. As total land area increases, it is more and more likely that a full-time adviser is needed. The hiring of such a person may be highly profitable when combined with the use of contractors for housekeeping chores. The adviser can supervise the contractors from time to time to ensure that his recommendations are carried out and spend the majority of his time considering the problems and possibilties of the enterprise.

Some landowner cooperatives exist, and more are suggested, but you can see from discussion here and elsewhere in this book that the idea has no advantages for you unless ownerships are contiguous or unless the total area managed by the cooperative is large enough to hire the best brains. Even then, cooperatives reduce your freedom of action (and complete independence is one great advantage of individual ownership) and may result in more expensive operations. You should not become part of one without serious thought.

# 3

# Sale of Timber

One of the most frequent questions I receive is, "What extra work can I do on my timberland to increase my income from it?" Without trying to be humorous, I always reply, "Stay home and study HOW and WHEN to sell timber." The reason for this answer is that nothing you can do will increase the amount of your timber growth as much as 50%, whereas knowing how and when to sell timber can increase the amount of money you get for it by 100% or more. You can spend 50 years growing a crop of trees and then lose most of the profit in it in 50 minutes by mistakes at this point. Selling timber is far more important than any other timberland operation and deserves all the study you can give it. You should start by considering whether the product you have for sale is scarce or plentiful.

## THE MYTH OF TIMBER SCARCITY

Timber is *not* scarce. No matter what you have heard, we are not running out of it. But acting as if we were can reduce your profit almost to nothing. The things you would do if timber were scarce are ridiculous if it is not.

How can we tell that timber is not scarce? My firm gets this message loud and clear from timber buyers, for we sell timber for landowners about 60 times each month.

Government reports tell the same story. The U.S. Forest Service inventories of timber by states have been showing for years a surplus of growth over removals or a near-balance between them in most eastern states. Although some types of trees are less plentiful in certain areas and although our forests are clearly not producing all they could even with our present limited knowledge, the picture is definitely one of increasing abundance.

A 1975 study sheds additional light. In "Is Timber Scarce? The Economics of a Renewable Resource," Dr. Lloyd C. Irland stated,

No *general* timber scarcity has existed in this country since 1950. . . . Recent decades have brought persistent declines in real prices of major forest products. Our balance of foreign trade in timber products has steadily improved since 1950. And despite rising consumption of industrial wood, the quantity, quality, and accessibility of our forest resources have been steadily improving for the last 30 years. . . . It appears that the United States enjoys a timber-producing capacity equal to the needs of a population double its present size.

Therefore, you are not dealing with desperate buyers who will fight to get what you have. You are competing with a horde of sellers who want the same dollars you are after. When any product is plentiful, it must be marketed with skill if you want a good price for it. The first step in your marketing is to learn the mechanics of the timber market.

## HOW THE TIMBER MARKET WORKS

No market I know of is like the timber market. A phone call can get you a firm price on many common items: stocks, bonds, groceries, clothing, commodities, autos, and so on. But a phone call to 20 timber buyers will likely get you 20 different estimates, and each buyer will want to see your timber before making a firm offer.

Many forces cause this market to be so entirely different. Some are obvious to all; other powerful ones are known only to a few. You must first understand how complex the market is, and second learn how to cope with this complexity.

The first step is to discover who the buyers are and what they want. There are many. Our list for Mississippi alone contains 642 names. Each uses trees of some sort, and all buy on the open market.

Each buyer, in turn, manufactures the trees he buys into products for his market, and there are many markets. To illustrate the situation, Table 3.1 gives the 16 buyers in one county and what they want.

Some of these buyers buy from and sell to each other at times, and all buyers also have a hookup with buyers of forest products that they do not want.

This is the situation today, but it changes constantly. Some buyers will disappear and be replaced by others. Others will change their

**TABLE 3-1**
**Buyers and Their Products in One County**

| Buyer | Wants Trees That Can Be Made into |
|-------|-----------------------------------|
| A | Small-size pine lumber |
| B | Pulpwood and logs of all species |
| C | Pulpwood |
| D | Pine lumber |
| E | Pulpwood |
| F | Pine and hardwood logs |
| G | All forest products |
| H | Small-size pine lumber |
| I | All forest products except poles |
| J | Tree-length pulpwood |
| K | Pine plywood |
| L | Pulpwood and pine and hardwood lumber |
| M | Pine poles and piling |
| N | Hardwood veneer |
| O | Pulpwood and poles and piling |
| P | Pine and hardwood lumber |

requirements; paper companies, for example, formerly bought only pulpwood, but now they want everything.

Our next step is to determine where these buyers are. Timber can be hauled economically about 75 miles from woods to mill. Therefore, the buyers listed want timber in several other counties, and buyers at many other places want timber in this county.

All buyers have limits on the kind of tree they can use. For example, a pulpwood buyer can use anything that can be reduced to chips; a plywood mill can use only fair-quality trees large enough to be peeled on a lathe; a pole buyer can use only trees of a certain size, taper, species, and straightness. But when you consider the whole spectrum of desires, you can see that almost all can use a reasonably straight 12-inch-DBH pine tree.

Such trees, acceptable to many, are worth quite different amounts to each buyer, however, and the difference depends on what the buyer plans to make from the tree. Such a tree on today's market brings about $1.90 for pulpwood, $4.50 for sawtimber, $5.70 for plywood, and $7.30 for poles in one county.

I say "today's market" because prices are never stable, and markets for manufactured trees are independent of each other. Pulpwood

### TABLE 3-2
### Results of Timber Purchases

| Percent of Requirements | Method of Buying | Price per MBF | Total Price |
|---|---|---|---|
| 10 | Distress sales | $ 75 | $ 750 |
| 30 | Negotiations | 100 | 3000 |
| 20 | Delivered logs | 125 | 2500 |
| 20 | Cutting contracts | 150 | 3000 |
| 80 | | | 9250 |

demand fluctuates with demand for paper, which fluctuates with general business conditions and the exchange rate of the dollar. Sawtimber demand fluctuates with demand for new housing and remodeling or repair of existing houses. Plywood demand fluctuates with demand for many products. Pole demand fluctuates with level of utility construction.

Another factor, unrelated to those just mentioned, also causes wide differences in prices. So far as we know, no buyer owns enough land to grow all the timber needed. All must buy much of their raw material on the open market. Although there are many sellers and although total supply of timber is greater than total demand, open-market buyers can never know in advance where all their timber will come from or what each tract will cost. They know only that their average manufacturing costs are so much and their average selling prices are so much; therefore, average timber cost must be less than the difference between them.

Therefore, the open-market buyer starts each year trying to buy timber as cheaply as possible. First he looks for distress sales (rights of way that must be cleared quickly, damage from windstorms or insects) where timber is cheapest. Next he negotiates directly with timber owners, many of whom know little about how to sell timber. Next he posts notice that he will pay so much per thousand board feet (MBF) for logs of certain specifications delivered to his mill. Next he tries to negotiate long-term cutting contracts in which the prices he must pay are set according to a published index of prices, preferably of the product he manufactures.

Each tactic produces some timber. Over the course of a year, results might be as in Table 3.2.

His *average* cost for 80% of his needs is thus $9250 divided by 80 =

$115.63/MBF. But his mill will not be profitable if he runs only 80% of the time; his fixed costs must be spread over a larger production, and his workers cannot earn a decent living from part-time work. Therefore, he cannot stop buying at this point. But since these tactics have succeeded so well, he has a lot of room to maneuver in. If he can pay an average of $140/MBF and still make a profit, arithmetic shows that he can pay as much as $237.50/MBF for the last 20%.

This is a hypothetical case. I used these figures just to illustrate my point. But something like this happens to every buyer every year. All buy timber by every means they can think of and pay a different price every time.

To get the remaining 20%, our open-market buyer must now turn to the professional market. Here competition is much stiffer. Not only are sellers much better at their business, but he also encounters other buyers whose situations are like his. He cannot tell in advance what they will do, and he may not get a second chance to buy what he needs. His only alternative is to make his best offer the first time.

Further information about the timber market appears in an interview with two timber buyers in Appendix III.


## ILLUSIONS ABOUT MARKET PRICES

In an interview just before retiring as librarian of Congress, Dr. Daniel Boorstin said, "The great obstacle to progress is not ignorance, but the illusion of knowledge." Every participant in timber markets should read, mark, learn, and inwardly digest these profound words, for the most common mistake is the illusion of knowledge. Here are some illustrations.

In clear-cut sales just one week apart, we received the bids in Table 3.3 for blocks of timber on the same large tract.


### TABLE 3-3
### Bids for Blocks of Timber

| Bidder | Block 1 | Block 2 |
|---|---|---|
| Timber dealer A | $141,000 | $136,748 |
| Timber dealer B | 110,200 | 147,700 |
| Major company A | 102,099 | 128,899 |
| Major company B | 93,430 | — |
| Timber dealer C | 80,579 | 90,056 |

All bidders were under the illusion that they knew what the market price was, and four of them, especially timber dealer B, were astonished at the high bid on block 1. Shortly before the sale, as we learned later, timber dealer A discovered that, because of past mistakes in procurement, one sawmill near the tract was about to shut down because of a lack of logs and would pay a premium of $30/MBF for immediate delivery. Because of this private knowledge, timber dealer A was the easy winner at no cost to itself.

Suspecting the reason for timber dealer A's remarkable bid, timber dealer B quickly canvassed all mills, discovered the same shortage, worked out the same premium, bid accordingly on block 2, and won. Timber dealer A, under the illusion that its knowledge was still private, tried to increase its profit by reducing its bid and lost.

In these market actions, the most important factor was one that most persons never think about: the past mistakes of a single buyer somewhere near the timber. This knowledge is almost impossible for a seller to obtain in advance. It is also not necessary. If the seller sends out about 250 invitations to bid on his tract, he will expose it to every possible buyer and reap a profit from another's mistakes.

The powerful forces at work in this market are further illustrated in Table 3.4, the list of bids we received on three other tracts. Even an old hand like me was amazed at the bids on tract B, and I still do not know what happened. Our client does not know either, but he smiled all the way to the bank.

You can now see that the timber market is huge and extremely varied. There is no "market price" in the sense that there is a market

### TABLE 3-4
### Bids on Three Tracts

| Tract A<br>Winter-Logging Pine | Tract B<br>High-Quality Hardwood | Tract C<br>Medium-Quality Hardwood |
|---|---|---|
| $496,613 | $338,283 | $202,569 |
| 404,440 | 236,657 | 168,117 |
| 375,375 | 204,762 | 157,597 |
| 276,083 | 195,101 | 152,185 |
| 275,000 | 165,048 | 133,870 |
| 269,907 | 128,768 | 112,554 |
|  | 120,000 | 104,922 |
|  |  | 101,000 |

price for General Motors stock. On most trading days, the high for General Motors is not 5% above the low, whereas the bids just listed show that the high often exceeds the low by more than 100%. Furthermore, the market is changing all the time, and this means that the timing of sales is important.

## TIMING

Compared to many other businesses, timberland management has a unique advantage. If you do not like the market this year, you can postpone sales, and conditions may improve. Even if they do not, growth during the waiting period will increase the size of the harvest. So you have some leeway as to when to sell, and good timing can pay handsome dividends. One aspect of timing is to sell at market peaks. No one will ever know whether prices will go up or down or stay the same. If your sales are infrequent, however, you must make some decision, and several groups can help you.

First are the timber buyers. They are in the market every day and can give you good information on prices. They can give you more than opinions; they can offer you money you can spend. As your timber becomes more desirable, you will see more and more of these buyers as they call upon you in efforts to buy it. When the market is good and their mills are running full blast, these visits become more frequent; this is a sign of excellent markets. They are not nearly so eager to buy when markets are poor.

Second are other private owners, some of whom operate larger tracts on a full-time basis. They sell timber of all kinds every month or so and have done so for years. They constantly compare notes with other owners and will gladly talk shop with you. You should look for someone with 5000 to 10,000 acres who is not engaged in forest-products manufacturing. You should also realize that the private owner is an expert only in his particular situation, and his situation may not be the same as yours.

Third are the consulting foresters. Consulting foresters make most of their living from timber sales, and probably no group knows as much about prices of so many different forest products as they do.

Fourth are those foresters with the U.S. Forest Service and state forestry departments who work directly in the management of federal and state forests; the district ranger of a U.S. national forest is an example. These foresters often sell timber and have personal knowledge of market conditions, which is far better than information passed around in the organization.

Fifth is your state forestry association. All persons and companies interested in forestry belong to such an association, and it is a good source of data on present and future markets. Many private conversations at meetings are about markets. Memberships are available at moderate cost and provide information on all forestry subjects. Additional data are available from the Forest Farmers Association and national and local associations of manufacturers.

If your timber sales occur at frequent intervals, this aspect of timing, selling at market peaks, is not so vital, since the law of averages works for you. Another aspect of timing then becomes more important, that of selling each tree when it is no longer a profitable investment.

Value of an individual tree changes constantly throughout its life. In general, its annual percentage increase in value is very high just after it reaches merchantable size and declines gradually as the tree grows larger, until the rate eventually dips below that commonly paid on savings accounts. Therefore, within certain limits, a young tree is a highly profitable investment, and an old one should be liquidated. For instance, a 6-in. pulpwood tree, by growing 4 in. in diameter, often increases in value 433%, and this growth may take place in as few as 12 years. On the other hand, a 16-in. sawtimber tree, by growing the same 4 in., often increases in value only 71%, and this growth can take place in 12 years only under good management.

The first cut from your tract will probably be a selective one, and it goes without saying that you will remove diseased, crooked, forked, defective, and suppressed trees. Biology will select these for you. After they have been cut, you may notice that the remaining trees are still too crowded. Which of these should be cut?

You can answer the question for each tree by a slight modification of the procedure described under "Growth Study" in Chapter 7. Measure the tree's diameter now, and calculate its present value. Then calculate its value when it becomes 2 in. larger. Divide the increase in value by the present value to get the percentage increase the tree will make by this growth. Now take an increment core, and count the number of rings in the outside inch. This shows how many years it took the tree to put on the last 2 in. in diameter, a growth rate it will probably maintain in putting on the next 2 in. Using a compound-interest table, determine the annual rate that corresponds with the percentage increase and the number of years just obtained. Let us suppose that a tree has a value today of $2.00 and will be worth $3.00

when it is 2 in. larger, and that the increment core shows eight rings in the outside inch. The tree will thus increase in value 50% and will probably do so in eight years; the compound-interest table shows that its annual growth rate is 5.2%. If the interest rate you selected for your financial forecast is more than this, the tree should be cut.

Performing the steps outlined above for each tree is not feasible but also is not necessary. If the timber marker does the calculation a few times each morning and repeats it occasionally during the day, he will find that the general appearance of the tree and its relation to its neighbors are reliable indicators of its growth rate, and that from these indications he can predict almost exactly what the increment core will show.

You must use judgment when you come to clumps of good trees so closely spaced that none is growing at a satisfactory rate. It is reasonable to assume that removing two trees from a crowded clump of six will speed up the growth of the remaining four to an adequate rate. Training and experience in biology are necessary to make sound judgments of this type; this explains why foresters spend such a long time in school and continue study after graduation. You must also be sure that the trees left after cutting are sufficient to make full utilization of the soil's productive capacity. If they are not, it is usually time to liquidate everything and start again. Removal of less than 45% of the trees generally means that the remaining trees will expand to cover the ground; removal of more than 75% probably means that the stand should be liquidated. The area between these guideposts requires expert advice. A partial cut is not always good; it can be bad business and biological practice. Let us move on to a discussion of how to sell timber once you have decided that the timing is right.

## SEALED BIDS VERSUS NEGOTIATION

Selling timber by sealed bids is the superior method by far compared to selling by negotiation. It is mandatory in some cases and highly desirable in most others, and has advantages for both buyer and seller.

The biggest plus for the seller is the higher price that usually results. As you saw in Tables 3.3 and 3.4, the high bid is often far above the second highest; this is not possible at an auction. A well-prepared and properly advertised sale of this type definitely establishes the market price even if there is only one bid. The method also treats all bidders fairly and impartially, and, when properly conducted, eliminates the suspicion that sometimes arises from private negotiations. It is most satisfactory for estates with scattered heirs of all ages. It eliminates negotiation on price, and since the bids are written and sometimes accompanied by good-faith deposits, the buyer's commitment is firm.

The system has some advantages for buyers. Where it is well-established, the buyers are somewhat like shoppers at a supermarket. They receive a steady stream of sale announcements and can pick tracts they want from a wide assortment. They save money on timber inventories, since preparation of the sale is properly the seller's responsibility and includes an independent inventory. A prudent buyer can spot-check this independent inventory without the expense of a complete inventory. He benefits from fair and impartial treatment of all bidders. He meets his competitors in this market place and checks prices of timber in his area.

The sealed-bid method will not always work. The market is active where individual sale volumes range from $30,000 to $300,000, but the number of bidders may decrease rapidly as amounts grow larger. Many sales involving $1,000,000 or more must be negotiated. Negotiation is also the only way to sell poor timber, since demand for it is always weak. It is often the only solution when specifications for the item sold are varied and complicated, a situation common in poles and piling, oak-stave logs, walnut, dogwood, persimmon, and so forth.

Popularity of the sealed-bid sale has increased rapidly as sellers have become more experienced, but some owners are excellent traders and prefer negotiation. If you want to try this, remember that a timber buyer is a skilled professional. As a veteran buyer once said, "A seller may think he can outtrade me. This won't happen one percent of the time. He and I are like a dog chasing a rabbit, with me being the rabbit. The dog's after a good meal, but the rabbit's running for its life."

## LUMP-SUM SALES VERSUS PAY-AS-YOU-GO SALES

A sale for a lump sum is usually superior to a pay-as-you-go sale. It is clear, fast, and definite, permitting flexibility for tax purposes in most cases and eliminating much of the negotiation and argument that all too often are part of pay-as-you-go sales. Title passes immediately to the buyer, who then has a certain time to remove the timber; this transfers to the buyer the risk of loss by fire, insects, weather, theft, and so on. When combined with sealed bids, lump-sum sales render timber almost as liquid as many stocks. One frequent dispute in the sale of timber by previously discussed methods arises over how it will be measured, and this is often combined with fear that the timber will not be paid for at all. Lump-sum sales eliminate these problems.

You will be able to sell most of your timber for lump sums, but in several cases you will have to use the pay-as-you-go method. You will certainly want to do so in selling large, overmature timber where values per unit are high and where the presence of many defects makes it impossible to determine the volume of standing trees. You should do so when selling timber so inaccessible that no buyer will risk paying a lump sum for it except at bargain prices. You will also have to use the pay-as-you-go method when the market is made up primarily of small operators, which may be the case in the sale of pulpwood. Many pulpwood buyers are capable, but their capital is just sufficient for trucks and other production equipment, and they have nothing left over with which to buy timber. Insistence on lump-sum sales in this kind of market means that you must take a licking on price.

If you are forced to make pay-as-you-go sales, you should require buyers to put up a deposit large enough to ensure that they will fulfill the contract. Twenty-five percent of the anticipated sale volume is common. The sale agreement should specify in an unmistakable manner the timber to be cut and the time allowed for cutting, and buyers should forfeit the deposit if they fail to meet these conditions. The air is always full of sweet reasonableness and good intentions during negotiation of a contract, but they vanish when the hard work of logging is made harder by bad weather. A buyer who starts logging should be compelled to finish, since you will probably not be able to get another to clean up the mess.

## SEALED-BID AND LUMP-SUM SALES: A COMBINATION TO COPE WITH COMPLEXITY

As I pointed out earlier, the timber market is huge, extremely varied, and changing all the time. Nobody can ever know enough to predict what it will do. Location of a buyer is easy to determine, but his hopes, fears, and present financial status can only be guessed at. Anyone trying to predict which buyer will be the highest bidder on a given tract is sure to be surprised. Two examples will give you an idea of how analysis can fail.

Two sales were equal in area and pine volume and were held nine days apart. Both contained trees suitable for a wide variety of products and were located in the same market area. We prepared both in the way described in the next section and sent invitations to bid to the same 250 buyers. We received the bids shown in Table 3.5.

Several results surprised us. Why was plywood plant A the high bidder on sale 1 when it was 41 miles farther from the tract than plant B? Why did plywood plant C fail to bid on sale 1 and yet become a strong contender for sale 2? How could lumber company B almost win sale 2 and yet be so far away? How could pulpwood dealer A bid more than paper company A on sale 2 when he was farther away and normally would sell the timber to paper company A?

The changing-all-the-time characteristic affects different buyers in such different ways that no single buyer can or will pay top dollar all the time. Each January for five straight years we bid off one block of timber from the same tract. Listed in Table 3.6 are all bids for each year. As you can see, only two buyers bid every year, and although their five-year totals were higher than the others, neither succeeded in buying any of the timber. No single buyer bid a total that was more than 85.7% of the highest total. The bids are in Table 3.6.

When results are so unpredictable, and when you can never predict what will happen, what can you do? There is only one solution to the problem: Make your sales both sealed-bid *and* lump-sum. The sealed-bid feature makes all buyers compete against each other. The lump-sum feature puts all of them on an equal footing and eliminates the need for understanding technicalities of all products.

### TABLE 3-5
### Bids on Two Sales

| | Sale 1 | | Sale 2 | |
| Bidder | Miles from Tract | Bid | Miles from Tract | Bid |
|---|---|---|---|---|
| Plywood plant A | 49 | $80,240 | 65 | $ — |
| Plywood plant B | 8 | 77,124 | 35 | 79,353 |
| Plywood plant C | 73 | — | 59 | 84,910 |
| Lumber company A | 50 | 74,440 | 15 | 80,151 |
| Lumber company B | 63 | — | 80 | 86,656 |
| Paper company A | 25 | 69,308 | 30 | 60,475 |
| Pulpwood dealer A | 30 | 66,334 | 60 | 63,641 |
| Pole company A | 45 | — | 10 | 92,812 |
| Pole company B | 45 | — | 10 | 90,286 |

**TABLE 3-6**
**Bids for Five Year Period**

| Buyer | Year 1 | Year 2 | Year 3 | Year 4 | Year 5 | Total |
|---|---|---|---|---|---|---|
| Highest | $89,331 | $97,587* | $228,432 | $92,812 | $101,705 | $609,867 |
| A | 88,350 | 92,705 | 195,965 | 79,353 | 66,406 | 522,779 |
| B | 71,672 | 92,613 | 179,082 | 60,475 | 66,613 | 470,455 |
| C | 89,331 | 48,492 | 195,424 | — | 74,745 | 407,992 |
| D | — | 77,100 | 166,772 | 84,910 | — | 328,782 |
| E | — | — | 228,432 | 90,286 | — | 318,718 |
| F | 62,040 | — | 142,689 | 80,151 | — | 284,880 |
| G | — | 87,000 | 179,200 | — | — | 266,200 |
| H | — | — | 166,739 | — | 71,477 | 238,216 |
| I | — | — | 194,560 | — | — | 194,560 |
| J | — | 52,459 | — | — | 101,705 | 154,164 |
| K | — | 33,000 | — | 92,812 | — | 125,812 |
| L | — | — | — | 86,656 | — | 86,656 |
| M | 83,333 | — | — | — | — | 83,333 |
| N | — | 67,753 | — | — | — | 67,753 |
| O | — | — | — | 63,641 | — | 63,641 |
| P | — | — | — | — | 44,000 | 44,000 |
| Q | — | 10,034 | — | — | — | 10,034 |

* Sum of bids on three separate parcels.

## PREPARATION OF SALE

The most important item in preparing a sale is to determine *exactly* what you are selling. I emphasize *exactly* because this is where many sellers fail. They estimate timber volumes by measuring samples of the tract and then multiplying them by a factor to get the total. And since woods work is hard and may be expensive, they spend a lot of time figuring out how to reduce the size of sample theorectically needed.

This fancy figuring is perfect in theory, but wrong in practice. Theorists forget that ordinary people measure the sample, that ordinary people make mistakes, and that many mistakes cause an underestimate of the actual volume.

The most common mistake in practice is to measure a sample that is not representative of the whole. This mistake is so common and causes such serious errors that I want to emphasize it by citing two cases. A timber buyer made a 10% sample inventory of a tract and estimated the volume to be 393,717 board feet. In a cursory examina-

**TABLE 3-7**
**Differences Between 100% Counts and Sample Estimates**

| Tract | MBF by 100% Count | MBF by Sample Estimate | Percent Error of Sample Estimate |
|---|---|---|---|
| A | 139.3 | 182.0 | + 30.7 |
| B | 1,415.9 | 877.0 | − 38.1 |
| C | 135.9 | 72.0 | − 47.0 |
| D | 375.4 | 813.0 | +116.6 |
| E | 3,293.5 | 1,974.5 | − 40.0 |
| F | 393.2 | 764.6 | + 94.5 |
| G | 1,666.7 | 2,112.0 | + 26.7 |
| H | 1,536.1 | 1,149.0 | − 25.2 |
| I | 599.2 | 1,075.0 | + 79.4 |
| J | 1,532.6 | 2,044.0 | + 33.3 |
| K | 579.8 | 244.4 | − 57.8 |
| L | 464.3 | 265.2 | − 42.9 |

tion of the tract, one of our managers made a 2% sample inventory and estimated 602,800 board feet; in preparing the tract for sale later, he measured 100% of the trees and found 502,200 board feet. Shortly thereafter, the timber was cut and hauled to a mill where the volume was measured to be 510,143 board feet. If the mill measurement determined the correct volume, errors of the other estimates were 22.8% for the 10% sample, 18.2% for the 2% sample, and only 1.6% for the 100% sample.

In 1983 we measured 499,028 trees containing 50,000,000 board feet of sawtimber in 66 separate tracts comprising 10,281 acres in a joint inventory for two big timber companies. One of them had earlier made sample estimates of each tract and gave them to us to help in planning our work. To illustrate the differences between 100% counts and sample estimates, Table 3.7 shows results on 12 of the 66 tracts: The sample-estimate error was *less* than 10% on only 11 tracts, between 25% and 30% on most of them, and more than 10% on two.

Another common mistake is to measure the sample incorrectly. I have worked in the woods for 45 years and know how easy it is to make mistakes when the weather is terrible, you are very tired, the tract is a huge briar patch, you step on a snake, or you are being eaten alive by mosquitoes.

Finally, for reasons we have never understood, mistakes in measuring a sample usually cause an underestimate. Perhaps timber cruisers think that the worst mistake is an overestimate and are therefore unconsciously conservative. Perhaps it is easier to miss a tree *on* the sample than to include one *outside* it. At any rate, our experience reveals that by far the largest number of mistakes cause an underestimate and that this error can easily be 25%.

The way to avoid such mistakes is to measure 100% of the trees (not a sample) and to measure them with a steel tape (not a Biltmore stick). This requires a lot more work. But you can pay for it by finding 5% more timber, and you may find 25% more.

The measurement should be made by a person of unquestioned competence, integrity, and independence. (For obvious reasons, most timber buyers will not bid on measurements made by a competitor, especially when the competitor might bid on the same sale. Buyers are also very wary of measurements obviously made by a amateur and of results that contradict common sense.) The report must show the number of trees by species, DBH classes, and lengths, and also the estimate of the volumes they contain. These facts are especially important because trees of certain sizes can be manufactured into several different products, and because many buyers now determine volumes by weight. Even if buyers do not agree with the forester's volumes, they can calculate their own from the tally of tree numbers and sizes.

The second step in preparing a sale is to make the terms as attractive as possible to buyers. You should certainly furnish them with a copy of the forester's report. This makes it easy for them to decide whether they are interested, and to check the figures, something they must do. They also know how accurate a 100% count is, and the reputation and experience of the forester will go a long way toward convincing them that the volume is actually there.

You should also try to meet the other terms buyers want. For example, although 12 months' time is usually long enough to allow for cutting some tracts, an unsettled economy or difficult logging conditions may cause buyers to lose interest unless they are allowed 24 months. Severe restrictions on logging can reduce value of a tract to zero, so you must strike a happy medium here. Access to the tract is essential; if you do not provide it, you force each buyer to work out his own access and thereby reduce his interest by raising his cost of bidding. Finally, you must allow time for buyers to appraise the tract; three weeks is usually enough.

The third step is to advertise the sale thoroughly. You should send an invitation to bid to every buyer with 75 miles. In much of eastern

United States, a circle of this size will contain 250 buyers. If you do not have their names and addresses, the next best thing is to advertise the sale in classified sections of nearby newspapers.

The invitation to bid should include maps of the property that can be followed by timber buyers of reasonable competence. A map with the scale common to most state road maps will help them locate the tract and the meeting place for the show-me trip. A larger-scale map of the tract itself will help them greatly in their appraisal work.

The invitation should contain such details as time allowed for cutting, penalties for cutting trees not included in the sale, instructions on how to submit a bid (including place, date, and hour), a copy of the conveyance to be used (if buyers are not familiar with your sales), provision to allow seller to reject bids, and any special conditions of the sale that might be important to buyers. Requiring bidders to attach to their bids a good-faith deposit in cash or equivalent increases the cost of bidding and should be avoided if possible. You must provide a qualified person to show the timber to buyers and answer questions about it, and the invitation should contain the time and meeting place for such a show-me trip.

All of this information tells nothing about timber quality or logging conditions, and of course all of the information is supplied by the seller. Consequently, buyers must spend money for an on-the-ground examination of the tract including a check of the seller's volumes. Since such costs frequently range upward from $500, no buyer will knowingly bid when another buyer has the right of first refusal on the timber.

## OPENING BIDS

The best strategy on bid-opening day is: "Operate in a goldfish bowl." In the past some sellers, who hate to be cheated themselves, have figured that any trick played on a timber buyer was fair, so buyers have good reason to be suspicious of secrecy. Their appraisal cost them time and money, and they want a fair chance to get the tract. The more open your conduct is, the more convinced they will be that they received fair treatment, and the more anxious they will be to deal with you again.

No bid should be considered except those that arrive before the specified time. Taking bids over the phone is acceptable in these days of poor mail service, but be sure that they arrive on time.

You should open all bids publicly and announce them. If no bidder is present or if some of the sellers are absent, you would be wise to have the bids opened by a third party, perhaps an officer of a nearby bank. Soon after the opening, you should tell all bidders about the results of the sale.

Although the bid-opening should be public, deliberations about the bids are usually private. Sellers might want a short time to think over a bid that is less than expected, or they may want to consult forestry or tax advisers about certain aspects of the sale. Occasionally, approval of all members of a joint ownership may be required. Nevertheless, bids are like marriage proposals; they usually expire if not accepted quickly. If there must be a delay in acting on the bids, you should tell the successful bidder what your problem is and ask for a reasonable time to solve it.

Some sellers attempt to use a sealed-bid sale merely to establish a floor from which to start an auction or negotiation after bids are opened. This practice infuriates buyers, and no one can blame them. It destroys the ability to make future sealed-bid sales and may destroy the sale at which it is attempted. If you do not like the bids, reject them all, and then do what you like. Everyone's customers deserve fair treatment.

## CLOSING THE SALE

After the best bid has been accepted, you should prepare the conveyance and submit it to the buyer for approval. By taking the initiative here, you can usually assure that the language in the conveyance is what you want; this is often much quicker and easier than trying to rework a fill-in-the-blanks form used by many buyers. You can not close the sale until the buyer approves the conveyance, but most buyers will go along with any reasonable form.

While this is going on, the buyer's lawyer will check your title. Although you do not intend to convey something you do not own, you may not know about some flaws in your title. Such an outside check, which is free, can help you find and cure them. This title work usually takes about three or four weeks.

You cannot get your money until the sale is closed, so there is not a minute to be wasted. Many things can happen to upset a sale: a tornado may rip up the timber; the buyer may die or go bankrupt; one member of a joint ownership may die. You can prevent closing delays by working with your lawyer before the sale to remove any obstacles.

## WHAT TO DO AND WHAT NOT TO DO

As I said in the beginning, timber is not scarce, so those who want good prices must act like good merchants in other fields: make it easy on the buyer. This means presenting the timber in a clear and concise manner that creates confidence in the inventory, and submitting a conveyance with a minimum of restrictions and words. JMV&CO's inventory methods demonstrate what to do (other consultants may do as well or better); U.S. Forest Service (USFS) inventory methods in one national forest demonstrate what *not* to do.

JMV&CO measures the DBH of *all* sawtimber trees with a steel tape, and this work on one typical, clearcut tract produced a stand table shown in Table 3.8, column 2. USFS makes an ocular estimate of DBH on all sawtimber trees, but measures only 10% or less of them, and this work on another typical, clearcut tract produced the other stand shown in Table 3.8, column 3. Looking at Table 3.8, we may compare them.

Although JMV&CO used 2-in. classes and USFS used 1-in. classes, one stand table is certain to destroy the confidence of all buyers. The

### TABLE 3-8
### Results of Inventory Methods Compared

| DBH Class | Number of Trees | |
| --- | --- | --- |
| | JMV & CO | USFS |
| 10 | 3020 | 930 |
| 11 | | 368 |
| 12 | 2446 | 1595 |
| 13 | | 649 |
| 14 | 1569 | 1457 |
| 15 | | 1099 |
| 16 | 969 | 1562 |
| 17 | | 715 |
| 18 | 437 | 732 |
| 19 | | 587 |
| 20 | 230 | 98 |
| 21 | | 97 |
| 22 | 66 | 78 |
| 23 | | 28 |
| 24 | 17 | 34 |
| 25 | | 24 |
| 26 + | 1 | 67 |

JMV&CO table (Table 3.8, column 2) is believable because the number of trees in each DBH class decreases steadily as DBH increases, a natural situation in most stands. Although the total volume estimate may actually be correct, the USFS table (Table 3.8, column 3) is not believable because, in many cases, the number of trees in even-numbered classes is larger than the number in odd-numbered classes on *both* sides. All buyers know that there are never more trees with even diameters than trees with odd diameters; therefore they know that something is peculiar about the USFS inventory and that they must check it at greater-than-normal cost in time and money.

Both agencies use a prospectus to solicit bids. JMV&CO's contains four pages; USFS's contains 18.

Since all JMV&CO sales are for private landowners, there is no standard form for conveyances, but most owners need only one, two, or three pages. The USFS conveyance has been standard across the South since 1971 and requires 69 pages. A comparison of provisions in conveyances of the two sample tracts is shown in Table 3.9.

The 69 pages of the USFS conveyance contains additional restrictions that may apply to tracts that differ from the sample. When any good merchandiser of timber reviews the last three paragraphs, he understands why USFS timber, which is usually larger and of better quality than private timber, does not bring premium prices and sometimes sells at a discount.

## INSPECTION OF THE LOGGING OPERATION

It is essential to inspect the logging operation until the last tree has been removed. All sale agreements should provide penalties for cutting trees not included in the sale, and these penalties must be strictly enforced. The reason is obvious in lump-sum sales of marked timber. You should also watch logging operations in pay-as-you-go sales where some of the timber to be cut is relatively inaccessible. Many loggers want to cut what is easy to get and leave the rest. Inspection is equally important in complete liquidations. It is expensive to harvest trees passed over in the main logging operation, and such scattered trees may impede development of the next crop. Most buyers are responsible, ethical business people who will not countenance any violation of a sale agreement, but they cannot supervise every movement of every woods employee or contractor. Loggers and their employees are often short of money, and even today some timber strays into the hands of unauthorized persons. Proper inspection of logging minimizes these problems.

TABLE 3-9
Comparison of Provisions in Conveyances

| Private Landowner | USFS |
|---|---|
| Payment in full at closing | 10% due at closing, remainder in advance of starting on each unit. |
| 24 months for logging | 28 months for logging |
| Double stumpage for cutting unmarked trees | Double stumpage for cutting unmarked trees |
| No requirement | Road-building required |
| No requirement | Maximum stump height specified |
| No requirement | Buyer to furnish crews for fire-fighting |
| No requirement | Performance bond necessary |
| No requirement | Buyer to submit operating plan for approval |
| No requirement | Buyer to confer with USFS representative before starting logging |
| No requirement | Four-page bid form specified |
| No requirement | Buyer must remove all merchantable wood |
| No requirement | Traffic-control plan for nearby roads to be submitted and approved |
| No requirement | No vehicles to enter and no trees to be felled into designated streamcourses |
| No requirement | Strict specifications for temporary roads |
| No requirement | Treatment of slash required |
| No requirement | Effective mufflers on trucks, tractors, powersaws |

## MISCELLANEOUS CONSIDERATIONS

Much timber sold today is marked for selective cutting, and you can get a good idea of the experience of the timber marker by looking at paint marks on the trees to be cut. There are always at least two marks, one at eye level and one below stump height. An experienced marker puts all marks facing the same direction, uses plenty of paint in a bold and unmistakable manner, and applies the bottom mark after scraping away the litter so that some paint sprays on the ground around the stump. Much of today's felling is done with hydraulic shears flush with the ground. If your marker applies little dribbles of paint first on one side and then another, or puts the bottom mark so high that it will not be there after the tree has been removed, the marker is an amateur who will scare buyers or cause you grief. An experienced marker often uses so much paint that a casual observer may think that the marker has cut the stand too heavily. Do not be alarmed if this optical illusion occurs on your tract; just be thankful that you selected a marker who knows what he is doing. The tendency is usually to mark too few trees.

A desirable sale contains trees with a larger average volume, and you should keep this in mind when selecting areas to be cut, method of cutting, and future objectives in your forest-management plan. It is quite common for 9-in. pulpwood trees to sell for 100% more per cord than 6-in. trees. The larger the average tree or stick, the smaller is the cost of logging, as every pulpwood producer and logging contractor well knows. Foresters are anxious to thin a stand as soon as possible to speed up or maintain the percentage growth rate, and inexperience leads some to attempt thinning too early. It is sometimes better to suffer some overcrowding temporarily in order to get an increased price per unit of volume. Timing of thinnings is a complex matter and requires an experienced adviser.

You may hear talk about managing stands on a pulpwood rotation or a sawlog rotation and wonder what this means to you. The answer is almost nothing. The decision about this is of primary importance only to a timber company growing raw material for a manufacturing plant. Your main objective is money, and you have to maintain flexibility to reach it. Insofar as possible, you must be able to change your forest-management plan quickly and often. It is not necessary, and may be a big mistake, to make fixed plans for 20 or more years into the future. Your task is to keep your productive acres busy growing something—reproduction, pulpwood, or sawtimber—and the only thing to fear is idle land.

It is difficult to sell timber by contracting with a logger to deliver logs to various markets. Determination of proper logging cost is a complex problem even for professionals. Logging depends greatly on weather, and what starts out to be a job requiring one month sometimes requires one year. Log-storage capacity at each mill is limited and varies with the season of the year; therefore, log production must be coordinated with mill production. Log specifications vary from mill to mill, and it is often hard to see subtle but significant differences between them. These considerations alone make a sale of this kind a management job of major proportions. In addition, the legal relationship between you and the logging contractor may not be clear; this can be dangerous if there are accidents involving people or property. You should not attempt such sales without expert advice.

## TIMBER-DAMAGE APPRAISAL

Related in many ways to the sale of timber is the destruction or damage of it. The party causing damage expects, and may be required, to pay for it, and determination of the proper dollar value is hard. Damaged timber is not often sold and may include such unsalable items as reproduction. If it is sold, the amount received is more likely to be its salvage value than its value under normal circumstances. In some cases, destruction is total, but it is often only partial. Forest fires kill some trees and reduce growth and resistance to decay of many others. Timber damage may be only part of the total damage to a tract; for instance, construction of a limited-access road will destroy trees on the right of way itself and may reduce the value of the remaining timber and land. Destructive agents such as salt water from oil wells may not only kill existing timber but also reduce or eliminate the productive capacity of the affected area for a variable period of time. Timber may be killed at a time when its owner would not consider selling, such as during temporary market dips or while trees are small and growing rapidy into products of high value.

In most such cases, these factors make it necessary to substitute an expert appraiser for the market itself. His job requires thorough knowledge of both forestry and finance, and he must be able to explain his procedure in convincing terms, since he will often testify before a jury whose members know little about timber operations. Damage claims in thousands of dollars are common, and they run into millions in large forest fires. If you are on either side of a damage claim, you should see your lawyer and, with his assistance, choose someone to appraise the damage. Although many feel competent to do this, most are not qualified by either training or experience, and few make good witnesses in a courtroom. Your lawyer probably has some experience with appraisers in this field and knows which ones can be qualified as expert witnesses. In many cases, such as rights of way of all kinds, you will be able to determine much of the damage before it occurs, and most appraisers prefer to inspect the trees standing on the area to be cleared rather than to estimate what has already been removed by sampling an adjacent area.

Money received for timber damage gets much the same treatment as income from sales, but you should consult your tax adviser about this.

## THE DANGER IN TREATING TIMBER LIKE A BANK ACCOUNT

Some landowners look upon their timber as a bank account that can be held indefinitely and will always be there whenever they need it.

They cite several reasons for doing this, but as their trees get older, such a policy becomes ever more dangerous.

One reason it does is biological, and a recent study showed why and revealed other interesting facts about how forests develop. All energy originates in radiation from the sun, but we cannot use most of this until it has been converted by photosynthesis in the cells of green plants. Your forest does a lot of this work.

Scientists studied the flow of energy in a New Hampshire forest and came up with this accounting of yearly radiation per square foot:

|  | Calories |
|---|---|
| Total received from the sun | 116,499 |
| Received outside growing season and not converted | −71,906 |
| Reflected back into atmosphere during growing season | −6,689 |
| Used to heat forest to permit growth | −18,358 |
| Used for evaporation of water | −18,580 |
| Total converted into plant form | 966 |
| Used by plant for their own maintenance | −531 |
| Deposited as litter on forest floor | −324 |
| Growth of roots | −23 |
| Total growth of trunks, limbs, twigs, etc. | 88 |

Since there had been no fire or logging for 55 years, this was an impressive forest. The scientists calculated that the stored energy per square foot was located as follows:

|  | Calories |
|---|---|
| Living trunks, limbs, twigs, etc. | 5,546 |
| Living roots | 1,089 |
| Litter on forest floor | 3,189 |
| Organic matter in top 14 in. of soil | 8,187 |
| Total stored energy per square foot | 18,011 |

You cannot use your store of this energy until you cut the parts of living trees suitable for logs or pulpwood. Although the scientists did not calculate the volume of such material, I guess it to be about two thirds of the visible forest. Therefore, even if you clearcut your forest, remove all sound sticks of wood as big as your arm, you will remove only 20% of its stored energy. And replacement will begin the following spring.

The forest on the study area was old. Growth was slow. Total calories added per square foot each year were less than the total in an ordinary soft drink. Total living material in it was increasing in volume only 1.7% each year. Even this small addition will gradually decrease until it just equals mortality and the forest is biologically mature.

Sometime between the start of a forest and its biological maturity, annual energy storage reaches a peak in volume and percentage. My guess is that this occurs when the forest is 40 to 50 years old. If I am correct, you can utilize this energy source most efficiently by selling your timber before it gets much older than this. If you treat it as a bank account for longer periods, your earnings from timber growth will become zero.

On 13 September 1979 Hurricane Frederic demonstrated the other reason why you cannot treat timber as a bank account. In a few hours it did severe damage to many timber stands in a strip 40 miles wide running from Mobile, Alabama, 50 miles to the northwest. Some trees were shattered by hundreds of small tornadoes around the eye; others were broken off; most were blown over and attacked by insects and fungi. I estimate that many stands suffered a 50% drop in value.

The hurricane temporarily glutted markets in the area. Although mill operators worked day and night on the salvage job, there were too few loggers to handle such huge volumes of timber, and storage space at each mill was limited to that needed for normal operations. Timber owners who did not move quickly were not able to arrange any salvage. The glut ended the following spring because all down timber not salvaged became worthless.

Owners of small, well-spaced, fast-growing trees were small losers. Their trees suffered little damage from the winds, and even when damage did occur, they could look back on annual growth rates of 10% or more that had made it worthwhile to run some risk. Owners of big, crowded, slow-growing trees were big losers. Their trees suffered great wind damage, and their past growth rates of 4% to 6% were very small in proportion to the risks they had run. My firm had about $1,000,000 of timber on the market in the area, and the bid date of the sale was September 15; of course, we got no bids and eventually salvaged only about $300,000.

# 4
# Miscellaneous Income

Although managing a timberland investment is often called *forest management*, the term does not include the whole task. Trees are surely the primary product of the factory, and most income arises from their sale. But the task before the investor is better described as applying brains and money to natural resources, and its major attraction is that it offers him many ways to make a profit. The average tract is a grab bag of several natural resources, and many owners were experts in *multiple use* before foresters discovered the term. Income from sources besides trees is always important and sometimes may provide spectacular profits. We will consider some possibilities and the problems they present.

## RIGHTS OF WAY

Rights of way (ROWs) now occupy millions of acres of our land. A casual glance at an aerial photograph of many sections reveals a striking pattern of strips occupied by roads, pipelines, powerlines, highways, and railroads. Nearly every owner has had some contact with ROWs or soon will have. Our expanding population requires goods and services in enormous quantities, and many of these move to market over ROWs of one kind or another.

Sale of ROWs is one of the plus factors that cannot be measured (see Chapter 8), and you need the profit offered by sales of this kind. This old ROW buyer's jingle suggests how big it can be:

> I thought that I would never see
> A twenty-thousand-dollar tree,
> But I saw one just the other day,
> Standing on a right of way.

The price per acre is often three or four times the market price of the land through which the ROW passes. This makes the sale attractive, but there are good reasons for the premium price. Although each ROW agreement must be investigated thoroughly with your lawyer, there are several considerations that apply to all agreements.

First, ROWs often damage parts of the property outside the ROW itself. For example, they may obstruct free travel from one side to the other. Second, they increase administrative costs. It takes time to study and negotiate proposed ROW sales, and you are often left with an annual ad valorem tax burden on land you cannot use. Third, they may limit future chances for profit. A large pipeline ROW through your land may greatly restrict its development for residential or industrial subdivisions. Fourth, certain phrases in the usual agreements may cloud the title to other parts of the property. Fifth, the usual agreement often contains conveyances of certain rights you may want to keep for future trading. Although some ROWs may increase the value of your tract, any ROW may have far-reaching effects, and proposed sales should be carefully studied. Let us look at factors that vary with the purpose for which the ROW is used.

**Pipelines.**    Construction of pipelines usually involves burying the pipe and, consequently, disturbing the soil and its cover. In hilly country, subsequent erosion is possible. Gullies are obvious dangers, and trees adjacent to the ROW may be killed by heavy deposits of silt on them. The pipeline company has an interest in preventing erosion, since it may expose the pipe, and the company's self-interest may protect you from this hazard, but it is far better to provide for erosion control in the ROW agreement.

Usual agreements prepared by companies grant them rights to construct additional pipelines on the property either on the present ROW, approximately parallel to it, or in unspecified places. Many owners assume that additional lines will be laid on the existing ROW and as close to the original line as possible. Under certain agreements, however, the company may have the right to construct a second line at right angles to the first. The agreement may also grant the company rights of access across all land described therein. Such agreements may limit future development of the entire tract, and you should avoid them. These rights cannot be acquired by eminent-domain suits, and you should save them for future trading.

Buyers usually offer a certain amount for the ROW plus an additional amount for damages done to the surface, such as destruction of timber. Total consideration is the important thing. You can usually settle damages either in advance or after construction is completed; the better alternative depends on the situation, but you should remember two things. First, settlement of damages after construction delays payment, opens the door for interminable haggling, and may necessitate a lawsuit to determine the amount of damages. Second, settlement of damages in advance requires that you sign a release. Be sure that it covers only damage on the ROW itself, for additional damage may be done to adjoining portions of the property.

After much trading, you may find that the company will settle for a permanent ROW of narrow width for the pipeline itself plus use of an adjacent strip for the period of construction, which will revert to you afterward. You can often make this trade without reducing the amount of money you receive. This depends mainly on your trading ability; the company can probably acquire by eminent domain a permanent easement over the entire width.

**Powerlines.** The most important characteristics of powerline ROWs is the provision allowing the company to cut danger trees. Ordinarily, a danger tree is one standing outside the ROW that would hit, or come within 5 feet of hitting, a structure or conductor if it fell directly toward it. Such a provision is essential for the company; your only concern is to see that the agreement requires payment for these trees. They will be cut as long as the powerline is used, and it will be almost impossible to salvage them. Some old agreements may not contain this danger tree provision.

**Roads and Highways.** Generally, construction of a new road through any tract adds value to it by improving access and increasing development possibilities. Obviously, this is not true of the limited-access road. Such roads cannot be crossed except at designated points, and their construction may eliminate access to certain portions of your property. In addition to studying the agreement, you should thoroughly inspect the proposed ROW on the ground. Minor logging barriers such as streams may become major ones after the road is constructed.

Highway departments and private companies have one thing in common: both try to acquire by agreement rights that they cannot acquire by eminent-domain suits. Highway departments are particularly anxious to obtain access over other parts of the tract in order to reduce construction costs. It is a good idea to treat highway departments and private companies equally and never convey anything that cannot be taken from you unless the grantee pays for it.

Many existing highway ROWs contain substantial amounts of merchantable timber, and ownership of this is often of interest to you when you harvest yours. Your lawyer can determine this ownership. When the timber is on the ROW, the highway department probably controls its disposition, but may have to give you the proceeds from its sale.

**Logging Roads.** Requests for logging ROWs are common and generally granted without charge. Many parcels do not touch a public road, and giving logging ROWs to your landlocked neighbors may pay handsome dividends in goodwill. Someday you may want a logging ROW yourself. Such ROWs should be written and have a definite time limit. If properly prepared, they can be recorded and thereby eliminate easements by adverse possession. Details of this subject are too technical for this book; you should discuss them with your lawyer.

**Trading Pointers.** The time to settle difficulties involved in ROWs is before you sign the agreement, not after. Pressure is on the buyer, and you should keep it there until all details are settled satisfactorily. In particular, you should avoid provisions that permit future operations on your property with only damages to be negotiated. You should insist that anyone desiring to enter your property negotiate with you each time entry is desired.

Occasionally, ROWs are used and later abandoned; in rare cases, ROWs are obtained and never used. Agreements should provide for reversion to you after use is discontinued or unless construction or use begins by a specified date.

In many printed forms used for agreements, location of the ROW is described only in general terms, and indefinite language often leads to trouble by casting a cloud on the title to all land described in the instrument. The ROW should be surveyed and marked with stakes, and the agreement should contain an exact legal description of its location.

The ROW to be cleared often contains merchantable timber, and what to do with it is a subject of negotiation. As a general rule, it is wise to sell it to the ROW buyer and let him worry about it. Difficulties of salvaging any money from it are many. The time allowed for salvage is limited, the total volume is relatively small, and the area on which it is located is a long narrow strip to which all salvage operations must be confined. These factors reduce prices substantially.

Some ROWs are easements only, and some are conveyances of land. If the ROW is an actual transfer of title, it can probably be removed from your ad valorem tax assessment. If it is an easement, you should leave it on your assessment, since you still own the land and the ROW may revert to you in later years. You have some grounds for a reduction in assessment in such cases, but tax assessors are hard to convince. The best solution is to see that the consideration for the ROW includes an amount on which interest will be sufficient to pay ad valorem taxes forever. Only your lawyer is qualified to explain differences between easements and transfers of title.

Eminent-domain suits take time and cost money for all parties, and most agencies prefer to avoid them if possible. This fact may enhance your trading position. Because ROW buyers are professional traders, it would be most unusual if their initial offer were their best. Since buyers know that the law will always require them to pay the fair market price, an offer once made will seldom be withdrawn or reduced. The time element involved or a desire to save expense of litigation will sometimes make the buyer more eager. Therefore, take plenty of time to study the agreement; you may be repaid in more ways than one. Under certain circumstances, it may be advisable for you to defend an eminent-domain suit, but this decision requires expert legal advice.

These considerations add emphasis to the discussion of title work in Chapter 10. You can control your position on ROWs that come up after you acquire the tract, but you must investigate the provisions of ROWs existing at the time of acquisition. Previous owners may have signed away many rights that you want to keep. Do not forget that, as long as it is used, the ROW cannot be used for growing trees.


## LEASES OF CULTIVABLE LAND

Presence of cultivable land including pastures offers chances for immediate, substantial cash income, and such possibilities should be carefully analyzed. Some cropland produces an annual cash rental three or more times the value of timber that can be grown on it; this money is available now and not 30 years from now. Your first task is to find out how much rent the cropland will produce.

The best way is to ask for bids from capable farmers of recognized financial ability. Chances are that they are already familiar with the productivity of your fields, and that they are experts in making use of information available from the Soil Conservation Service. They are usually willing to bid on leasing your fields, since the cost of bidding is small. You can solicit bids by means of a letter stating what you want. The local bank can give you names and addresses of farmers who might be interested. If you get several bids on your land, you probably do not need further information about prices. If you receive only one bid, you might check the price with the local county agent. Remember, however, that the best appraisal of value is usually a firm, written offer of money, not an opinion of a third party.

Once you have an offer in hand, you should compare it with the income that might be obtained from planting the land in trees. A consulting forester with some knowledge of soil capabilities can help you here. He knows how much it will cost to establish the plantation, how much volume it will produce in a given period of time, how much this volume is likely to be worth when it is ready to harvest, and what annual taxes are now and what changes might be made in them after planting; he is an expert in using compound interest to bring all these costs and values to the same time for comparison. Although this procedure may seem complicated and expensive, it is not. Annual cash incomes are generally very effective in raising the value of a property since the money comes now, not later; therefore, you will usually decide to lease whatever cultivable land you have.

Then you should ask your lawyer to draw up or review the lease, since it is an important contract and may have a longer term than most. As always, all details should be covered in writing so that there will be few arguments later. The lawyer may be familiar with provisions that vary with the kind of crop involved, but it is a good idea to compare notes with other lessors in your situation. Your bank can help you locate other lessors also. Some leases should be for nothing less than cash in advance; others may call for some cash now and more after harvest; still others may be based on a share arrangement. Customary practices in the area usually establish a broad framework, and the experience of others will help you decide on the best plan.

Many small tracts were farms at one time, and the owner (usually an ancestor of the present owner) raised crops or livestock on 25% to 30% of the total area. Such properties may generate no interest among today's farmers. They are no longer farmed because it has long since been uneconomical to do so, and this trend is not likely to be reversed. Since converting land from forests to crops is obviously costly, the present owner thinks that cultivable land is more valuable and will be worth more in the event of a sale, so he often agrees to agricultural leases at nominal rates merely to keep the land open. This is usually a mistake. The sooner the land is put into trees, the sooner it will become more valuable, whereas the nominal lease merely postpones profit.


## RECREATION LEASES

Hunting and fishing leases often provide rentals that are small, about equal to annual ad valorem taxes, but timberland investment is a penny-pinching business and no annual cash income is unimportant. In addition to paying rentals, lessees of this kind often help prevent forest fires, trash-dumping, and trespass, since these things are contrary to their interests also. As a general rule, good hunting and fishing are by-products of timberland operation, and neither the game nor the lessees interfere with the main business.

You should consult your lawyer about these leases also; they usually run for several or many years and may make it difficult to sell the land at some later date. You may also encounter a change in your public liability risk. The lessee is often a club or association with many members, and a well-drawn lease will prevent many future arguments.

Our population is expanding rapidly, and demand for such leases seems to increase even more rapidly. There are more people with more spare time and more money to spend on leisure; you should at least give some thought to providing a service they will pay for. Lakes for fishing and duck-hunting and ranges for hunting doves and quail are obvious possibilities on small tracts. Long-term, low-interest loans for some recreational purposes are available through the Area Redevelopment Administration and other federal agencies; you can get necessary information from the local agency office. Such development may cause some loss of timber income; your consulting forester can help you analyze this.

Other opportunities are limited only by the landowner's imagination, but developments of this sort are often highly specialized businesses requiring active participation of the owner. The call of the wild is still strong today, and none can predict where it will lead. The only sure thing is that recreation in forests will expand, and alert managers should capitalize on these chances for profit.

## GRAZING LEASES

Domestic animals have grazed the woods since early times, and although research has demonstrated the superiority of improved pastures, many stockmen allow their animals to run on timbered land, at least during some seasons. This practice can be profitable for both cattlemen and timberland owners. The first grazing leases probably came about more to cure adverse possession than to produce revenue, but the shrinking land area available for grazing has made revenue more of a factor. In many cases, rental from grazing leases is enough to pay annual ad valorem taxes.

Grazing is also beneficial because it reduces fire hazard. Hungry animals eat grass and shrubs that would otherwise serve as fuel. They may also eat young trees or trample them, but this can be prevented by proper management. Your consulting forester can help you determine how many animals your land will support without damage to timber.

The rental is ordinary income, but it is payable annually in cash and may be the only source of income during early life of the stand. Although necessary fences restrict free movement of loggers and firefighters, logging operations are infrequent, fences keep down trespass, and lessees can be persuaded or required to help fight or prevent fires. Demand for grazing leases is not large at present. I think that advantages so far outweigh disadvantages that you should keep alert for the chance to negotiate them. As usual, leases should be prepared or reviewed by your lawyer.

## MINERALS ON OR NEAR THE SURFACE

Chapter 5 covers minerals, but does not include substances not considered minerals in the legal sense. By this I mean sand, gravel, dirt, bauxite, limestone, or any other substance found near the surface and extracted by open-pit mining, which causes severe surface damage. Deposits of this kind may produce large profits for you. Locating them is the major task. The top of such a deposit may be visible, or its presence may cause enough difference in appearance of the timber so that it will be discovered in timber inventory or operations. General information about minerals of your state is available from the state geological department. Specific information about your property must be obtained by drilling for sample cores, which requires expert guidance from a geologist.

Commercial value of such a deposit depends upon many things. First, how much soil must be removed to get at it? Second, how far is it from the point of use? Third, what are the quality and extent of the deposit? These are complicated problems beyond the scope of this book, but some general principles are worth mention.

Importance of a location changes. For example, construction of a new road near you may make a gravel deposit suddenly valuable because distance to the point of use is reduced. The gravel may be used on the new road itself, or it may allow a shorter haul to other places. In addition, deposits nearer the market than yours may be gradually exhausted, which would enhance the value of yours.

As a general rule, material of this kind is paid for per unit as it is removed, since it is hard to determine size of a deposit before operations begin. This makes the character of the mineral operator important. The average landowner does not have time to be present constantly to check how much is removed. Other owners nearby usually have had some experience with the operators and will share it with you.

A written agreement between you and the operator is a must, and your lawyer should prepare or review it. He may be necessary also to determine whether you actually own the material, since definition of minerals is tricky business. Your tax adviser can tell you about tax treatment of this income. Percentage depletion usually applies to these minerals, and the percentage varies with kind of material. Your consulting forester can advise you about the effect of such operations upon the surface. They will prohibit tree-growing during actual mining and may cause a permanent reduction in, or elimination of, the productive capacity of the mined area. Some rehabilitation may be feasible after deposits are exhausted, and the contract covering operations should provide for this if possible.


## OTHER SPECIAL SITUATIONS

Stumps and fragments from virgin-timber trees on some lands are impregnated with resin and are desirable because steam distillation can recover chemicals they contain. Their presence can be easily detected in a timber inventory. Sale of such stumps provides extra income and causes more bare ground to be exposed, thereby assisting in establishing a new crop of trees. They are sold by the ton or in a lump-sum sale; the first method is usually preferable, because most of a stump is underground and its weight is hard to estimate. Their commercial value depends upon their size, weight per acre, and accessibility. Any consulting forester can tell you the going price for them and give you information about the character and operating methods of buyers in your area. Although stump removal seems likely to cause damage to standing trees, you will be surprised at how little is done by experienced buyers.

Certain species of trees supply valuable products from sap extracted by scraping away the bark or boring into the tree; income from this source may fit into your program. Sweetgums produce storax, maples produce sugar, and certain pines produce resin. Rights to work trees for these products are usually leased to specialists. Payment is according to number of trees worked, depending on their size. Leases vary in length, but commonly run three years. These cash incomes are always important, but there are disadvantages. The lease prohibits any other disposal of timber during its term. The lessee's operations usually reduce the incidence of wildfires, but injury to the tree as part of the production process may increase mortality and damage if a fire occurs, and decrease growth and market value of the tree when it is finally harvested. Metal objects are often driven into the tree in this work, and operators sometimes leave a few there, thereby decreasing the tree's value for such a product as sawtimber. You should discuss these factors at length with an experienced forester before leasing your timber for these purposes.

Many landowners are tempted to grow Christmas trees. The trees are beautiful and have a wonderful smell; they give great joy to buyers and their children; and they may be highly profitable. Few businesses have such desirable characteristics. Nevertheless, this is a tough business for the average owner unless he sells trees to an experienced dealer. Selling trees to individuals or retail stores is a specialized art. Buyers will bid against each other for your ordinary timber, but you must use persuasion and salesmanship to sell Christmas trees. Growing a tree that will sell well usually requires pruning and cultivation, for few trees are naturally well-shaped and full enough. Deliveries to market must be precisely timed. Dried-out trees are undesirable, and no one wants a Christmas tree on December 26. If you plan to produce more trees than are needed to supply your family and friends, you should discuss the project with someone who is or has been active in the business.

# 5
# Minerals

Minerals are important to all timberland owners, whether they own those under their land or the minerals have been reserved entirely or in part by previous owners. Minerals may be extremely valuable or nearly worthless, and their values can change almost overnight. In recent years, the political structure of much of the world has undergone radical change. Because of the threat of nationalization, oppressive taxation, or political instability, mineral development in many overseas countries is no longer attractive; consequently, exploitation of lower-grade deposits in our own country is increasing. You must do all you can to enhance their value, provided these actions do not cause an equal amount of damage to other parts of the property. Huge industries are based on minerals alone, and the subject is broad and complex. Here I can only discuss some reasons why minerals are important to you and point the way to further information. First, we need to know what we are talking about.

## DEFINITION OF MINERALS

One dictionary defines a mineral as"a solid, homogeneous, crystalline, chemical element or compound that results from the inorganic processes of nature," and we generally think of minerals as materials of which rocks of the earth's crust are made. Some believe that a mineral is anything that is neither animal nor vegetable. For your purposes, the important consideration is what the law determines a mineral to be, and this is a real wilderness. In one important case, the court's opinion stated,

"Mineral" is a word of general language, and not per se a term of art or trade. It is not a definite term, and is used in so many senses, dependent on the context, that the ordinary definitions of the dictionaries throw but little light on its signification in a given case, and therefore it is not capable of a definition of universal application, but is susceptible of limitation or expansion according to the intention with which it is used in the particular instrument or statute.

The question of defining minerals has been before courts for years and probably will continue to be decided for many more years. When minerals are sold or leased, the seller, or grantor, usually knows what he is conveying, or thinks he does, but the buyer, or grantee, may not have the same idea. These differences, often caused by careless wording or new mineralogical developments, may not be presented to the court for solution until many years later, when it is almost impossible to determine exactly what was intended. This causes trouble. Water, sand, and gravel are considered minerals by some authorities, and they would be so classified under definitions in some dictionaries. Nevertheless, many courts have decided that these are not included under the term *minerals,* and most landowners do not consider them such. Other true minerals such as bauxite and limestone do not come under the legal meaning of minerals under certain conditions. This is often the case with minerals whose removal not only deprives the surface owner of the use of the land, but also destroys the surface. Other substances, formed by organic processes and thus excluded by the dictionary definition, are considered minerals by the courts. This is true of oil, gas, and coal, substances of primary importance to many landowners.

Other major difficulties are that the definition varies from state to state and even from county to county, and that courts have decided the same question in different ways at different times. This complicated situation surrounding items of great actual or potential value is a strong argument for consulting an expert lawyer when you plan to buy a tract with a mineral reservation or plan to reserve minerals in a sale. Exact wording of the reservation may not become vital until years later, when it is impossible to change it. Your position depends to a great extent on what fraction of the minerals you own; the simplest situation exists when you own them all.

## FULL MINERAL OWNERSHIP

Theoretically, if you want to exploit the minerals yourself, all you have to do is dig a hole or drill a well to get at them, bring them to the surface, and sell them. This is seldom feasible because of the technical difficulties and capital requirements involved; you will probably sell the right to exploit them under certain terms and conditions to specialists in the business. This is a whole new world, and you must understand some of its language.

**Common Mineral Terms.** The most common way to keep an interest in minerals and yet have them developed is to enter into a *mineral lease.* This is a written contract by which the mineral owner, or lessor, allows the developer, or lessee, to explore for and extract specified minerals from certain lands for a limited period of time and for certain considerations. It is often a lengthy printed form with blank spaces for the proper insertions; and you should read all of the lease carefully in spite of its length.

One blank space is for the legal desription of the land, and it is often followed by the "Mother Hubbard" clause. This clause provides that the lease covers all land owned or claimed by lessor that is adjacent to, although not included within the boundaries of, the land described in the lease. It is normally inserted to take care of those small areas around the boundaries that the lessor may own by adverse possession only. The clause can have serious consequences, and you should consult your lawyer about its meaning to you.

The period of time may be of any length, but is commonly five to ten years, and is known as the primary term. Moreover, in the paragraph about the term, there is usually a provision extending the lease for as long after the primary term as minerals in commercial quantities are produced. In other words, the lessee has so many years to search for minerals and, if successful, may extract them as long as the operation is profitable. Many landowners want immediate development of minerals on the assumption that production will make them more money than lease rentals, and this is generally the case. On the other hand, if exploration reveals that minerals in commercial quantities are absent, the lessee immediately drops the lease, and rental income stops. Large sums have been paid to lessors in bonuses and rentals on minerals whose value has never been determined, and such payments may be sizable in your case. For reasons discussed below, a short-term lease is better than a long-term one.

Consideration may take several forms. First is the *bonus,* a sum paid by the lessee to induce the lessor to sign the lease in the first place, and it usually gives the lessee the right to conduct development operations for a certain period, often one year. The amount of the bonus is important, for it may be all that the lessor ever gets. Upon receiving the lease, the lessee must begin operations within the specified period, and the lease is automatically terminated if he does not. The lessee can buy the privilege of delaying operations for 12 months by paying the lessor in advance another form of consideration, commonly called rental or delay rental. The lessee can repeat this process each year during the primary term of the lease. Failure either to begin operations or to pay rentals terminates the lease. Therefore, leases are one-way streets; the lessee binds the lessor for the term of the lease by paying rental, but can cancel the lease merely by failing to pay the rental. You should not count on the rental until it actually arrives. Many lessees send a release to the lessor whenever a lease is terminated, and you should make sure that this procedure is followed. The lease is usually recorded in public records and is an encumbrance on the land until a release is recorded. Bonus and rental payments are usually expressed as a certain amount per acre of minerals; when you own a full mineral interest, the number of mineral acres and surface area acres are equal.

The amount of the bonus is generally far more important than the amount of the rental. The bonus, paid when the lease is signed, is a sure thing; the rental, paid later if the lessee wants to continue the lease, is an unsure thing. In areas of interest, the bonus tends to be a much larger sum than the rental. In addition, most mineral operations are speculative ventures, and new data obtained on an area may change opinions of lessees rapidly. Leases on the same property have sometimes been bought and dropped several times within a five-year period. The good trader puts himself in position to negotiate for bonuses as often as he can.

Consideration will take a third form if everything goes well and production of minerals begins. This is known as royalty and is the portion of production that remains the property of the lessor and may be stated as a fraction of production or as a certain price per unit. Although the lessor may receive his payment in kind, settlement is usually monetary. Royalty means the right to receive a share of the minerals produced, free of all cost and risk, whether the operator makes money in their production or not, so it is usually a small fraction. Amount of the royalty is negotiated by the lessor and lessee and is set forth in the lease. As development of certain minerals proceeds, the royalty fraction often becomes the same in all leases over a wide area; for example, most oil and gas leases provide three-sixteenths royalty. Local inquiry will reveal what these usual fractions are, and customary practice is usually based on the distilled experience of years of such operations. Once production begins, royalty payments usually keep the lease in force after the primary term expires, and this explains why releases must be recorded. A title lawyer looks only at the public records and has no way of knowing whether there was or is any production under the lease. After production begins, royalty payments are slightly delayed to allow time to prepare a division order, an agreement prepared by the operator stating the ownership of each interested party. As soon as the order is signed by everyone, checks come regularly as long as minerals are produced.

The foregoing discussion of bonus, rental, and royalty applies primarily to oil and gas leases. There are slight differences in the case of "hard" minerals like coal. The bonus is paid for the exploration period; it is based on the area involved and is to compensate you for damages that might arise from prospecting and for the inconvenience of having your land tied up. The usual exploration period is one year. If the lessee then exercises his option to lease, there are annual payments in the form of advance-production royalties, which are deducted from future royalties. Royalties are paid on the basis of a percentage of the price of the product or so much for each ton or cubic yard extracted.

Royalties for different minerals vary widely, and you should investigate the prevailing prices paid in the nearest area where a particular mineral is being mined. Royalties of most common minerals range upward from $0.50 per cubic yard. One acre of a deposit 1 ft thick contains 1613 cubic yards, so with a 10-ft deposit and a royalty of $0.50 per cubic yard, you would receive $8065 for each acre mined.

Your lease should require that you be notified well before mining operations begin. Such notice should give you time to sell the timber on the area without great sacrifice; six months is enough, one year is better.

**Surface Damages Due to Operations Under the Lease.** The process of searching for and extracting minerals causes some damage to the surface and, usually, removal or destruction of the timber on it. By-products of the production process may have the same effect. For example, oil wells often yield salt water along with oil, and salt water usually kills trees if it is allowed to flow on the land. Although lessees try hard to dispose of harmful by-products, they are not always successful. Actual wording of the lease governs the payment to be made for this damage. Most lessees feel, and the printed form provides, that the consideration under the lease is sufficient to cover all damages caused in a normal operation. Lessees do not believe that they should be required to pay additional sums except in the case of extraordinary or unnecessary damage. Nevertheless, to avoid nuisance lawsuits and to build goodwill among surface owners, many lessees customarily pay reasonable damages for the disturbance caused by their operations. When damage occurs, you may have an argument, or even a lawsuit, over whether it was part of normal operations or due to negligence. The best way to eliminate uncertainty is to write into the lease a provision requiring the lessee to pay for *all* damage done to the surface.

**Exploration Permits.**  A lease normally permits all activities necessary to explore for minerals, and the lease should provide for payment of damages caused by exploring. You might be asked for an exploration permit, usually to conduct seismic or coring operations, even though your minerals are not leased. This would bring other factors into play. Exploration may reveal mineral possibilties that will cause a flurry of leasing activity and development, or it may show such negative results that all interest is killed. Only a mineral expert is qualified to advise you on the probable results of exploration, but many landowners think that fees should be charged for such operations. The fee may be a flat rate per acre, or it may be based on the amount of damage caused to the surface plus the cost of appraising it. In rare cases, owners may offer exploration permits in exchange for data gathered by the exploration party, but since most lessees will not make this trade and since the data may be meaningless to a layman, payment in money is usually preferable.

**Customary Buying Practices.**  The possibility of acquiring quick riches from minerals brings a swarm of buyers to areas of interest. They are usually self-employed; some are outright speculators; many represent major companies or substantial independents. All are aggressive, hard-working persons who want to buy leases, minerals, royalty, or any other mineral interest available. The pressure is on, and there is no time to find out whether the seller owns what he is selling. Most buyers are familiar with title work but are not expert at it. Therefore, they pay for what they buy with drafts of a ten-day-or-longer time limit. This period allows lawyers working with them to examine titles; if the titles prove faulty, buyers do not honor their drafts. Occasionally, a buyer will use this practice when he thinks he knows where he can sell a lease but has no specific order for it. He will pay for the lease with a draft and try to sell it before the draft must be honored. Drafts not honored always make people angry, and reputable buyers do everything possible to avoid this practice.

Drafts are for the buyer's convenience, not the seller's, and you can avoid difficulty here by insisting on payment in cash. You may discourage some buyers, but a serious one will usually agree to this plan. Insistence on cash is especially important at times of intense interest, such as when a well is being drilled and is near the zone of expected production. Mineral values may fluctuate by hundreds or thousands of dollars per acre in several hours; by accepting a draft, you have given a free option on your minerals without any assurance that it will be exercised.

The decision about cash or draft depends to a great extent upon activity in the area and the buyers involved, and either method may be quite satisfactory. If you accept a draft, however, you should present it to your bank with the lease attached to it. If buyer honors the draft, his bank will give him the lease when it sends you the money. If you give the lease directly to buyer, he may record it, sell it to an innocent third party, and also fail to honor the draft. Your minerals may then be under lease, and you may have great difficulty recovering money from the original buyer. This is an unlikely occurrence, but it can be precluded altogether by keeping the two documents attached until the draft is honored.

## PARTIAL OR NO MINERAL OWNERSHIP

Mineral ownership can be separated from ownership of the surface, and the situation can be further complicated by separation of minerals and royalty. Separation may be permanent or temporary and may be the result of state mineral laws or agreement between parties. It is accomplished by what are commonly called reservations.

**Provisions of the Reservation.**   The foregoing section shows how important the language of the reservation is and how much you need a good lawyer to study and explain it. You must have the answers to many questions.

What minerals are reserved? Were they reserved in general terms or was the previous owner an expert mineral operator who used a detailed and all-inclusive reservation? The reservation may be quite specific so far as oil and gas are concerned, but may make no actual or implied mention of other minerals. In unusual cases, wording of the reservation may cover sand, gravel, and other surface deposits.

What fraction has been reserved? It is common for each successive owner of a property to reserve part of the minerals, and some persons are not as careful or as good at arithmetic as you are. For example, A sells to B and reserves half the minerals; B sells to C, reserving half of what he owns; C sells to D, reserving half of what he owns; D, thinking that he owns one-quarter, sells to E and reserves one-eighth, thereby separating the last fraction, so E gets nothing. Proper choice of words in mineral reservations is a technical legal problem, and any of these four may not have reserved what he intended to reserve. Was the full mineral interest reserved or perhaps only the royalty?

What is the length of the reservation? Is it permanent? Some state laws prohibit permanent reservations under certain conditions, and the variety of limited reservations that can be made is endless. Many properties were owned at one time by the Federal Land Bank, and it is common to find reservation of half the minerals for 25 years by the Land Bank.

What access rights, implied or specified, accompany the reserved minerals? As a general rule, the law allows some access to reserved minerals even though the reserving words do not mention access specifically; you need to explore this facet. The owner of reserved minerals may be able to lease them under such conditions that the lessee will be required to pay only for unusual or unnecessary damage done in operations.

These questions point out the value of even a small fraction of minerals to the surface owner. A lessee must lease all minerals under a tract to develop it, since the owner of an unleased fraction may be entitled to his pro rata share of minerals extracted without paying the costs of extraction. Ownership of any portion of the minerals enables a surface owner to make sure that mineral leases require the lessee to pay for all damage to the surface and, therefore, to protect the owner's trees. In addition, ownership of minerals may have a great effect on future land values, since few investors are willing to build houses, service stations, or factories on land where they have little control over mineral operations.

We have discussed this as if the owner sold the surface and reserved the minerals. Of course, while retaining the surface, he can convey the minerals. All of the above applies in either situation.

**Exploration Permits.** Mineral exploration is usually performed for major companies by specialists who do the work on a contractual or other basis. These specialists have an assigned work area and often contact surface owners there by telephone to ask permission to enter their lands for exploration. As a general rule, they have no knowledge of mineral ownership in the area, including whether the minerals are leased by their client. If the surface owner allows them to enter, all is well; they are then concerned only with claims for any damages they might cause.

Your trading position determines what response you should make to such a request, and it depends on the language of the mineral reservation. Under certain circumstances, you may have no trading position at all, and it is wise to investigate this with your lawyer. If you can not do this, you can quote a reasonable fee to the next person requesting entry and see what happens. He might agree to pay it, since his operations may cause some damage for which he is liable, and his agreement solves your problem.

## TRADING IN LEASED MINERALS

When buying minerals under lease, you must know the terms of the lease, since the lessee has prior rights, and a title opinion usually gives this information. You also want to receive your pro rata share of rentals. Most leases provide that no change in mineral ownership shall be binding on the lessee until 30 days after he has been furnished by registered mail at his principal place of business with a certified copy of the recorded instrument as evidence of the change. Title examination may reveal the proper address, or you might be able to get it from the lessee's local office.

The lessee usually sends lease rentals to a bank designated by the lessor. The lessee needs proof that the money is received; the lessor may move or die or be careless about endorsing checks or signing receipts. Using a bank to receive these payments is a satisfactory solution. You must notify the bank to send the money to you. Rentals are usually paid annually in advance, and you may be entitled to a pro rata share of the rental for the year in which you buy the minerals. This is something you must work out with the seller; since you are buying the minerals subject to the lease, the lessee cannot help you.

## AD VALOREM TAX ON MINERALS

When minerals are owned by the surface owner, they are ordinarily assessed separately for ad valorem tax purposes, but this situation can change when they are separated. Treatment by taxing authorities varies from county to county, and you should investigate this. Many states allow owners of separated minerals, at the time of separation, to buy documentary stamps in lieu of all future ad valorem taxes. They are usually sold in the county where the minerals are located and must be affixed to the deed. In theory at least, failure to buy and affix stamps means that minerals will be sold for taxes along with the surface if taxes on the surface are not paid. Tax sales require public notice, but notice is given in the county where the minerals are located, and an absentee owner may be unaware of an impending sale if he does not subscribe to the local paper. I have also found instances in which the minerals were still on the tax rolls because of a clerical error in the tax assessor's office even though stamps were bought and affixed. County officials are conscientious persons, but they sometimes make mistakes, and looking after your business is your responsibility. Ad valorem taxes paid by mistake are seldom refunded.

## MINERALS AND ADVERSE POSSESSION

We have seen that separated minerals still have some effect on the surface, and the reverse is also true. Minerals can be acquired by adverse possession under unusual circumstances. Suppose that adverse possession begins on a parcel in 1930 before the minerals are separated. The record owner sells the minerals 10 years later and sells the surface 20 years later. Eventually, the adverse claimant makes his claim effective and acquires the surface. Chances are he acquires the minerals too, since his claim dates from a time the minerals and surface were together. This is one more good argument for using a good lawyer and for diligent management of timberland. I have said elsewhere that adverse possession is a difficult and sneaky problem; now you can see that it may affect areas not normally considered to be in danger.

## WHO CAN HELP YOU WITH MINERALS?

One obvious answer to this question is, "A geologist." He specializes in minerals, and the field is so large that specialization is essential. Most principles used in selecting any professional adviser can be applied to selecting a geologist. Your state geologist can give you a list of those practicing in the state, and you can assay the competence of each individual by inquiry around the business community.

General information about minerals of your area is available from the U.S. Geological Survey, which has offices in every state, and from your state geological department. The amount of this information is tremendous, and you will probably need some help in interpreting it. It makes interesting reading, for it describes the wealth that may be yours.

One difficulty here is that geologists are often primarily concerned with development of minerals, whereas you merely want to make money from them as part of your whole operation. The two objectives are not always in harmony. Your best adviser is an owner who has extensive, successful experience in minerals management. These persons are rare, and the value of their experience and knowledge is often unappreciated. You should search for and listen to them. Landowners often sell their properties and retain a fraction of the minerals, thereby gradually building a substantial mineral estate. Good advice is even more important here. Mineral ownership offers you a chance at extraordinary profits and deserves serious study.

# 6
# Management Costs

The value of a timber tract as an investment depends on the net income it produces. It is difficult to raise gross income by increasing timber growth, because it takes 15 years or longer to grow a tree that can be sold. Since income tends to be fixed, the role of management costs is vital. You should study these costs thoroughly in order to predict them for your initial financial forecast, and you should appraise them at regular intervals to determine what reductions may be possible. As I have pointed out, a successful forest manager is necessarily a penny-pincher. The business is a long-term one, and a small cost has a large effect when repeated every year forever. Let us examine these management costs.

## AD VALOREM TAXES

Ad valorem taxes are unavoidable, constantly increasing, and often the biggest item in annual costs. Furthermore, you might be saddled with an inequitable tax burden that was inherited from previous owners or that has become inequitable because of changes you have wrought.

Ad valorem taxes are primarily for the support of county government and are the main source of its income. The method of calculating these taxes varies from one county to another, and even by districts within the county, so it is impossible to go into detail on your personal situation. The general method of taxation is usually established on a statewide basis, however, and there are many similarities among states. A close look at the procedure in Mississippi will illustrate several important features.

The owner of property on January 1 is assessed with taxes for the coming year. He declares the property he owns to the tax assessor before April 1, using forms provided by the assessor. This official spends the next three months entering assessments on the land roll, making sure that every acre of the county is on the roll and assessed at its proper value. The owner sets a value on the property when he declares it, but the tax assessor can change this if he disagrees and, for the time being, wins any arguments on this subject. Shortly after July 1, the assessor presents the completed land roll to the board of supervisors, the county governing body, which then makes it available for examination by all citizens. On the first Monday in August, the board meets to hear complaints of those who object to their assessments. After making whatever changes seem justified, the board forwards the roll to the State Tax Commission, which reviews the assessments to see that they are in line with adjoining counties. Although it cannot adjust individual assessments, it can order the board to raise or lower the level of assessments on one or more classes of property. After completing its task, the commission returns the land roll to the county, where it is delivered to the tax collector. Taxes must be paid during the following January to avoid penalties, but they may be paid in late December if the taxpayer desires. If the owner fails to pay taxes, title to his property eventually passes to the county and, through it, to other individuals or the state.

The state constitution provides that all property be assessed in proportion to its value, and because timberland values vary so widely, this causes a big administrative problem. Taxing authorities have solved it in a rough but workable way by dividing all land into either cultivable or uncultivable classes and assigning a value to each class. For example, the county may assess all cultivable land at $50 per acre and all uncultivable land at $22 per acre. Improvements such as houses and barns are assessed separately and added to the land assessment. The tax rate, which varies slightly each year, is applied to the assessment, and the amount of annual taxes depends mainly on the assessment.

The system works surprisingly well, considering its obvious inequities. Nevertheless, as years go by, timberland assessments gradually approach the level of farmland assessments, whereas the market price of the former is often less than half that of the latter. This means that timberland bears a disproportionate part of the tax burden. Although they are illegal and uncommon, there are sometimes discriminatory assessments against larger landowners who live outside the county. Assessments of some properties were made long ago and repeated without change. Houses that disappeared years ago and former cultivated fields that now contain a stand of trees 30 ft tall are still on assessment rolls at their old values. The administrative burden on the tax assessor is heavy, and some errors are inevitable. An owner who makes a thorough inspection of his assessment can often reduce his taxes considerably.

Early in this century, standing timber in Mississippi was taxed at higher and higher rates, and it was a race to see whether taxing authorities or sawmill operators would actually harvest the value of trees. This led to destructive cutting practices, idle land, and idle people. In an effort to place the main tax burden on the timberland owner when he was most able to bear it, the legislature exempted timber from ad valorem tax in 1940 and substituted a severance tax due when the timber is cut. Other states have similar laws, some of which allow the owner several options. Such taxes must be included by the owner in his financial forecast. They receive different treatment under federal tax laws. Severance or yield taxes reduce the total consideration in a sale; ad valorem taxes are a deductible expense.

Your state tax commission and county tax assessor will supply any necessary information about ad valorem taxes on your tract. It is worth serious study, for saving only $1 per year on taxes increases net income by that amount and adds more than $14 to the tract's value.


## FIRE PREVENTION AND SUPPRESSION

Most forest owners rely on the state for fire protection, just as most urban residents rely on the city fire department. Fire-suppression activities are out of the question for them because of the heavy expense. State fire-fighting organizations usually provide protection only in counties where help has been requested by the county government. If your county has fire protection, look up the telephone number of the dispatcher in your area, and report all fires. It is a good idea to call the person in charge of the effort, describe where your land is located, and ask for all the help available. Personal contact always helps.

To supplement the state effort, you may want to do something in the way of fire prevention on your own. One obvious thing is to construct firebreaks. This is expensive, and construction costs must be weighed against resulting benefits. Many owners build a firebreak by making one or two passes with a farm tractor and a disc plow, on the theory that doing something is better than doing nothing. Since doing this costs money and may not be effective, it *can* be worse than doing nothing. Plowing two furrows 40 to 50 ft apart and burning the strip between them are often necessary to afford any protection at all. Each situation demands a separate analysis, but you will probably find that construction of firebreaks is not economical except to protect plantations during early stages. This is particularly true when you use controlled burning as described below.

Another apparently helpful tool is the offer of a sizable reward for information leading to conviction of anyone for setting a forest fire. The reward is usually offered by a state or local forestry association, and the funds to pay rewards are pledged by interested individuals.

## CONTROLLED BURNING

Controlled burning is a common practice in many areas and promises both financial and biological results. The practice is good business because it reduces risk of loss from wild fires. This applies particularly to plantations, and you should use it as soon as possible after planting. As trees approach 15 ft in height and begin to form a solid canopy, there is a large accumulation of fuel on the ground which can support a fire hot enough to kill everything. Removal of this threat is highly desirable. As trees grow taller and larger, they become less susceptible to ground fires, but periodic removal of fuel is still helpful. Wildfire always threatens disaster, and you should reduce your exposure whenever it is economically possible. As you will see later in this chapter, fire insurance on timber is expensive. Many investors make allowance for fire hazard by increasing the interest rate used in the financial forecast; any decrease in fire hazard raises the value of the investment.

Controlled burning also reduces costs because it prevents establishment and development of some undesirable species. Hardwoods, for instance, frequently invade pine plantations and must be removed eventually. Periodic fires usually prevent their establishment, thereby reducing or eliminating the cost of removal later. If allowed to grow unchecked, hardwoods may seize a significant portion of available growing space, thereby reducing value of the harvest; this biological fact adds weight in favor of fire. But controlled burning still costs money, and small expenses grow to large sums when they are increased by interest for many years. The Burkhart programs mentioned in Chapter 17 will help you determine whether you can justify controlled burning for hardwood control alone.

The cost of controlled burning is a deductible expense, but the practice may be helpful even when its cost must be capitalized, as is the case when it is used in establishing a plantation. A fire just before planting releases some minerals that are tied up in vegetation on the site, may kill some undesirable vegetation, permits better spacing by providing better visibility, and eliminates the possibility that the plantation will be destroyed by fire immediately after planting.

Fire is a very dangerous tool, however, and should be used only by experienced people. It may consume what you are trying to protect and even escape to adjacent properties. There are also very serious liability risks. In several cases, smoke from controlled burns obscured vision on public highways, and the resulting accidents killed motorists. You must make sure that anyone using fire on your land is adequately covered by liability insurance. Before setting fires, you must notify the local fire-fighting organization and obtain a permit if necessary. Any fire at all is highly destructive in managing hardwoods. Controlled burning may not have a place in the management of some other forest types and may be illegal under certain conditions. For many reasons, you should use it only after careful planning with expert help.

## BOUNDARY LINES

It is difficult to overestimate the importance of knowing exactly where your property is. Much of the United States was originally surveyed 150 or more years ago and maybe dozens of times since, but boundary-line disputes still cause much friction and some violence. You can eliminate most disputes with a simple, inexpensive program.

First, you must locate the lines. This may be no task at all, since most owners have done some work on their boundary lines, and the evidence (old blazes or hacks or strands of barbed wire) may be still visible on the ground even though the work was done many years ago. The original inventory should tell something about the condition of the lines. Your neighbors can often supply much more information, since your boundaries and theirs are the same; this is particularly true if your neighbor is a big timber company. A competent consulting forester or surveyor can check information obtained from these sources within reasonable limits of accuracy by pacing or other inexpensive measuring methods on the ground. If such checks show that the accepted lines are approximately correct, you should accept them too. This saves the expense of an accurate survey and a heated argument if the survey shows that any line should be moved a few feet onto the property your neighbor thought he owned. Moving your neighbor's line or fence may be harder than stealing the neighbor's spouse.

If a survey appears to be the only or best solution to your problem, choose the surveyor carefully. The best arrangement is a joint survey with both parties selecting the surveyor and sharing the cost. If you must act on your own, select a surveyor whose competence is well known to your neighbors, and notify them of your plans. He should have common sense and a cool head, and be able to explain what he is doing in a convincing manner. Many states require that surveyors be licensed, and any surveyor can tell you how to get a list of licensees. Many counties have an elected surveyor, but the qualification for this job is all too often charm instead of competence. Beware of incompetents; they cause problems where none exists.

Once the line is located, it must be established in some permanent fashion. The most common method of doing so is to blaze trees on or near it, showing by a cut or hack in the bark the side on which the line passes. Some such system must be used to show location of the line in relation to nearby trees, for as a general rule of law, trees whose trunks are entirely on your side are yours and those through which the line passes belong to both you and your neighbor. You may eventually want to cut all your trees even if they help to establish line locations; you can usually blaze or hack other nearby trees if necessary. Marks of this kind are long lasting and easily visible to an experienced woodsman, but most good managers paint blazes and hacks a striking color for emphasis. White, yellow, blue, and red are often used. Since a gallon of paint is sufficient for 1 or 2 miles, paint costs much less than the labor to apply it; therefore, you should use a brand that will last up to 10 years, perhaps a good grade of outside white or paint made especially for boundary lines. Many owners always use the same color, but this is not mandatory. The important thing is to get the necessary quality as cheaply as possible. Before applying paint, shave off loose outer bark so that growth of the tree will not make it shed the paint rapidly.

Points at which lines turn should be marked. A short length of 1-in. iron pipe is satisfactory, since it is relatively permanent, cheap, and easy to transport. Wooden stakes that resist decay, rocks, concrete monuments, and other markers may be used; you should select whatever is barely adequate for the job. Elaborate corner markers and aluminum tags nailed to a nearby tree are needless refinements.

Five to ten years later, the paint will be dim, and the line will be obscured by the growth of trees and shrubs. Nevertheless, corners, blazes, and hacks will be visible, and they can be renewed and repainted cheaply. They should be renewed in exactly the same place, and the same trees should be blazed and painted if possible; this procedure is important as legal evidence of possession. Reports on boundary-line maintenance should be dated, should state specifically that this method was followed, and should include detailed information about fences on or near the line.

Legal or other reasons may make it desirable to erect along your lines signs warning against trespass. Durability of these signs is important because the cost of erecting them is much greater than the cost of the signs. The manufacturer of state automobile license plates usually makes suitable signs the same size as license plates.


## TRESPASS AND ADVERSE POSSESSION

The seriousness of trespass has decreased markedly with steady improvement of the national economy, but the main factor in reducing it is maintenance of boundary lines as described. A well-painted boundary makes it almost impossible for a trespasser to plead ignorance, and elimination of timber theft almost pays for maintaining the lines. The only other necessity is to have some competent person make irregularly periodic inspections of the tract in such a manner that residents of the community know he is doing so. Your neighbors can be a big help by informing you or your agent of unusual activities on your land, and they will be glad to do so if you discuss your need with them.

Adverse possession is a more insidious problem because it often begins innocently as an accommodation to a neighbor. For example, he may desire to fence part of your land so that his cows will stay off the road or will be able to get to a convenient watering place, and as a friendly gesture, you allow him to do so. As years pass, he may feel that he has acquired some right and begin to use your property as if it were his. If he later sells his property, the situation becomes more complicated, since the new owner has no knowledge of how the fence came about and tends to accept the situation as it is. Eventually, you may have a full-fledged dispute if you want the fence removed to prevent its damage by timber cutters, to provide better access for other purposes, or to meet the requirements of a future buyer. A fence enclosing any part of your land must be covered by a lease or some other document showing clearly that it is there with your knowledge and permission and covering all other legal aspects. Requests for fencing privileges deserve thoughtful consideration by you and your lawyer, and unauthorized fences discovered by regular boundary-line maintenance should be acted upon quickly.

Possession has been the subject of many books and countless lawsuits, and I can stress its importance only by a greatly simplified description of what is involved. As referred to in this book, *possession* is the condition under which the record owner exercises his power over a tract to the exclusion of other persons, and *adverse possession* is the exercise of the same power over a tract by someone else against the record owner. Therefore, possession is possession; whether it is adverse depends on your viewpoint. It may be all the title that is necessary, and it adds great strength to any title. To be effective under the law, it must have certain characteristics.

Possession must be consistent with type of use. It is your only title to the money in your pocket, and you exert it by carrying the money with you. Since you cannot carry a tract of land, you must exert possession in other ways. One of the best is cutting and removing timber, but equally effective may be TSI work, planting, payment of taxes, fencing, painting of boundary lines, and so forth. It must be uninterrupted. There is no interruption when title passes from one person to another, so long as each carries out whatever acts constitute possession. Possession must be exerted against everyone without exception. For example, if you fence your boundary line to keep everybody out and then tell your neighbor that you are unsure about the boundary line and that he can disregard the fence, your possession is not legally effective. It must be open in the sense that the property is held without concealment or attempt at secrecy, its ownership is not covered up in the name of a third party, and there is no attempt to withdraw it from sight. It must be held in such a manner that any interested person can ascertain by proper observation or inquiry who is actually in possession. It must be continued for a certain period of time as established by law.

The principle of possession exists to prevent difficulties, not to make wrongdoing easy, and it solves several problems associated with boundary lines. First, when continued long enough, it firmly establishes their location. Although surveying can be done very accurately, the low per acre values involved in timberland do not warrant the expense of extreme accuracy. Consequently, three surveyors may survey the same line and put it in three different places, each varying from the others by a few feet. Changing line locations every time a new surveyor comes along is expensive, and it is unnecessary if you establish your lines and then exert possession on everything inside them. Eventually, all the surveyors in the world will not be able to change them. Do not, for instance, leave a strip of uncut timber along the line just to be sure that you avoid a squabble with your neighbor. Doing so is a clear indication that you are unsure of your ownership and acknowledges to a certain extent the interests of another. Do not erect a boundary fence anywhere except exactly on the line. Backing off for any reason means idle land, wasted financial resources, and lower profits, and may cause you eventually to lose the unused strip.

Second, it settles worries about minor variations in area. Suppose you own a tract that, according to the public land survey, contains exactly 160 acres, but is found by an accurate survey actually to contain 163 acres. Although the mistake may have been made in the original survey, chances are the extra 3 acres came from an unintentional encroachment many years ago on land belonging to your neighbors. It is often costly to discover where the encroachment is and then relocate all boundary lines in the area in an effort to correct it. Some adjoining owners may object to such a procedure. Your adverse possession against your neighbor makes this unnecessary.

Lawyers have much less trouble with the law regarding possession than they do with the facts. Facts, particularly those concerning the distant past, are hard to prove, and a record of facts is what you must accumulate as time passes. Prompt recording of all forest-management activities is a must for this reason alone. Your record of possession is also helped by proper assessment of your land and by recording all timber deeds, oil leases, and mortgages in which you are grantor or mortgagor. Put these things on record as they happen, not years later, when it might appear that you are doing so in an effort to fight a case of potential adverse possession. Get time on your side by making your record as you go.

Although adverse possession is a bugaboo for most owners and can be a sticky problem, the good management and maximum use I have been urging all along will eliminate most dangers from it. Fulfillment of legal requirements of possession is good forest management, since it means full use of the land. A timber inventory will reveal most cases of adverse possession, and you can act promptly to interrupt them.

The foregoing is simplified and general; the whole matter of possession is complicated and varies from state to state. Under no circumstances should you attempt operations in this field without consulting your lawyer. People are sensitive about location of lines and fences.

## FOREST MANAGEMENT

The necessity for good forest management has been hammered home to all landowners recently. As long as prices rise steadily, everyone seems to be a good forest manager, but return to normal up-and-down movement demonstrates the cost of incompetence and places a premium on sound judgment. Timberland investment is a long-term venture, and there is a tendency to think that there is no hurry, that a job unfinished today can be finished next month, next year, or during the next cutting operation, that growth will compensate for any mistakes, and that each individual decision is unimportant. The effect of interest points out the danger of these fallacies. The long-term nature of the business *increases* the importance of each decision.

Part of good management requires a thorough knowledge of how trees grow, and although this book concentrates on the business of forestry, I want to give you an example to show why biological knowledge is important. Professor T. T. Koslowski is the author of an outstanding text on tree physiology, and the following are excerpts from an interview with him published in my firm's newsletter.

JMV: What is the most important factor in tree growth?

TTK: Water is the one factor that affects tree growth most; more trees die from lack of water than from any other single cause. This is because a tree, with its large crown, is admirably constructed to lose water through evaporation from the leaves and to do so faster than its roots can take it up. Whenever water loss becomes too great, however, the stomata, millions of tiny pores in the leaves, close to protect the tree from death by dessication. This normally happens during short periods of water stress about noon every day even when the soil is fully charged with water, and stems, leaves, and roots shrink, as can be shown with special instruments. The stomata stay closed all night, and the roots continue to take up enough water to restore the tree to its original condition by the next morning.

Temporary closing of stomata during midday stops the manufacture of carbohydrates even though there is plenty of sunlight. When the stomata close, carbon dioxide from the air cannot get into the leaves, and photosynthesis ceases. So water deficiency in the leaves, which leads to closing of stomata, is the big problem.

JMV: Therefore, what happens in a plantation depends more on competition for water than for light?

TTK: Yes. Soil water doesn't move to the roots fast enough, so they have to grow toward wet soil, and they start growing toward the roots of neighboring seedlings. As soon as roots from two seedlings reach the same volume of soil, competition for water (and also for minerals) begins. How long it takes to cause reduction of growth rates depends on how fast the species grows and how close the spacing is. In loblolly pine planted at a spacing of 12 ft by 12 ft, competition could begin in five years and would probably be severe in ten years.

JMV: If it starts this soon, most of us probably wouldn't notice it.

TTK: That's right. Most of us make the mistake of assuming that competition starts only when we can see that some trees have large crowns and others have small ones, visible signs of suppression. To bring about that suppression, however, there must have been a whole series of sequential physiological events. Competition that causes suppression actually starts several years before there are visible signs, such as reduced diameter growth; by the time you can see the signs, you have already suffered growth losses.

JMV: Why is the response to thinning often delayed?

TTK: This is because the crown must first get more light, water, and minerals so it can produce more leaves and buds so they can produce more carbohydrates and hormones to be pumped down the stem eventually to be converted into wood. All of this takes time. Even in fast-growing southern pines, the delay can be one or two years.

Forest managers who understand what Dr. Koslowski said realize what poor business it is to plant trees too close together in the beginning and to leave them too crowded until only a small fraction of the trees contain live limbs. Other mistakes may occur when removing trees in a thinning. Some foresters, particularly inexperienced ones, use the marking gun with timidity when boldness is required. They leave trees that should come out and rationalize this by saying that they can correct errors of this type the next time around. Thus they postpone income that should be captured now, slow down the growth of the remaining stand, and reduce the value of later thinnings by reducing the size of trees that will be cut then. The combined effect of these errors is large enough to alter the profit picture substantially.

Experienced forest managers can prevent losses caused by premature or improper application of research findings. Forest scientists discover some exciting new techniques, and these discoveries often receive great publicity. The scientists state exactly what has been found and are especially careful to point out the limitations of their experiments. These precautions are often overlooked by landowners, however, and the temptation to pioneer is strong if big profits seem possible. Failure is almost inevitable, and failure costs money. You should go slow with new techniques and seek expert advice even then.

Good forest management is mandatory, and you must provide for it in your financial forecast. Although you do all other work yourself, you will probably need help from an experienced adviser. If you elect the do-it-yourself method, estimate the cost of your time, your car, temporary labor, and other expenses, and put all of this in your financial forecast. Management costs money regardless of who does the work, and successful investments require good management.

## ON-THE-GROUND INSPECTIONS OF THE PROPERTY

Inspections of the property at least once a year are essential to good management. The sooner you know about incipient adverse possession or damage from fire or insects, the better you can avoid losses from them. The best inspections are made by the owner himself. As the old saying goes, "The best fertilizer is the footsteps of the gardener." Those who live far from their tracts or cannot visit them should arrange for inspections by others.

Our annual inspection service is an example of what is needed. We first verify that the assessment is correct and then report when taxes are due. Next we walk the perimeter to check on condition of boundary lines. We also walk into the tract at intervals to examine timber conditions. Finally, we recommend actions needed and report on stumpage prices in the area. On the back side of the report sheet we sketch a map of the tract and add names of adjoining landowners as shown by the tax roll. In most cases these inspections are done annually, but timing is up to the landowner.

The form of the report is shown in Figures 6.1a and 6.1b. The questions to be answered force the inspector to look at important matters. He writes in the answers by hand; those shown are typical.

You can use this as a model to develop a form of your own, and your lawyer might suggest ways to improve it. Each year's report should be filed as part of the forest-management records.

## FOREST-MANAGEMENT RECORDS

It is imperative to record all forest-management activities on your land. The record may be quite simple, but must be continuous and all-inclusive. You should require a written report from everyone performing work on your property and put this report where it can be inspected from time to time.

An effective way to keep these records is to use copies of the map that is part of timberland inventory. The mapmaker undoubtedly prepared a tracing, and you can obtain additional copies for a pittance. Select a symbol for each activity such as thinning, harvesting, planting, TSI work, boundary-line maintenance, and so forth. For each year select a color or combination of color and number, and plot each activity on the map as it is completed. Usually you will be able to record many years' activities on the same map.

Time passes faster than you think, and without records you cannot remember when you performed certain work. How can you appraise its results if you do not know when it was done? Records of boundary-line maintenance are especially useful. They not only serve as a guide for the next crew reworking them; they may also be invaluable in fighting adverse possession. You may use different people in management because people die, move away, or change employment. You will lose valuable history if the only records were in their memories. Each new manager must gather complete new data if there are no past records, and this process is far more expensive than keeping records.

## PLANTING AND CULTURAL WORK

Everyone who plants seedlings loses lots of them during the first growing season, and every year some lose most of them. Most persons blame this "bad luck" on the weather, because over the course of every year every area suffers at least one period that *could* have caused it. I do not think this is fair, although it is convenient to blame something that cannot talk back. I suspect that 50% and maybe 75% of

**JAMES M. VARDAMAN & CO., INC.**
FOREST MANAGEMENT SPECIALISTS
P.O. DRAWER 22766
JACKSON, MISSISSIPPI 39225
601-354-3123

ANNUAL INSPECTION REPORT

Inspector: _Brown C. Hairston_ Date: _18 Oct. 1989_
Title: _Manager, Jackson District_

Owner of Tract: _James A. Ross_
Address: _Box 1500, Memphis, Tenn. 38102_
Legal Description: _NE 1/4, Section 31, Township 10 North, Range 8 East,_
_Johnson County, Mississippi_

1. **Assessment:** Description correct? _yes_ Why not? _____
   No. of uncultivatable A. _160_ Assessment/A. _$24.00_ Correct? _yes_
   No. of cultivatable A. _none_ Assessment/A. _____ Correct? _yes_
   Assessment of improvements _none_ What are they? _____ Correct? _yes_
   If there are errors, what action is needed? _____

2. **Ad Valorem Taxes:** When is next payment due? _January 1990. Penalties begin Feb. 1_
   If it is not made, when will land be sold for taxes? _mid-September 1992_
   If sale is made on this date, when will title mature in new owner? _September 1994_

3. **Perimeter Inspection:** How are boundaries marked? Show on map on reverse.
   What additional work is needed? _Boundary lines should be brushed out, blazed_
   _and painted a conspicuous color. Total length is 2 miles._ Estimated cost? _$800_

   Who are adjoining landowners? Show on map on reverse.
   What evidence of trespass is there? Show on map and describe here: _none_

   What action is needed? _____
   What evidence of adverse possession is there? Show on map and describe here:
   _Fence as shown. They are not platted to scale. Total encroachment is less than 1/10 A._
   What action is needed? _Ask owners to remove them or sign lease._

4. **Timber Conditions:**
   What kind of timber is predominant? Pine _65_ % Hardwood _35_ %
   Sawtimber: Large (16" & up DBH) _____ Small (10"- 16" DBH) _✓_
   Small sawtimber and pulpwood _____ Pulpwood and young growth _____

   Is a sale desirable now? _yes_ What kind? _Sawtimber_
   How much in volume? _200-300 MBF_ In $ _36,000 - 39,000_ Why? _Growth rate of_
   _these trees has dropped below 6% annually. Market prices are very strong._
   Is TSI work needed? _yes_ Planting? _no_ Controlled burning? _no_
   Where are they needed? Show on map and describe here: _After sawtimber sale_
   _to remove cull trees. Entire tract should be treated._
   What is estimated cost? _$1,000_

   Is there evidence of damage by insects? _no_ Fire? _no_ Disease? _no_ Wind? _no_
   Animals? _no_ Ice? _no_ What corrective action is needed? _____

   What are approximate stumpage prices in the area?
   Sawtimber per MBF: (Doyle)
   (circle one)       Scribner
                      International scale: Pine _$125-150_ Hardwood _$50-60_
   Pulpwood per cord: Pine _$12_ Soft Hardwood _$6_ Hard Hardwood _$5_

**Figure 6.1a.** Typical inspection report form.

the loss is due to human error, for even a cursory investigation will reveal that not all seedlings and planters are created equal.

Let us start with the seedlings. The next time you receive bare-root seedlings from a nursery, pick out the best-looking one, and examine it carefully. All the needles you will see will lose water to keep the

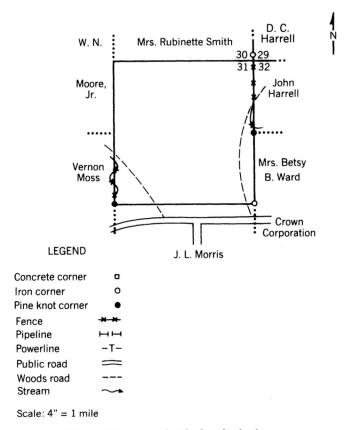

W. N.

Moore, Jr.

Mrs. Rubinette Smith

D. C. Harrell

30 29
31 32

John Harrell

N

Vernon Moss

Mrs. Betsy B. Ward

Crown Corporation

LEGEND

J. L. Morris

| Concrete corner | ▫ |
| Iron corner | ○ |
| Pine knot corner | ● |
| Fence | ✕✕ |
| Pipeline | ⊢⊢ |
| Powerline | –T– |
| Public road | ⩵ |
| Woods road | --- |
| Stream | ∿ |

Scale: 4″ = 1 mile

**Figure 6.1b.  Map sketched on back of report.**

seedling at the right temperature and will use water to make food. Most of the roots you will see will absorb some water, but the main water-absorbing roots, the hairlike, almost transparent kind, have all been broken off during lifting. As long as conditions are favorable for the seedling, that is, its water consumption is no more than its water absorption, it will live. But the balance is precarious when you receive the seedlings and is only temporary. When spring brings high temperatures, fresh breezes, and the start of growth, water consumption shoots up, and unless the seedling can grow a new set of water-absorbing roots, the loss of water through the needles will kill it.

The catch is that the seedling can grow these new roots only with food made by the needles. The very needles that deal death by losing water give life by making food for new root growth. Consequently, to do well in its new life in the wild, where it must compete for water, sunlight, and nutrients, a seedling must have plenty of secondary needles and plenty of lateral roots. In other words, it must be big enough to have the resources to overcome the various shocks of transplanting.

To qualify as "big" by my standards, a seedling must have a diameter of 1/4 in. at the root collar; 3/8 in. would be better. Any big seedling will automatically have a large root system. Height above root collar will probably be over 12 in., but is not the critical factor; all you must beware of is a tall, spindly seedling, which may have too much ability to lose water and too little ability to take it up. Big seedlings require at least 1/20 square foot of growing space in the nursery bed. For many reasons, most nursery managers allocate only 1/30 square foot or less and thus cannot produce seedlings more than 1/8 in. in diameter (smaller than a pencil). I do not quarrel with their reasons; all I say is that every landowner who wants good survival must be concerned about the size of seedlings to be planted on his land.

There is a more important reason for using big seedlings. Everyone who has watched plantations develop has noticed that height growth in the first summer is often very small. This is because the seedlings are waiting for their water-absorbing roots to develop; until these roots are in place, the seedlings will not endanger their lives by using more than the minimum of water for height growth. But while the seedlings are marking time, all other plants on a cutover site, especially hardwood sprouts whose roots are already in place, are growing vigorously in response to new growing space. Usually any plant with a one-year head start on its neighbors will soon overtop them. To take away this head start (or to try to), some landowners spend a bundle on site preparation. The more profitable way by far is to use big seedlings, first to improve survival and second to begin height growth sooner.

The importance of big seedlings has been established for decades. P. C. Wakeley, the South's greatest expert on planting trees, emphasized it for years and presented mountains of data in support of his recommendations. As long ago as 1954 he suggested for southern pines three seedling grades based on root-collar diameter: Grade 1 = more than 1/5 in., Grade 2 = between 1/5 and 1/8 in., and Cull = less than 1/8 in.

In spite of his great contributions, big seedlings are hard to find. No southern pine nursery that I know of grades seedlings in this way;

most of them produce few Grade 1 seedlings. A survey of 53 nurseries by the Auburn University Southern Forest Nursery Management Cooperative indicated that 44 nurseries were producing less than 20% Grade 1 seedlings and about 35 were producing more than 30% culls in the mid-1980s.

Nursery managers affect survival and early growth next when the seedlings are lifted and transported to their ultimate home. Most nursery managers are highly qualified and dedicated to producing superior trees, but since nurseries are usually part of larger organizations that decide on capital investments and operating budgets, their managers have limited resources and must adjust their practices to their individual situations. Some lift by hand, others by machine; some cull runts before packing, others do not; some have cold-storage facilities, others do not; some pack seedlings in paper-and-plastic bags, others in open-end bundles with roots in sphagnum moss or similar material; some rarely experience a killing frost. And when the higher authority insists on seedlings that are cheap to grow and plant, the manager must sow seed for a stocking of 30 per square foot. Because of the sheer volume of work needed to handle millions of seedlings, most carry on lifting operations over several months, and the deadly risk of water loss increases if seedlings are lifted before they have "hardened off" or after growth has started in the spring.

The differential impact of two common nursery practices was demonstrated by tests at W. W. Ashe Nursery operated by the U.S. Forest Service near Brooklyn, Mississippi. Researchers took two batches of seedlings from the same bed, put one in a test chamber immediately, packaged the other in a paper-and-plastic bag, placed it in cold storage for 21 days, and then put it in the test chamber. The test chamber is a large, ingenious apparatus by which root growth of individual seedlings can be measured every 24 hours. During the 21 days that each batch eventually spent in the test chamber, the average seedling put in immediately grew about *20 ft* of new roots (the kind that absorb water), whereas the average seedling put in after cold storage grew about *3 in.* Those growing 20 ft could have survived much stress and still have started height growth soon after planting. The others might have been killed by the periods of dry weather that occur every spring, but even under ideal conditions, would have produced very little height growth.

As you can see, landowners who want good results in planting have a vital interest in what goes on in the nursery, but since few nurseries are perfect, some compromises are inevitable. In the regeneration work of my firm, we plant the biggest seedlings available, require that they be lifted only in January or February, rush them to the planting site in our own vehicles, plant them in less than 96 hours after lifting, and cull all runts. On sites with special problems, we strongly consider using containerized seedlings, which make up for lack of size by having undisturbed roots.

The person who plants the seedling can harm its future more than all the people involved in nursery work combined. The list of things he can do wrong is limited only by the ingenuity of persons who are usually paid by the number planted, but have little interest in first-year survival and growth; one machine-planting contractor was reported to have cut off most of the roots so that planting would be easier. When you find a single row in which every seedling died, I think you can blame the planter.

Considering the foregoing blunders, I am surprised, not by the amount of mortality, but by the survival and growth of so many seedlings. If pine seedlings can do so well in spite of people's mistakes, think of what they can do with a little help. The best solution to the regeneration problem is an enforceable guarantee of a suitable survival rate at the end of the first summer. If big seedlings are available, some planting contractors will make such a guarantee.

Use of controlled burning to reduce undesirable species in the stand was discussed earlier in this chapter, but many tracts contain excellent stands of desirable reproduction stock that are completely overtopped by worthless trees. Such acres, apparently productive, are almost totally idle and must be released. Methods of release are varied, and some are very expensive. You must select one that is barely adequate for the job. Everyone has seen thick stands of pure pine reproduction stock from which every hardwood sprig was painstakingly removed. The financial analyst cringes at the sight; the high cost of producing this eyewash so early in the crop virtually eliminates the possibility of future profit. You must seek expert advice before attempting cultural work.

## CASUALTY LOSSES

By definition, casualty losses are unpredictable, but you should give some thought to these management costs. To help you evaluate this risk of loss and react to it after it happens, I have described below the typical events in a Southern Pine Beetle (SPB) epidemic.

In 1985 there were 16,000 SPB sites of infection in Texas; SPBs were estimated to have killed the pines on 50,000 acres. Because SPBs attack better-than-average timber, I estimate that the loss was

$500 per acre at prices then; a $25,000,000 loss is big enough to hurt many owners. But in percentage of total volume, it is very small. Texas contains 7,000,000 acres of pine timberlands, so if the *average* stand on them is worth only $250, total value is $1,750,000,000. Total SPB loss was 1.4%, about one-fifth of annual growth. Since 1985 was a year of heavy SPB infestation, the annual loss projected over a decade is probably much less than 1.0%.

SPB infestations usually start from a single tree-in-trouble, often one struck by lightning. This means that nearly everyone with trees of merchantable size suffers some loss every year, and in an epidemic, the widespread and random incidence of attacks sets the stage for much larger losses than trees actually killed by SPBs. Ignorance loads the gun; panic pulls the trigger.

When many landowners discover SPBs in their timber, they assume that the infestation will gradually spread and consume everything. (In fact, many infestations die out from natural causes.) They then attempt to carry out the standard control practice, which calls for cutting and removing all infested trees plus all bug-free trees in a buffer strip surrounding them. Those with an infected acre containing 3 MBF soon learn that loggers cannot move in equipment to salvage such a small amount, but must have four to five times more volume, and are not willing to disrupt their normal operations unless they can buy the trees at a big discount. In a situation like this, the bugs force onto the market in a distress sale five to six times as much as they kill. If the 3 MBF is normally worth $150/MBF, SPBs cause a death loss of $450; if the forced-sale discount is 50% (in Louisiana in 1985 it was 90% to 100%), the landowner salvages $75 on 3 MBF, but loses $75 on 12 to 15 more MBF. In trying to control the bugs by a salvage cut, he increases his loss from $450 to $657 or $800. Sometimes panic takes over, the landowner decides to sell everything on the infested tract, and the bugs cause a distress sale of 50 to 100 times as much as they destroy. Since all landowners have a few bugs, opportunities for panic are legion.

The clear winners in SPB outbreaks are timber-consuming industries. Prices of the products they make are set in national or world markets, their manufacturing costs remain unchanged, and yet their raw material costs drop 50% or more. (They should not be charged with taking advantage of the misfortunes of landowners. They cannot do otherwise; when panic-stricken sellers flood the market, buyers with limited storage space and bugs in their log decks must try to stop the flood by cutting prices.) Loggers are also winners, for they stay furiously busy until all storage yards are chock full.

The clear losers are landowners with bug infestations and especially those who panic. The not-so-obvious losers are SPB-free landowners who, for reasons such as paying estate taxes, must sell on markets flooded by others. Other losers are those who can delay sales, but must therefore delay dividends, pay for extra planning, and disrupt work schedules.

SPBs in infested trees continue to develop even after the trees are felled. Therefore, the most important control activity is to move infested trees off your land to places where emerging SPBs cannot easily attack a new host. I suggest that you forget about trying to salvage money from these trees and that you hire a logger to haul them away (be sure he gets them all) or at least to drag each bole to a separate location in a nearby hardwood area. I also suggest that you cut no bug-free trees at all. If they are not later attacked by SPBs (and many will not be), you will have cleaned up the spot without selling anything at a big discount. Finally, I suggest that you keep your cool and postpone sales of large volumes until the SPB outbreak subsides, as all of them have done over the past 50,000,000 years.

No one that I know of keeps records of how much is lost each year from the various types of casualties, but my guess is that SPB outbreaks cause much more loss than any other casualty and that all of them put together amount to an insignificant figure. Averages do not help much, however, if you are the victim. Then the best way to minimize losses is to keep your cool and minimize cutting. Any good consulting forester can help you in this situation.

## INSURANCE

Timberland owners are subject to risks. Some are so small, and others so very large, that they must be assumed; most, however, can be transferred.

The common method of transferring risk is to buy insurance. Many companies offer insurance applicable to timberlands, and they are usually represented by independent agents. Choosing the right company and agent is important. You must consider experience, reputation, loss-adjustment records, and cost. You will find some specialization among agents, for the field is so broad. It is wise to consult an agent familiar with timberland operations, even if he lives in another part of the state. Since insurance regulations vary widely from state to state, you should consult an agent in the state where your land is located.

The average owner needs only some form of public liability insurance, since his exposure to loss is slight. The cost is very low, and you may already have adequate coverage under policies you bought for other purposes. One great value in all insurance lies in the agreement by the insurer to defend you in all lawsuits. Anyone can sue you, even if the allegations in the suit are groundless, and you must either spend money to defend yourself or allow the plaintiff to obtain a default judgment against you. The cost of such a defense is many times the cost of insurance.

Workmen's compensation insurance laws usually vary by states and constitute a tangled wilderness. The normal owner is not subject to them, but you should investigate this matter, since certain activities, such as hiring people to work on your land, may make them apply to you. Your agent can tell you.

Insurance to cover loss on standing timber from fire and lightning is available from some companies and may cover all trees larger than 1 ft tall. Rates are calculated by increasing or decreasing a base rate because of certain unfavorable or favorable conditions. Increases are caused by naval-stores operations, lack of fire-control organizations, recreational use of land, presence of unmerchantable trees, heavy underbrush, steep terrain, and other recognizable hazards. Decreases are caused by state fire protection, large tree size, fire resistance of species, heavy forest, light underbrush, and so on. This calculation of rates is a complicated one and must be made for each tract. Policies must contain the exact legal description of the tract and the species covered. You cannot insure timber so inaccessible that it cannot be logged by usual methods at ordinary profit margins. Reproduction stock is usually valued at a flat figure per acre and cannot be insured if it located under a fully stocked stand of merchantable timber. The company often requires that the amount of insurance equal 90% of the value of the timber, and for each loss it is liable only for the difference in value before the fire and salvage value immediately after the fire. In order to reduce the number of small claims, policies usually contain a deductible clause that eliminates liability for losses less than 1% of the face amount of the policy. A dry-season charge allows the insurer to earn most of the annual premium during hazardous months of the year. Your insurance agent can give you all the details you may require. The base rate is usually over 2% annually, and it is quite common for the total rate to be 3%. Therefore, the cost of this insurance can easily be a third of annual income and explains why it is seldom used.

Most owners provide their own fire insurance by increasing the interest rate used in the financial forecast, constructing firebreaks during critical periods, offering rewards for firebugs, or gambling that they will not have a fire. The increasing effectiveness of state fire-control organizations has greatly reduced risks, and a continuation of this trend is essential to successful forest management. Fire insurance can also be carried under special programs by associations or loss-sharing arrangements among individuals. There has been some study of expanding the federal crop-insurance program to include timberlands. Rates have already been well-established by private industry, however; they cannot be made much more attractive without public subsidies of some type.

## SUMMARY

The value of timberlands as investments fluctuates with their net return, and reduction of management costs, wherever possible, increases net return. At a 7% rate of return, an increase of $1 in net annual income raises the value by more than $14. Frugality must be a day-to-day companion in timberland investment and is a prerequisite for success.

# 7

# Timberland Inventory

The first step in any business is to find out what it owns, and what it has to sell. Many stock-market investors can recite from memory the exact number of shares they hold, but some landowners have only a vague idea of what they own and often make no effort to find out. They neglect this step because these inventories are sometimes called timber estimates, and many tracts contain little or no merchantable timber. Actually, the kind of inventory needed covers many things other than merchantable timber and is essential to success. It should include several items, which are discussed below.

## TIMBER INVENTORY

First in importance is the timber inventory. You may take it by measuring every tree on the property, but usually you measure an adequate sample of them. You need to know something about sampling procedure. Sampling is based on the law of probablility, and this law works well if you give it a chance to operate. If your tract contains 40 acres—15 open and 25 timbered—there is an obvious danger in basing your inventory on the measurement of only one sample. If the sample falls in the open area, you will show no timber at all, and you will overestimate the timber volume if the sample falls in the timbered area. If you measure 40 or 400 samples distributed evenly over the tract, you can see that the law of probability has a chance to work and will produce a much more accurate answer. Inventories are described by the percentage of total area measured, such as a 10% or a 20% inventory. When you take a 20% inventory of a 40-acre tract, you measure every tree on a total of 8 acres.

The sample must be properly distributed over the tract, and this is usually done by measuring strips or plots in a grid pattern. Statistical theory shows that samples taken at random may be used under certain conditions and may be superior for some purposes, but this practice is for experts. The important thing for you is to be sure that the sampling percentage is large enough to give a reliable answer. Size of the sample depends on total area, purpose for which the inventory is made, and species, size, distribution, and value of the timber. Generally speaking, the comprehensive inventory we are talking about demands a 20% sample for areas under 300 acres and a 10% sample for larger areas. All distances and the diameters of more valuable trees should be measured with steel tapes. Smaller samples may be used when timber volumes alone are required. The report must show the sampling percentage and how it was obtained. All other specifications must be covered in detail.

After selecting the sampling procedure, you must decide how much information to gather. A simple statement that the tract contains a certain amount of pulpwood and sawtimber is suitable only for elementary purposes. The inventory must show volumes by products, species or groups of species, and DBH classes. If the tract contains more than several hundred acres, it should be divided into smaller blocks for inventory; you need to know where the timber is in order to plan future operations. The report should clearly describe the units of volume measurement.

It is most important to know the number of trees by DBH classes and species. Size of a tree has a big effect on its value, and you might need this information to take advantage of fleeting market opportunities. It is essential for growth studies and is valuable in comparing the present inventory with others that might be taken later. The inventory should give this information for all trees 6 in. DBH and larger (generally considered merchantable timber); it is helpful to have some data on smaller trees since they will eventually become merchantable. General comments on small reproduction are sufficient.

## VOLUME MEASURES

**Pulpwood Volume Measures.**  The standard measure is the cord, a stack of wood 4 ft x 4 ft x 8 ft containing a gross volume of 128 cubic feet. To determine the number of cords on a truck when the sticks are cut in short lengths, the scaler makes several measurements of height, length of load, and length of sticks, averages them, multiplies the

**TABLE 7-1**
**Comparison of Volume, Measuring Rules**

| DBH Class | Board Foot Volumes Under Common Rules | | |
|---|---|---|---|
| | Doyle | Scribner | International |
| 10 | 1000 | 1468 | 1580 |
| 11 | 1000 | 1444 | 1576 |
| 12 | 1000 | 1388 | 1539 |
| 13 | 1000 | 1310 | 1478 |
| 14 | 1000 | 1253 | 1430 |
| 15 | 1000 | 1169 | 1358 |

averages to obtain cubic contents, deducts an estimated amount for cull, and then divides the remainder by 128. The method is slow and not highly accurate.

**Sawtimber Volume Measures.** For more than 100 years, we have wrestled with the problem of measuring logs or trees to determine how much lumber might be manufactured from them. The task is complex because a round log must be made into square or rectangular pieces and the pieces must be separated from each other. Using either formula or diagram, we have developed three scales or rules for doing this that are commonly used today, namely, Doyle rule, Scribner rule, and International rule. Each rule gives a different answer for the same tree, and to add complications, the relationship between volumes shown by these rules varies with tree size. Volumes under the rules for trees of common sizes and diameters are revealed in Table 7.1.

The rule used to measure logs has no effect on their value, for this depends on what products they will yield. It does affect calculation of the selling price. You must specify what rule is to be used in your timber sales.

Other problems arise in actually measuring or scaling logs. This usually is done by measuring the length and the average diameter inside the bark at the small end, determining the volume by the rule, and adjusting it for whatever defects the log contains. Scaling of logs is not an exact science, however, and you may find wide variations among scalers. Some measure one or both bark thicknesses at the small end; some measure diameter at other points on the log; some have difficulty in determining the average diameter when the log is relatively flat on one or more sides instead of round; some raise the measured diameter an inch or two to adjust for extra-long logs; all have difficulty in judging the extent of defect and the deduction that should be made for it. Accurate scaling of logs requires skill and experience.

**Determining Volume by Weight.**   Every year more timber is sold by weight, and the trend seems likely to continue. Weighing to determine quantity is easy, accurate, and less susceptible to fraud and disputes than the former methods of scaling volumes with a stick. Nevertheless, its apparent exactness is a trap for the unwary, and considering some facts about the two main classes of products reveals that determining volume of timber by weight is tricky business.

*Pulpwood.*   In pulpwood the trap develops because, in discussing volumes, sellers and buyers are talking about apples and oranges. When sellers refer to cords, they mean the *total space occupied by the stack of wood*. In other words, they think that a cord is a stack containing 128 cubic feet of space. Most foresters and the scientists who construct volume tables express themselves in the same way. They cannot weigh a standing tree; they can only measure its dimensions.

On the other hand, buyers are interested only in the cord's *solid material* and what they can make out of it; they obviously cannot afford to pay for the air in it. Weight measurement serves them very well, for weight of a cord depends on its solid content. The solid content, in turn, depends on diameter of the sticks; the smaller the diameter, the smaller the solid content. (If you doubt this, think of a cord that is a single block of wood having a solid content of 128 cubic feet. Now imagine splitting it in two with a wedge. Once you have done this, you cannot squeeze the pieces back together as tightly as they grew originally, so to get them into the 4 ft by 4 ft by 8 ft space, you must shave off some of the solid wood.)

The larger the DBH of a tree is, the larger the average diameter of the sticks and the greater the solid content of cords produced will be. Tables showing this appear on page 4 of *Yields of Old-Field Loblolly Pine Plantations* by Harold E. Burkhart et al., Publication FWS-3-72, Division of Forestry and Wildlife Resources, Virginia Polytechnic Institute and State University. Using these data and a wood-and-bark weight of 53 lb per cubic foot, I calculated the weight of cords by DBH classes to be as shown in Table 7.2.

The weight of a cubic foot of rough wood varies with many factors,

**TABLE 7-2**
**Weight of Cords by DBH Class**

| DBH Class, inches | Solid Content per Cord, Cubic Feet | Pounds per Cord |
|---|---|---|
| 5 | 84 | 4452 |
| 6 | 85 | 4505 |
| 7 | 87 | 4611 |
| 8 | 90 | 4770 |
| 9 | 91 | 4823 |
| 10 | 92 | 4876 |
| 11 | 93 | 4929 |
| 12 | 94 | 4982 |
| 13+ | 95 | 5035 |

but weights equivalent to a cord adopted by all buyers in a locality are similar. One buyer reported that his cord-equivalent weight was 5200 lb. Therefore, a seller who delivered a stack of wood containing 128 cubic feet and produced from 6-in.-DBH trees would be paid for only 4,505 lb divided by 5200 lb = 86.6% of a cord. If he had calculated by the usual method that his stack contained a full cord, he would suspect that he had been cheated. But there would have been no cheating here; for just so many apples, he would get just so many oranges.

*Sawtimber.* In sawtimber the trap develops because, in discussing volumes, sellers and buyers are often talking about pineapples and lemons. When sellers refer to MBF, they mean the volume of logs or trees calculated by measuring the dimensions and applying one of the common rules discussed previously. In spite of the obvious inaccuracy of this method, it is still the most practicable one available to most sellers.

On the other hand, buyers are interested only in how much product they can make from a tree. For a century or more they used the same procedure used by sellers, measuring individual logs or trees and then calculating output by one of the rules. Although there were wide differences between calculated and produced volumes at different diameters, buyers discovered the relationship between them by measuring logs at one end of the mill and lumber output at the other. They adjusted their prices accordingly, which communicated the knowledge to sellers. Over the decades, both adjusted their practices to make these differences irrelevant.

Two developments increased the potential difference between calculated and produced volumes. One was tree-length logging; this greatly decreased logging costs, but made it impracticable to measure logs or trees individually. The other was weight measurement or scaling; this greatly decreased measuring costs, but added a new element of confusion. Since there was only one measurement for a truckload containing several MBF and tree sizes and since it measured weight and not tree dimensions or lumber output, each buyer had to establish an *average weight per MBF*, even though variation from the average by individual trees might be large. Sellers whose tracts exactly matched the average suffered not at all; those whose tracts differed from the average found that volumes estimated by measuring standing trees often differed very much from volumes estimated by weighing at the mill.

Magnitude of these variations can be demonstrated by analysis of trees in a typical pine stand, such as the one in Table 7.3.

Weight of an MBF varies with many factors, but weights equivalent to an MBF adopted by all buyers in a locality are usually similar. One buyer where Scribner is the prevailing rule reported that his MBF-equivalent weight was 17,500 lb. Therefore, a seller who delivered material cut from trees 15 in. DBH would be paid at the rate of 13,130 lb divided by 17,500 lb = 75% of the MBF-equivalent price. If he had calculated by the usual method that his material contained a full MBF, he would suspect that he had been cheated. But there would have been no cheating; for just so many pineapples, he would get just so many lemons.


## MAPS

The report should include a map on a convenient scale such as 2 in. or 4 in. to the mile. The map should show everything that might be useful to the forest manager, should fit readily into an ordinary file folder, and be easily taken into the woods. A satisfactory solution is to prepare it on standard 8½ x 11 in. sheets, even if several sheets are required to show the entire property. Maps are made to be used and *will* be used if the design is convenient. The report must contain the correct legal description. It may include aerial photographs of the tract, since these are available through the U.S. Department of Agriculture at modest cost. The local office of Agricultural Stabilization and Conservation Service (ASCS) can tell you how to get them. An excellent scale for all purposes is 1/20,000; larger sizes are needed

## TABLE 7-3
### Analysis of Trees in Typical Pine Stand

| DBH Class | Volume Cubic Foot | Weight, lb at 53/Cubic Foot | Doyle | | Scribner | | International | |
|---|---|---|---|---|---|---|---|---|
| | | | MBF | lb/MBF | MBF | lb/MBF | MBF | lb/MBF |
| 10 | 151 | 8,003 | 0.333 | 24,033 | 0.489 | 16,366 | 0.526 | 15,215 |
| 11 | 607 | 32,171 | 1.472 | 21,855 | 2.126 | 15,132 | 2.320 | 13,867 |
| 12 | 557 | 29,521 | 1.483 | 19,906 | 2.058 | 14,213 | 2.282 | 12,818 |
| 13 | 488 | 25,864 | 1.438 | 17,986 | 1.884 | 13,728 | 2.126 | 12,166 |
| 14 | 339 | 17,967 | 1.065 | 16,870 | 1.334 | 13,469 | 1.523 | 11,797 |
| 15 | 219 | 11,607 | .756 | 15,353 | .884 | 13,130 | 1.027 | 11,302 |
| Total | 2,361 | 125,133 | 6.547 | | 8.775 | | 9.804 | |
| Average | | | | 19,113 | | 14,260 | | 12,763 |

only if you want a wall display. The ASCS can provide stereoscopic views cheaply, but you will probably need expert help in ordering the proper photographs and viewing equipment.

## GROWTH STUDY

Another important part of the inventory is the growth study. Accurate calculation of growth can be a very technical process, but reveals valuable information. My firm developed a computer program that can predict the volume of timber on any tract on any day of the year. The sampling pattern and procedure were designed for us by the late Dr. Jerry Clutter of the University of Georgia, one of our best forest statisticians. When we enter data for each tract in the computer, we label them with the date we measured the trees in the woods. Part of Dr. Clutter's work included an estimate, for the southeastern United States as a whole, of how much of the annual growth takes place in each month. Since our data base contains both the date of measurement and the percentage of growth that takes place each day, the computer takes only a few seconds to predict the situation on the tract at the end of each day. Here is the annual growth pattern from the program:

| Month of Year | Percentage of Annual Growth |
|---|---|
| April | 39 |
| May | 19 |
| June | 15 |
| July | 12 |
| August | 8 |
| September | 7 |
| | 100 |

The program shows some important relationships. The prediction of the first tract run through the computer revealed differential growth rates by DBH classes as shown in Table 7.4.

Since each tract is unique, the relationships for yours may be completely different. But it is generally true that, as DBH increases, annual percentage growth rate decreases. You will raise your *average* growth percentage everytime you sell the *larger* trees.

Such accuracy is not essential for your purposes. Your primary concern is the rate your trees will grow for the next 10 years or less.

**TABLE 7-4**
**Differential Growth Rates by DBH Class**

| DBH Class | Volume per Tree, Board Feet | Annual growth per Tree, Board Feet | Annual Percentage Growth Rate |
|---|---|---|---|
| 8 | 0 | 9.5 | Infinity |
| 10 | 59.3 | 5.8 | 9.8 |
| 12 | 131.4 | 8.6 | 6.5 |
| 14 | 188.5 | 11.5 | 6.1 |
| 16 | 272.1 | 12.1 | 4.4 |
| 18 | 363.5 | 9.8 | 2.7 |

You can calculate this with enough accuracy by determining first how long it takes your average tree to grow 2 in. in diameter. Using an increment borer, take a core from enough trees of various diameters scattered over the tract, and count the number of rings in the outside inch. Taking increment cores is hard work, and you can reduce the amount of it if, by using your judgment, you take cores only from trees that appear to be average for the tract. Avoid suppressed trees and large, limby ones growing all by themselves. A few cores will show whether there is a significant difference in growth rate of the various species present and whether the exceptional species are important enough to warrant a separate prediction. It is usually adequate in the South to know how many years, on the average, it takes all pine trees on your property to grow 2 in. in diameter. Once you determine this figure, you are ready for the next step.

First, make a list of the trees you now have, showing for each class the number of trees, volume per tree, and total volume. Next, assume that every tree grows exactly 2 in. in diameter, and make a list showing number of trees by DBH classes after this growth has taken place. Now, insert the volume per tree for each DBH class, the same figures you used in the first list. Then calculate the volumes per DBH class as before, and add them. When you finish and put the lists side by side, you will have a table that looks like Table 7.5.

Table 7.5 shows a 94.8% increase in volume during the period. If the increment cores mentioned above determine that the average length of this period is nine years, your timber is growing at a simple interest rate of 10.5%. You should use the compound-interest rate, however, and reference to an interest table shows it to be 7.7% for this example. Application of this rate to the present volume (or timber capital) of 171,300 board feet indicates that your annual growth is

**TABLE 7-5**
**Calculating Growth**

| DBH Class Inches | Now | | | Then | | |
|---|---|---|---|---|---|---|
| | Number of Trees | Volume in Board Feet Per Tree | Total | Number of Trees | Volume in Board Feet Per Tree | Total |
| 6 | 5,000 | | | | | |
| 8 | 2,500 | | | 5,000 | | |
| 10 | 1,000 | 24 | 24,000 | 2,500 | 24 | 60,000 |
| 12 | 700 | 52 | 36,400 | 1,000 | 52 | 52,000 |
| 14 | 400 | 96 | 38,400 | 400 | 96 | 67,200 |
| 16 | 250 | 150 | 37,500 | 400 | 150 | 60,000 |
| 18 | 100 | 210 | 21,000 | 250 | 210 | 52,500 |
| 20+ | 50 | 280 | 14,000 | 150 | 280 | 42,000 |
| | 10,000 | | 171,300 | 10,000 | | 333,700 |

12,200 board feet. This volume can be removed each year without dipping into timber capital. If it is not removed, it is added to capital and increases the following year's growth, since the 7.7% applies to whatever timber capital you have.

Table 7.5 applies to sawtimber only, and there are no volume entries after 6 and 8 in., since these trees are below sawtimber size. They will grow to this size, however, and information about their number is essential. Note that 8-in. trees listed under "Now" moved into the 10-in. class under "Then." This method makes no allowance for trees that will die during the period. Although this loss is normally insignificant, mortality can be serious, and experience is necessary to evaluate this factor. Most of you will select a professional to take your inventory, and these calculations are properly part of his job. My intention here is to give you a general idea of what he will do and a simple, workable system if you want to do it yourself.

## SOIL ANALYSIS

An equally important part of the inventory is an evaluation of the soil's productivity. Farmers have recognized the great variation in productive capacity among farms for a long time, but timberland owners have generally assumed that one acre is about as good for growing trees as another. Nothing is farther from the truth. Some acres will grow twice as much as others; knowing this offers you excellent opportunities. You can use the general lack of appreciation either to dispose of unproductive areas you own or to acquire land of high productivity at bargain prices. More specific discussion of this appears in the last chapter.

Trouble comes in finding someone competent to make a soil analysis. The study of the effect of soils on tree growth is relatively new in forestry, and although many foresters have some knowledge of the subject, few have applied it extensively. Your consulting forester can do this work or refer you to a specialist. Many big timber companies use soil analysis in land appraisals, and you might be able to get helpful information from their foresters.

If no technical help is available, you can certainly use your own powers of observation. The most common measure of productivity of forest soils is what we call "site index." This is the total height in feet to which the main trees in a stand will grow in 50 years; for example, an acre with site index of 90 will grow a stand of trees 90 feet tall in 50 years. Other measures of site quality are used; terms and ages may vary with species and geography, but the principle is the same. Therefore, you can get some idea of the productive capacity of the soil by noting the height and general condition of the bigger trees on it. Tall trees growing along stream bottoms point to excellent investments; runts fighting for life on a gravel deposit or the top of a ridge indicate trouble.

This method does not work when there are no large trees at all; then you must use other methods. By studying the mechanical and chemical properties of soil samples, soil scientists can often predict their timber-growing capacities, but this is a complex process for experts only. The U.S. Soil Conservation Service, in cooperation with state agricultural experiment stations, is preparing soil surveys by counties for most of the nation. These reports are about 1 in. thick and contain much valuable information that can be understood by a layman. They include detailed descriptions of the county soils and a discussion of their suitability for crops, pasture, engineering applications, and wildlife food and cover. The newer surveys have a section on their suitability for timber. This section enables you to predict fairly well the yield you can expect from each soil. Most of the report is made up of aerial photographs on which the soil boundaries are plotted. These reports are useful for many purposes and are available at no cost. If the survey for your county has not been published, you will benefit from studying surveys of adjoining counties, especially if they contain the section on timber. The local Soil Conservation Service office can tell you which surveys are completed, and a consulting forester can help you interpret what these data mean to you in terms of money.

## NEED FOR CULTURAL TREATMENTS

Your inventory should include a report on stand conditions, particularly those that require cultural treatment. Successful investing demands that every productive acre be busy, and you need information on acres that are idle or nearly so. It is easy to gather this information while taking a sample on a grid pattern. Areas needing planting, TSI work, controlled burning, and thinning should be shown on the map. Information on thinning areas is most useful, since this leads to immediate income and more rapid growth or concentration of growth on better trees. Areas damaged by beavers or other animals, insects, or diseases must be shown. It is also helpful to have comments about areas ready for harvest, but the timber inventory will assist in showing this.

Although the map will show location and extent of these stand conditions, the comments of the person taking the inventory are needed to estimate the cost of performing cultural treatments and the benefits that will be obtained from them. Financial forecasts for this work will be discussed later; I want to point out now only the need for basic data.

## MARKET ANALYSIS

The report should show the market value of various products found on the tract. General comments on the prevailing price of stumpage in the county or state are not sufficient. Timber values vary widely with quality and accessibility, and you need specific information on your tract to make a financial forecast.

Many properties contain some material that is unmerchantable now but may become so in the near future, and other material that is unlikely ever to become merchantable. An example of the former is oak pulpwood. For decades it had few or no markets. Many paper mills are now buying it, and the market is expanding. The market for hardwood pulpwood is growing rapidly, and some hardwood sawtimber trees are now used for the inner parts of pine plywood. Any comments about such apparent trends are useful in a market analysis.

## OTHER CONSIDERATIONS

You need to know something about several other matters, and one of these is the prevalence of forest fires. Signs of repeated fires are easy to spot on the ground, and their presence threatens trouble for the investor. Fire statistics for the county or state are worth far less than a few comments about the particular tract.

Another is forest type. There may be several on the tract, each representing special problems requiring special solutions to obtain satisfactory profits. For example, fire may help in managing some pine species, but is always a disaster in bottomland hardwood types.

It is useful to know who the adjoining landowners are. Although a complete list of them is not a part of the normal inventory, some data can be gathered on the ground. The U.S. Forest Service and big timber companies make excellent neighbors, since both help with forest-fire and trespass problems; the latter may be good customers when you want to sell timber or land. Such neighbors usually keep their boundary lines painted and relieve you of this management cost.

Of great importance is information that indicates adverse possession. It can be a serious problem, and the person taking the inventory should be especially alert for and report in detail any evidence of it.

During inventory, the person must start at one boundary line, may touch others during the day, but spends most of the time in the interior, where the lines are not visible. Nevertheless, any information about their condition is useful, for they must be established eventually, and this cost must be predicted. Equally important is information about area. Although distances in inventory are not measured as accurately as those in surveys, they may reveal appreciable variations from the areas shown by the legal description.

The map should show and the report should discuss all ROWs on the tract. Location, width, and type of use are important for two reasons. First, the location should coincide with that shown by title records; otherwise, there may be a title problem. For many state, county, and private roads, ROW agreements do not appear in public records. Second, ROWs are ordinarily unavailable for growing timber. This wasted space may be a significant percentage of total area and reduce possible annual production. If such ROWs are still on the assessment, annual ad valorem taxes are higher than they should be.

All preceding comments point to the vital importance of intelligent observation during inventory. For this reason, the best season for this work is the period when many trees and shrubs are bare. Although an experienced person can do accurate work at any season, he has an easier job when visibility is excellent. It should be obvious that inventories based on aerial-photograph interpretation with little ground work are unsatisfactory for most purposes; too many important items must be visually inspected, and a camera in an aircraft $2\frac{1}{2}$ miles above ground is not good enough.

You may hear a lot about continuous forest inventory (CFI), a system requiring frequent and intensive measurement of sample plots with data tabulated for computer analysis; it is or was popular with some foresters. As a general rule, CFI is suitable only for tracts of over 10,000 acres, may not provide all the information an average investor needs, and may be more expensive than conventional methods.

## MANAGEMENT PLAN

To many foresters, a management plan is essential, and by management plan they mean a written document covering many years and describing all aspects of the operation, such as method of cutting, volumes to be removed from certain areas at certain times, cultural practices, and so forth. Plans of this kind may be desirable for properties of the U.S. Forest Service or big timber companies, but they are usually not necessary for you and are premature as part of inventory. Inventory only gathers data to determine what plans are possible.

Good management plans depend on many things besides forestry. Your tract may be only part of your assets, and although you expect it to produce an adequate return, you want it to do so in such a manner that the *combined* return from your investments fits your needs as well as possible. At times, you may want an annual income; in adversity you may need a large, quick, cash income; in prosperity you may choose to invest funds from other sources to produce future profits. Once you have an inventory, you can sit down with your advisers on forestry, accounting, and law to prepare a plan for tomorrow, next month, next year, or next decade. The more you tell them about your financial objectives, the better they are able to suggest a suitable plan. It should be as simple and flexible as possible, and you should review it at least annually to determine its suitability.

As you carry out your plan on the ground, you will work great changes in the inventory, and you should keep it up to date with office calculations and entries that show the effect of each action. Under such a system, it will serve as a sound guide for eight to ten years. Eventually, however, a calculated inventory will contain large errors and must be checked by another physical inventory. You will want to compare the next inventory with the present one as adjusted by the calculations, and you must use the same standards in both to allow this.

# 8
# The Financial Forecast

Everyone who buys timberland makes big money. They are not making any more land, so all you have to do is pay the market price and hang on; inflation and development will take care of you. This seems to be the lesson of the past. In the 45 years I have been watching the scene, timberland prices have always seemed to be too high today and then proved to be quite low when you looked back on them 10 years later.

But if making money is so easy, why are there so many disgruntled timberland investors who could have earned better returns on other investments? Why are there some losers?

There have been both winners and losers because timberland investment is like any other business. Success depends on attention to elementary business principles, one of the most important of which is preparation of financial forecasts. You can appreciate the importance of the forecast by looking at some past and present mistakes.

## FALLACIES OF COMMON APPRAISAL PRACTICE

A very common approach to buying a property is to break it down into its components, assign a value to each, and add these values to determine how much to pay for the whole property. Components usually listed are merchantable timber, reproduction, bare land, and minerals. Although each component has a definite value if it can be acquired separately, the components cannot be separated in the normal tract. They operate as a team, and their joint action is the only important thing to you.

The first weakness in this approach is that it is difficult to assign correct values to each component, especially since some of them do not even exist. There is nothing wrong with component-parts appraisals; the problem is poor valuation of components. It is easy to determine the market price of merchantable timber but hard to apply it. If this timber is present in very small volumes, less than two cords of pulpwood or 500 board feet of sawtimber per acre, you cannot assign the present market price to it, since it cannot be harvested even if you give it away. Nevertheless, this is often done. There is a market for minerals, but the tendency is to base mineral appraisals on professional opinions instead of cash offers. Although reproduction cannot be sold, it is worth something, but this value again must be an opinion or estimate. It is usually arrived at by predicting the value of the little trees at the time they reach merchantble size and then discounting this back to the present. The most nebulous component is bare land, devoid of minerals and merchantable timber and reproduction. It is almost impossible to find such an item; it can be evaluated only by an educated guess. For your purposes, bare land has a value only as a base for growing trees, although it might be worth something as a speculation. You often hear the remark that any land ought to be worth so many dollars per acre. Such an attitude in timberland purchases invites disaster.

Second, market prices reflect the opinions of others, whereas you are interested only in yourself. The market price of a new Cadillac is about twice that of a new Chevrolet; is it worth that much more to you? Market prices of timber tracts are strongly influenced by land-acquisition programs of big timber companies. When the programs begin, they exert a decided upward pressure on prices; once they end, prices drop rapidly to about the level where they offer a reasonable return on invested capital. This drop is hard to see because prices of timberlands are not quoted daily, as are those of listed stocks, and because sellers strongly resist the drop. Ownership of a tract is evidence in itself that the owner is a person of some means and can weather a period of weak prices for some time. When large concerns stop buying, and thereby decrease demand, the first result is a slowdown in trading activity until it almost stops. Buyers are unwilling to pay high prices, since adequate returns appear unlikely; sellers are reluctant to give up their previous ideas of the value of their properties and hang on, hoping for a rise in the market. Finally, pressure on some sellers gets so strong that they decide to meet current market conditions, and the price is often a surprising percentage below the peak. This process may take several years, but when trading is at a standstill, the usual explanation is a weak market where price reductions are a must. Proper appraisal practice will help you recognize such a situation and determine what a property is worth to you.

## THE CORRECT METHOD OF APPRAISAL

Let us demonstrate this by a study of an actual transaction. A lumber company offers for sale a 400-acre tract that has been under uneven-age management with trees of many sizes on each acre. It sets the initial offering price by the component-parts appraisal method, assigning per-acre values of $300 for sawtimber, $75 for pulpwood, $50 for reproduction, and $150 for bare land with a substantial mineral interest, for a total price of $230,000. Strenuous efforts by the company and its agents for 12 months produce many sightseers but no buyers. The company finally realizes that its tract must compete with investment opportunities available everywhere, so it solicits an offer from an experienced timberland investor.

First, the investor takes an inventory of the tract and gathers all data discussed in Chapter 7. Then he employs one of the great lessons from his experience: that a seller who wants the best price must ask his customers what they want and offer it to them. One of my professors in forestry school in 1940 hammered away at the truism that, merely because of the cost of processing them, big trees were more valuable per cubic foot than little ones even though they were manufactured into the same product, and that further differences in value arose from differences in the products that could be made from them. Even the most uneducated pulpwood cutter of that time knew that 10-in. trees were much more profitable for him than 6-in. trees. So our investor asks several local timber buyers about market prices by DBH classes and assigns them to his inventory data. (I followed his procedure in the examples in Chapter 17 and Appendix I, and they show the surprising magnitude of the differences.)

Next, he calculates annual revenue under the present type of management to be $13,600 less operating costs of $1360 = $12,240. Since his minimum real rate of return is 7%, the tract's value to him is $12,240 divided by 0.07 = $174,857, which he rounds up to $175,000 or $437.50 per acre. If you include reproduction as part of the timber component (because these small trees will eventually become merchantable), then the land is worth only $12.50 per acre. This is because land does not increase in volume as timber does and because the components are being used in an inefficient manner. But the important point is that the investor is taking them in their present combined form and is capitalizing only what they produce in this combination. He offers $175,000.

The lumber company is shocked; as you remember, it offered the tract at $230,000, establishing the price by component-parts appraisal. (The fact that, at this price, the return would be only 5.3% was not even considered.) Unfortunately, some parts of the property had been purchased using this appraisal method, and this is one reason why the board of directors was disappointed in the yield from this part of the company's assets. Surprisingly, purchases based on such reasoning are still commonly made by persons who ought to know better, and disappointment is inevitable. Nevertheless, looking forward and not backward, the company makes a financial forecast of its own, contrasts what it receives from the tract with what it might receive if the money offered were employed in manufacturing equipment or as working capital, and accepts the offer.


## TWO GUIDING PRINCIPLES FOR APPRAISALS

To put the lesson in this episode another way, you must recognize and accept two guiding principles in appraising timberland. One is this: *You do not make money from individual trees over a short period; you make it only from acres of trees over a rotation.* From observation of single trees or small clumps of them on your land or in your yard, or from reading research reports, you may have learned that you can cause spectacular growth increases by use of fertilizer, herbicides, irrigation, super trees, site-prep, controlled burning, wider spacing, and so on. This knowledge may lead you to believe that you can produce similar results with trees by the acre if you can treat them the same way. You cannot, and thinking you can may cost you a bundle.

The reason you cannot is that trees by the acre react with each other, and increases in one place usually cause offsetting losses in another. The common results of nitrogen fertilizer provide an illustration. On many sites, as soon as you apply the fertilizer, all trees begin to grow faster. Immediately thereafter, however, they begin to compete more fiercely with each other, and in no time this greater competition causes greater mortality. The greater mortality reduces the per-acre volume to the level that it would have reached without the fertilizer. (There may be, however, a shift of the volume into larger trees.)

Generally speaking, if you do not harvest the trees within five years of such fertilization, you will lose most of the benefits. It should be obvious that only so much rain and sunlight fall on any acre, so there are physical limits to what can be grown on it.

The second principle is this: *You do not make money from single management practices; you make it only from the surplus of incomes over expenses over the rotation.* As long as you are willing to pay the bills, you can create almost any desired condition on your land. The only trouble is that expenses in the beginning are much more important than incomes at the end, so you should never choose any practice until you test its impact on the whole.

To emphasize my point, I quote an observer outside the field of forestry. John Fowles, the British novelist, summed up the situation very well in these words from *The Tree* (Little, Brown and Company, Boston):

Evolution did not intend trees to grow singly. Far more than ourselves they are social creatures, and no more natural as isolated specimens than man is as a marooned sailor or a hermit. Their society in turn creates or supports other societies of plants, insects, birds, mammals, micro-organisms; all of which we may choose to isolate and section off, but which remain no less the ideal entity . . . of the wood. . . . Scientists restrict the word symbiotic to those relationships between species that bring some detectable mutual benefit; but the true wood, the true place of any kind, is the sum of all its phenomena. They are all in some sense symbiotic, being together in a togetherness of beings.

## WHAT RATE OF RETURN SHOULD YOU USE?

No one can tell you what rate of return to use. I can only point out several factors that come into play. Making the right choice brings out the artistry, as opposed to the science, of timberland investment. If you select too low a rate, your appraised value will be greater than the asking price of nearly every property offered. Almost every trade will appear advantageous, but of course you will earn little on invested capital. On the other hand, if you select too high a rate, every offering will appear overpriced, and you will make no trades at all.

Second, the rate depends on your assessment of the plus and minus factors discussed below and your ability to allow them time to work for you. One of the most successful investors I know believes that the long-term rise in the dollar price of land is so substantial that almost any purchase is a good one over a 10-year or 20-year period. Some studies of the history of land prices indicate that he may be correct. All of us know buyers who paid what appeared to be ridiculously high prices and then, within a short time, sold their purchases for a 100% profit. Nevertheless, this knowledge does not help if you pay such a price that interest and management costs force you into bankruptcy before long-term influences have time to work. Most successful investors give great attention to the near future and expect to receive at little or no cost whatever profits the distant future may hold.

Third, the figure you are choosing is the *real* rate of return, the rate produced by biological growth of trees, the rate that is independent of price changes or, in other words, over and above inflation. You will not find it quoted anywhere. The various rates that appear in the daily news are all *nominal* rates. They are combinations of real rates and the premiums that lenders tack on to protect themselves from expected inflation and are usually several points higher than real rates. There-fore, you cannot use them in your calculations because then you would be discounting real incomes by nominal rates and no tract would be good enough. I can only suggest that you look at history to help you choose a real rate. Over the past century or so, annual real rates of return produced by the safest investments (U.S. Government Bonds, for instance) have been 2% to 3%, with stocks and other bonds producing 3% to 5% and other media producing higher returns.

To get further insight into the level of nominal interest rates in 1987, I asked Leland Speed what discount or capitalization rates were prevalent in real estate and what rate should be used in timberland investments. He replied,

Declining interest rates have recently reduced the cap rate on all alternative investments. In commercial real estate today, the cap rates for income properties vary from a low of 7% on institutional office buildings to a high of 10.5% to 11% for motels. Considering the low risks involved, the nature of the investment, and the small amount of management needed, I think the cap rate for timberland would be on the low end of the spectrum, around 7%.

Although most timberland investors never consciously choose this rate and those who do do not announce it, I judge that most of them use a real rate of 6% to 8%. Big timber companies seem to use about 6% because they get the added benefit of more secure timber supplies; some professional traders seem to use 8% because they have limited capital and must make a big profit whenever they commit it;

everyone else seems to use about 7%. With no more guidance than this, you must choose your own.

Selection of the rate of return is equally important if you already own a tract. First, it enables you to determine whether it is performing as you desire. Using our investor's approach, appraise your property, and decide what you would pay for it if it were offered to you. If this value is less than the price at which it can be sold, you might be wise to sell it and invest the proceeds elsewhere. Second, the rate has a big effect on whether you cut a tree today or allow it to grow for additional years. The timber marker must have such a guide in order to choose trees to mark for cutting and which to leave. The general considerations above govern selection of the rate for this purpose. Some modifications to the rate may be necessary to reflect available opportunities for reinvestment of funds and how much of the sale proceeds will go for taxes.

## PLUS FACTORS THAT CANNOT BE MEASURED

Our investor has owned and studied timberlands for years, and he knows that they have substantial advantages that are hard to measure with a ruler or a dollar sign. These excite him once he finds a tract that passes his financial tests. First, timberland income and expenses receive slightly favorable treatment under tax laws. Second, timberlands produce profits from sources other than trees, and many of these sums cannot be anticipated. Third, he may have a chance to sell parts of the property for conversion to higher use, such as farms, pastures, or ROWs. Fourth, wood is a cheap and renewable resource (at present, the cheapest source of cellulose), which intrigues many scientists. New discoveries are frequent and will raise the value of his land. Fifth, research in tree genetics and in growth and yield of forests is just beginning to produce the kind of results that will greatly improve productivity of forests. Sixth, he cannot lose his entire investment, since land cannot be moved or destroyed and always has some residual value. An investor in an oil well buys an asset that will become worthless sooner or later.

Seventh and most important, he knows that land prices in the United States have risen continually since the Pilgrims landed. They may go up and down from year to year, but almost any 10-year period shows a sizable increase. It is reasonable to assume that this trend will continue. The pressure of people on land makes prices rise, and our population is expanding.

## MINUS FACTORS THAT CANNOT BE MEASURED

Our investor realizes that timberland investment has some disadvantages. First, it is not liquid. Investors prize liquidity and flexibility; they want to react quickly to sudden changes in conditions. Transactions in listed stocks are almost instantaneous, and market prices are in the paper every morning. Sale of a timberland tract may require several weeks or months, and the exact price cannot be determined until you find a buyer. Second, timber prices fluctuate, and since interest and management costs tend to remain fixed, a severe drop in timber prices that lasts a long time can hurt him. On the other hand, the investor knows that long-lasting declines do not occur suddenly, and he has enough financial resources to postpone sales for five or more years. Third, technological change and shifts in the rate and direction of our country's development may cause his property to fall in value. Fourth, over the long term, prices of some forest products have risen faster than those of competing materials, and this decreases the market for his crops. Nevertheless, if he buys at the right price, he should always be able to sell out without great loss. He believes that the effect of the last two factors will be so gradual that he will be able to react to them in time.

## WHOLESALE VERSUS RETAIL PURCHASES

The actual transaction described earlier in this chapter was many times larger and might be considered a wholesale purchase. This explains both the great care used by the investor and his insistence upon adequate return on capital. His approach is sound in every respect, however, and you should follow it even though your transactions are in what we might call the "retail market." This is the market familiar to most of us, where the normal transaction is less than $100,000. It is the land of dreams; romance, impulse, and desire for playthings have a real effect on prices, and market experts are found on every street corner. The market offers exceptional opportunities and exceptional risks. Component-parts appraisals are common, and the use of this method by others may help you sell to them. Nevertheless, our investor's objective analysis of income and expenses and his insistence upon a minimum rate of return should govern your actions even when you invest a small amount. If expectation of profits depends more on hope than facts, especially the hope of finding a greater-fool buyer, keep your money.

One half-truth believed by many foresters and timberland investors is that a big tract sells for a bigger price per acre than a little one. This is used as an excuse for paying premiums to acquire adjacent lands. Anyone who believes this fails to understand the genius of the developer of cemeteries who buys by the acre, but sells by the square foot. You will do well to remember this procedure. There are thousands of buyers for 40-acre tracts, hundreds of buyers for 4000-acre tracts, but very few buyers for 40,000-acre tracts. Competition decreases as the consideration increases. In addition, investors with large amounts of capital are shrewd and intelligent, know well the power of money, and use their great resources to make advantageous trades that persons with less capital cannot make. This is why they have so much money in the first place.

Another half-truth frequently repeated is that it is worth a sizable premium to acquire a small tract completely surrounded by your land. If you keep your boundary lines painted, if the tract improves access to your land, or if your neighbor is a constant source of trouble, there is at least something to this. Generally, however, a trading situation of this kind strongly favors the owner of the large tract; he is almost the only market for the small one and should be able to buy it on favorable terms if he is patient.

Trading in the retail market can be highly profitable, but it is several steps removed from pure timberland investment and thus beyond the scope of this book. I can only mention its existence to you and state that all principles covered herein will help you. Their application will establish the investment values of timberlands and reveal how much of their market price depends on other considerations.

## FINANCIAL FORECAST APPLIED TO CULTURAL WORK

We have discussed the financial forecast, with emphasis on the role of interest, only as it applies to purchases of tracts, but the procedure applies equally to such management activities as planting, TSI work, and seed-tree cuts.

Millions of trees are planted yearly, and their spacing on the ground has often violated two cardinal investment principles. First, it decreases the odds for success. The 6 ft × 6 ft spacing that once was the norm requires 1210 seedlings per acre. If the per-thousand cost of seedlings is $30 and of planting is $60, per-acre investment must be $108.90. By harvest time at age 25, this sum compounded at 7% will have grown to $591.00, so at an average stumpage of $20 per cord, the volume must be nearly 30 cords just to break even. At a spacing of

9 ft × 9 ft, the comparable figures are 538 seedlings per acre, initial investment of $48.42 increasing to $262.78, and a break-even volume of 13 cords. Everyone who has watched a 6 × 6 plantation develop has observed that the limited growing space per tree causes the average size to be smaller and thus less valuable per cord than in a 9 × 9 plantation. Therefore, if $20 per cord is average stumpage, 6 × 6 trees may bring only $17.50 when 9 × 9 trees bring $22.50, so the break-even volumes may actually be 34 cords and 12 cords.

Second, it increases the risk. Planting too many seedlings so that early mortality would leave the desired number has always been recognized as a bad idea by anyone who has watched plantations develop. Death from drought or poor planting technique does not strike seedlings alternately; these agencies take all or none, and so does fire. You cannot count on mortality to cure bad spacing.

Now that several growth and yield programs are available, you should choose spacing by predicting the net yield from each density, evaluating it according to DBH classes, and then discounting the total to today by the real rate you selected. The highest present value indicates how many seedlings to plant, but the calculation ignores value of the land involved and costs of management and taxes. If there is not a surplus after you recover planting costs, the land is not worth developing.

You should make the same forecast when considering TSI work. Once again interest makes size of the original investment critical. Spending $20 per acre to kill cull hardwoods overtopping young pines is one thing; spending $80 per acre to kill every undesirable bush and shrub is entirely different. Neither investment may be a wise one unless the growth and yield programs reveal that it can be later recovered.

Interest affects the practice of leaving seed trees to start the next crop. Seed from these trees is not free. Leaving an adequate stand of seed trees delays income that might be received from their sale; you must figure interest, perhaps for several years, on their value, which may be more than $200 per acre. They may continue to grow, perhaps faster than the interest rate, but some usually die because of great changes in the biological situation. They must be harvested to recover their value, and the future price per MBF may be lower because of small volumes per acre. They must be removed also to prevent interference with the new crop, and this commits you to a future cut when markets may not be favorable. Logging them will destroy some of the seedlings that came from them. In addition, spacing of natural reproduction cannot be controlled, and overcrowding is common. Choice of this method of regeneration requires careful consideration.

## FINANCIAL FORECAST APPLIED TO THINNING

The same procedure will help you decide whether to carry out a precommercial thinning. One of our Georgia clients has a five-year-old plantation that started at 990 seedlings per acre spaced 5.5 ft apart in rows 8.0 ft apart; an on-the-ground examination of it tempted us to recommend a precommercial thinning. Then we predicted yields at ages 20 and 25 for both unthinned and thinned stands and discounted them to the present. Per-acre differences between the two in favor of thinning was $14.05 at age 20 and $31.09 at age 25. Since the lowest bid for doing the work was $40.00 per acre, the client rightly decided to suffer the overcrowding, at least for the time being.

Using this approach in conjunction with a growth-and-yield program based on prediction of individual trees not only will change one common way of thinning, but also will demonstrate how research increases profits by enabling us truly to understand how trees grow. In the interview mentioned in Chapter 1 Arthur Temple also said that

### TABLE 8-1
### Stand Table Obtained Using Burkhart Program

| DBH Class | Number Trees | Average Height | Basal Area | Cubic Foot Volume o. b. | Volume Cords to 4 in. | Volume Doyle Board Feet |
|---|---|---|---|---|---|---|
| 4 | 5.3 | 38.5 | 0.5 | 10.1 | 0.0 | 0.0 |
| 5 | 13.5 | 42.4 | 1.9 | 38.9 | 0.3 | 0.0 |
| 6 | 21.8 | 45.7 | 4.4 | 96.4 | 0.9 | 0.0 |
| 7 | 39.0 | 49.6 | 10.4 | 244.7 | 2.4 | 0.0 |
| 8 | 44.3 | 51.0 | 15.4 | 369.6 | 3.8 | 0.0 |
| 9 | 52.5 | 53.2 | 23.1 | 572.5 | 5.9 | 0.0 |
| 10 | 41.3 | 53.9 | 22.5 | 563.5 | 5.9 | 1103.1 |
| 11 | 24.8 | 56.3 | 16.2 | 422.4 | 4.4 | 908.1 |
| 12 | 13.5 | 58.2 | 10.5 | 283.1 | 2.9 | 669.5 |
| 13 | .8 | 62.6 | .6 | 18.7 | .2 | 47.9 |
| | 256.5 | | 105.5 | 2619.6 | 26.7 | 2728.5 |

o.b. = outside bark

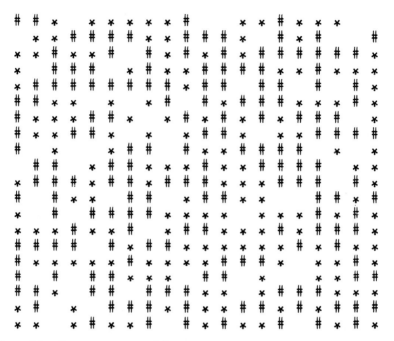

Figure 8.1.  Computer-generated diagram showing results of thinning 20 rows of 20 trees each. Blanks indicate trees that died before age 20 and asterisks indicate thinned trees.

Mother Nature may be the best forester of all, so I decided to test his theory. Most of us have recognized that the genetic variation from one tree to another can be large and that each cubic foot of soil is also unique, but we have often acted as if proper spacing would make up for these differences.

Using a Burkhart program (see Chapter 17), I ran a simulation for a 300-per-acre, site-index-80 plantation to age 20 and obtained Table 8.1.

The average heights clearly show that some trees are already suppressed, while others are growing rapidly. Since all were planted at the same spacing and most are still there, the differential growth must be due, not to spacing, but to a combination of genetics and soil. In other words, Mother Nature is telling us where the star performers are.

Following her direction, I removed in a thinning all trees smaller than the 9-in DBH class. At this point, the computer showed the diagram of 20 rows of 20 trees each, with blanks showing trees that

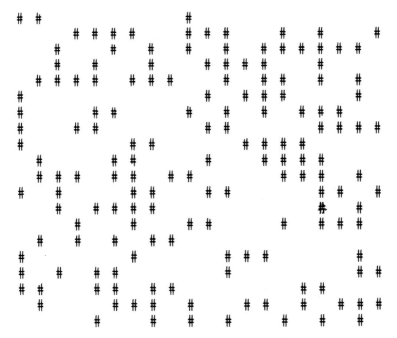

Figure 8.2. Computer-generated diagram showing stand at age 30.

died before age 20 and asterisks showing those thinned (Figure 8.1). I then projected the stand to age 30 and found the spacing pattern shown in Figure 8.2.

Many managers order thinnings by rows, and one thinning removing every third row would be very similar to the thinning as far as basal area is concerned. But it would nip in the bud one-third of Mother Nature's stars. Using our procedure and the values in the example in Chapter 17, I calculated the bare land value (BLV) for Mother Nature's system to be $81.23 and that of the third-row thinning to be $73.63. By adopting the natural system, you would raise BLV by more than 10%.

You need trees of merchantable size as quickly as possible, so you must space seedlings far enough apart to give them enough growing space from the beginning. As Dr. Koslowski pointed out in Chapter 6, it is hard to reverse growth slowdowns caused by competition. Once you have given the correct spacing, however, you should stay out of Mother Nature's way. She will show you from then on which trees she no longer needs in the stand.

Cultural practices on your tract depend mainly on biology, but financial considerations should govern which to undertake first. Some expenditures such as those for TSI work are deductible; others such as those for planting must be capitalized. Benefits from some practices may be realized 5 years later, while returns from others may be 15 years off. Need for practices like planting may be obvious, whereas need for other practices like pruning or precommercial thinning may require theorectical calculations by an expert. If development funds are limited, you must channel them into the most profitable practices.

Finally, you must recognize that many acres are inherently productive but are idle because of poor management in the past, whereas some acres are idle because they are inherently unproductive. Those in the first class can be put to work with varying success by cultural treatments; those in the second may justify no additional investment. In an extreme case, a landowner would be better off to give away his unproductive acres because they will not produce enough revenue to pay ad valorem taxes.

# 9

# Accounting and the Tax Laws

Accounting and taxation may be the least understood of the important aspects of timberland investment, and they are the most frustrating because Congress cannot resist the temptation to change them in every session. But you must have some grasp of them, for your understanding helps your tax adviser help you and makes it possible for you to appraise some investment opportunities without outside help. The following discussion touches only the high points.

## INCOME

**Capitalized Expenditures and Depletion.**  When you buy a tract of timberland, you swap dollars for natural resources. You have not changed the amount of your assets; you have merely changed their form. One day the list of them shows so much cash; the next day the cash is gone, and the list shows an equivalent amount of timberland. Transactions of this kind are capital expenditures. If you buy a property for $10,000, you capitalize the expenditure of $10,000.

The transaction is more complicated than swapping dollars for timberland. In the trade, you actually acquire some merchantable trees, some reproduction, some land, and perhaps some minerals; you must show the amount paid for each in order to establish your depletion basis. In such a trade, you establish a depletion basis by spending cash, but you must determine it whether you buy a tract, inherit one, or receive one as a gift.

Depletion basis is important because it determines what taxable income results from operating the tract. Let us suppose that, in the

$10,000 transaction above, you spend $9000 for merchantable timber and $1000 for reproduction, land, and minerals. If you sell all the timber for $9000 the day after your purchase, you merely swap dollars again and make no profit. In other words, you deplete your timber account by $9000; it has a balance of $9000, so there is no taxable gain. If you sell the timber for $10,000 or if you have no depletion basis at all, you have a taxable gain—a short-term gain if you owned the tract less than 12 months and a long-term one if you owned it more than 12 months. Short-term gain is ordinary income and receives the same tax treatment as your salary. Long-term gain is commonly called "capital gain," receives the same tax treatment as short-term gain, but may be useful in some situations.

Once you capitalize an expenditure and establish a depletion basis for part of a timberland investment, you cannot reduce or deplete the asset until you dispose of it. Depletion basis can never be more than actual cost, but whether the basis is in timber or in land means much to you. If it is in timber, you recover part of it every time you sell timber. If it is in land, you cannot recover any of it until you sell the land. Since you may sell timber frequently but dispose of the land only upon death, you should assign as much as possible of the total basis to timber. Nevertheless, it is common to find investors who buy a tract of cutover timberland for $250 per acre and assign $175 to land and minerals and $75 to timber. This is a bad practice and does not reflect the facts. In a timberland investment, land is nothing but soil without any trees at all, not even the smallest ones. When you pay $250 per acre, you certainly want more than bare soil (unless the soil is exceptionally productive and located in an outstanding market. You receive more than bare soil, because there are always some trees on it. Although they may not be merchantable, you expect them to become merchantable soon or you would not buy the tract at the price. Therefore, you pay some of your money for timber, and your records should show this. In this example, it is much more realistic to assign $175 to timber and $75 to land and minerals. Further illustration of this point appears in the table of plantation values in Chapter 17.

Let us return to the $10,000 example. If you assign $9000 to timber and sell all of it later, you deplete your timber account by $9000 and show whatever additional money you receive as a gain. Complete liquidations are rare, however; partial cuts are much more common and, for tax purposes, make things more complicated. You must determine how much timber of each kind you own at the time of sale and allocate part of the depletion basis to each. In this case, if you have 90 MBF of sawtimber and nothing else, your depletion basis is $100/MBF. If you sell any part of this timber immediately after purchase and receive $100/MBF, you have only depletion of $100/ MBF. Suppose, however, that the cut is delayed 10 years and that, during the delay, timber volume increases to 180 MBF. At this time your depletion basis is only $50/MBF, since the total cannot be changed from the original $9000. If you sell any part of this timber for $100/MBF, you have $50 of depletion and $50 of capital gain. You can see that calculations of this kind can go on forever and may become burdensome for owners of small tracts. The easiest solution for them is to ask their tax adivser whether they can deplete the entire timber account in early sales and show all future sales as pure capital gain.

Values assigned to land as a depletion basis usually include minerals, if any, and your tax adviser can tell you whether you should allocate a separate depletion basis to minerals. Your tract may contain fences, houses, barns, and similar improvements that can be depreciated. (Notice the difference between depreciation and depletion. Depreciation is reduction in the service capacity of a capital asset through use, obsolescence, or inadequacy. Depletion implies removal of a natural resource—a physical shrinkage or lessening of an estimated available quantity.) All of this makes establishment of the depletion basis a matter on which you must consult a tax adviser. The do-it-yourself method can get you in trouble with the Internal Revenue Service (IRS). If you failed to establish your depletion basis when you acquired your tract, perhaps by inheritance many years ago, you can do so at the time of the first timber sale with help from a consulting forester, and your tax adviser can tell you how.

**Tax Treatment.** The foregoing paragraphs cover nearly every aspect of the tax treament from timber sales, the main source of income. Some part of each sale is depletion, and some part is capital gain (or loss in unusual cases) if you have held the property 12 months or more.

Other revenues receive varying treatments. In general, sales of ROWs are like timber sales, but may also mean some depletion of the land account. Rentals under leases for turpentine operations, grazing, hunting, recreation, and so forth are ordinary income. Payments for damages are treated the same as timber sales. Option money is ordinary income, unless the option is exercised and the option money applies on the purchase price. Rentals under long-term timber leases require close scrutiny before they can be properly classified. These leases are so difficult to negotiate and administer that most lessees are interested only in tracts of 25,000 acres or more, so the problem may not concern you.

## EXPENSES

So far we have talked only about expenditures that change the form of your assets. Most of them, however, are not changes of form, but reductions of the size of your assets. These are expenses, many of which can be deducted against any of your income.

Some expenditures are deductible; some must be capitalized; a few may be treated in either way. Those in the last category are called "carrying charges" and "developmental expenditures." Rules about which items are deductible and which must be capitalized are not always clearly defined; there is a gray area where an item is deductible at one time and must be capitalized at another. Much hinges on the intent of the taxpayer and on timing. Some items are capital expenditures if incurred in connection with land acquisition or planting, but are deductible expenses if incurred several years after acquisition or in connection with TSI work as opposed to planting.

**Which Items Must Be Capitalized?**   Capital expenditures form depletion basis and include the following:

1. Acquistion cost of land and timber
   a. Lump-sum purchase price
   b. Inventory, boundary survey, legal and recording fees, and commissions, if connected with purchase
2. Direct costs in connection with reforestation by planting
   a. Preparation of planting site, including removal of cull trees or brush or other treatments to afford good growing conditions
   b. Cost of seedlings
   c. Labor and equipment expenses including depreciation or rental of tree planters, tractors, and so on, involved in planting
   d. Thinning and improvements to property, such as road construction, firebreak construction, grading, and ditching, if of a permanent nature with no determinable life

I mentioned earlier that capital expenditures must be allocated between land and timber accounts, and this applies to the three categories listed above. Your knowledge of timber operations probably gives you a general idea of the accounts in which the expenditures should be capitalized, but you should consult your tax adviser. You usually want to deduct as much as possible so far as total costs are concerned; if an expenditure must be capitalized, you usually want to capitalize as much as possible in the timber account.

**Which Items Are Deductible?** Deductible items are generally operating expenses incurred during the years a timber crop is being produced and include the following:

1. Expenses for TSI work, thinning, and improvement cutting in immature stands, where the work is not done in connection with planting
2. Cost of tools of short life (less than one year)
3. Cost of materials and supplies
4. Incidental repairs
5. Cost of temporary roads
6. Management expenses, such as use of your car for inspections
7. Professional fees paid, if not in connection with a sale
8. Inventories and boundary surveys, if not in connection with acquisition or timber sales
9. Ad valorem taxes
10. Interest paid on borrowed money (within certain limits)
11. Insurance premiums
12. Depreciation of improvements with limited and determinable life, such as roads, bridges, culverts, and fences—logging roads, as opposed to permanent roads, being generally depreciable by either of two methods:
    a. So much per year of an estimated useful life
    b. So much per unit volume of timber expected to be brought out over the roads
13. Depreciation of equipment used in operations (subject to the ordinary rules for capitalizing and depreciating equipment used in operations, such as trucks, tractors, power saws—generally, any equipment with a life of more than one year)
14. Maintenance of fire breaks
15. Protection expenses against fire, insects, disease, and so on

**Which Items Are Optional?** Certain expenditures just listed in the category of deductible expenses do not, from a technical income tax standpoint, come under the classification of deductible expenses; instead, they are classified as carrying charges and development expenditures. The government allows you either to deduct or to capitalize them. I have included them as deductible expenses because situations in which you wish to capitalize, rather than deduct, them are so rare as to be of no practical interest. Generally, carrying charges include such items as annual taxes or interest paid on a mortgage. How many times have you wanted to capitalize, rather than deduct, taxes and interest? Development expenditures are those incurred in caring for timber stands in the development stage, while they are not producing income, such as:

1. Thinning, girdling, poisoning, pruning, and improvement cuts
2. Protection against fire, insects, and diseases, including labor, materials, and tools used in maintenance of firebreaks, and contributions to fire-protection associations

**How Do You Treat Government Subsidies?**  Government subsidies for forest-management practices reduce the amount that can be deducted if the subsidies are for deductible items such as TSI work. Subsidies reduce the amount that must be capitalized if the subsidies are for such capital expenditures as planting.

**The Passive Loss Rules**  The Tax Reform Act of 1986 introduced a new dimension of uncertainty into an already complicated subject by limiting the deductibility of management expenses, taxes, and interest paid by investors whose timber-growing operations constitute a passive activity. To enable taxpayers to distinguish between what is and what is not a passive activity, the IRS in early 1988 issued 166 pages of temporary regulations on the subject. Since this situation is obviously in a state of flux and will be for some time, I shall not discuss it in detail now and shall recommend only that you talk to your tax adviser about it.

The regulations emphasize to some extent, however, what I have recommended throughout this book, that is, that investors take a very active role in managing their properties. The IRS sets up tests to qualify for material participation (and thereby allow full deductibility of expenses), most of which require spending more than 100 hours in the activity. Since this is 5% of the normal working year or $12\frac{1}{2}$ normal working days, I doubt that many investors will pass them. One test, however, requires only that the investor spend, by himself, substantially all the time spent by all individuals (including employees and consultants) in the activity, and I believe that, if you spend as much time studying and thinking as I have urged, you will pass this test.

Under the new law, deductions for passive losses are not lost, but are only suspended. They will be reinstated in years when you have income or when you dispose of the investment entirely, even at a loss. And some tax advisers think that you can deduct ad valorem taxes on real estate on the schedule of itemized deductions.

## CERTAIN ATTITUDES OF THE INTERNAL REVENUE SERVICE

Occasionally, IRS agents propose to disallow the entire tax loss claimed from timberland operations, usually in years when these losses are accompanied by little or no income. They contend that there is no expectation of profit and that the property is not being operated as a business. This attitude of the IRS may be due to some court cases it has won against part-time farmers, not timberland investors, who operated the farms as a sideline and in such a manner that the profit potential was remote. I believe you can win arguments of this sort, since the economics of the business dictate that there are likely to be periods of 20 or more years before merchantable timber can be produced. It also appears that the Internal Revenue Code has recognized this matter of timber economics by providing landowners an optional election, even though the option is seldom used, of treating carrying charges and development expenditures either as deductible expenses or as additions to capital investment. You just may have to prove to the IRS that you are a good forest manager.

The IRS is always anxious that your tax records show the true situation, but some agents might question values you place on bare land, since they usually seem low to everyone except experienced investors. One big trouble is that many persons confuse bare land with cutover timberland. Bare land is nothing but dirt; cutover timberland is bare land plus reproduction and perhaps a few scattered trees of merchantable size. As I pointed out earlier, bare land serves timberland investors only as a base on which to grow trees, and unless it is exceptionally productive and located in an outstanding timber market, spending much money for it dooms the enterprise to failure. Much of the money used to buy cutover timberland goes to buy reproduction, which will eventually become merchantable timber. The table of values of plantations by years in Chapter 17 emphasizes this truth. I believe that you can win an argument with the IRS on this subject also.

## CASUALTY LOSSES AND INVOLUNTARY CONVERSION

Another aspect of taxation important to you is treatment of casualty losses. Such losses are caused by fire, windstorm, ice, sleet, hail, unusually heavy rains, floods, freezing, drought, and insects.

For tax purposes, casualty loss is determined differently from an insurance loss or the amount of damages for which a negligent party can be sued. Such a loss is not necessarily your economic loss or decline in fair market value. You must have a depletion basis in timber to incur a deductible casualty loss. I have previously mentioned that this cost or depletion basis is composed of purchase price, inherited value, basis acquired by gift, or expenditures capitalized during the period of operations. If loss from casualty is complete, the loss for tax purposes is simply the amount of your timber depletion basis. If there is only partial loss with salvable timber remaining, the loss for tax purposes is the difference between the fair market value of the timber before the casualty and the fair market value after the casualty, with loss being limited to depletion basis. For example, if fire killed timber in which you have a depletion basis of $900 and such timber was worth $10,000 before the fire and nothing after it, you have suffered a $10,000 economic loss but a deductible loss for tax purposes of $900.

To support the claim for loss, an accurate appraisal of damage is needed. It may be made immediately after the casualty if there is no doubt the trees will die or delayed until after the next growing season if there is doubt. Waiting until the next growing season might require an amended income tax return, since a casualty loss can usually be deducted only in the year it is sustained, not in the year when its amount is determined. You should employ a consulting forester if the amount is large and likely to be contested by the IRS.

Involuntary conversion, a type of loss that differs from those just described but is treated in a similar manner, results from seizure by public authority through the power of eminent domain; it is becoming more frequent because of expanded highway-building programs and such projects as reservoirs, pipelines, and powerlines. Seizure by public authority often results in taxable gain rather than loss, however, because of accounting procedures for timberland. Depletion basis is usually greatest at the time of acquisition and falls gradually with each timber sale. Fair market value thus nearly always exceeds depletion basis by a wide margin, and condemnation proceeds are based on the former. In such a case, you have a taxable capital gain equal to the excess, just as if the timber or land had been sold in a

normal transaction. Condemnations are forced sales in the sense that
sellers have no control over timing and price; they may not plan to sell
or may be unwilling to sell. If the sale produces a gain, they may be
forced to pay taxes by being forced to receive income. The Internal
Revenue Code acknowledges the possible unfairness of this and
allows you to prevent this gain being recognized and taxed by
reinvesting the proceeds, within specified limits, in similar property.
The specified time limits, generally speaking, begin with the threat of
condemnation and end three years after the close of the taxable year in
which any part of the gain is realized. If only a portion of condemnation proceeds is reinvested in similar property, a gain is recognized
and tax paid to the extent that the amount of gain reinvested falls short
of total gain from condemnation.

IRS rules regarding investment in similar property are relatively
lenient, for the term "property of like kind" has been broadly
interpreted. It appears to be possible to take condemnation proceeds
from timberland and reinvest them in other real estate quite different
from the timber tract given up, such as office building, apartment
house, ordinary farm, or raw land to be held for future development as
a subdivision or shopping center, and still qualify for nonrecognition
of gain.

This tax provision helps to maintain the price of timber tracts, and
each condemnation has a nationwide effect. If, as is often true, the
property condemned has a very small depletion basis, most of the
consideration may be a capital gain. The owner must pay about a third
of the money received in taxes unless he acts within a relatively short
period, and he balks at this. As his time gets shorter, he thinks he can
afford to pay more than a property is worth, since he is spending
67-cent dollars. The effect is nationwide because an owner may lose a
property by condemnation in Oregon and replace it with one in
Pennsylvania. The alert seller should watch the progress of all large
projects where condemnation is substantial; he may find a buyer for
his property among those who have lost theirs and must spend the
money. This is one of the plus factors that cannot be measured.

## DEPLETION-BASIS PROBLEMS OF INHERITANCE AND GIFTS

Some problems arise with estate and gift tax matters. The first point
to keep in mind is that inherited property has a cost basis in the hands
of the new owner equal to the fair market value on the date of death or
the alternative valuation date, normally six months after date of death.

Therefore, if you inherit a timber tract, you should determine from the executor of the estate the fair market value of it and how much was applicable to land and to timber. It is also a good idea to have both the land and the timber valued separately so that the timber basis is established in the estate. Since it may be many years before inherited timber is ready to be sold and, therefore, many years before you need these values to determine your gain on a sale, it is a good idea to obtain this information while all facts are readily available and to make it part of your permanent records. This is especially true for estates of less than $600,000, which will owe no federal tax.

You may have the opposite problem of passing timberland to your eventual heirs in such a way that taxes will cause the least possible disturbance. If your tract contains much merchantable timber, your heirs can probably sell enough timber to pay the taxes. On the other hand, if it contains well-stocked stands of trees below merchantable size and is thus quite valuable, estate taxes may be sizable and force sale of the land itself, since income from timber sales is unavailable. Under present laws, farms and timberland may be valued for their present use, within certain limitations, rather than as property with a higher use. This is a very technical area, with numerous conditions to be met in order to qualify. Recent tax law changes have largely eliminated advantages of making lifetime gifts to individuals, except for annual gifts of $10,000 (market value) per donee.

You can give timber property to most charitable organizations and obtain a charitable-contribution deduction on your income tax return equal to the fair market value of the property at the date of gift, provided the deduction does not exceed certain limitations. It is often much cheaper, taxwise, to contribute property that has appreciated in value than to contribute cash, because appreciation in the value of the property escapes income taxation. Estate and gift tax problems are commingled and complicated; you should not make any moves without careful study with your lawyer, tax adviser, and consulting forester.

## IDEAS FOR YEAR-END TAX PLANNING

Tax laws add another attractive feature to timberland investment if you are on a cash basis and report your income by calendar years, a situation that includes almost everyone. You can influence each year's taxable income to some extent by timber operations. Annual growth is complete by the end of summer, and September is a good time to take stock and make plans. If your income for the year has been unusually large, you can schedule necessary deductible expenses for the last quarter of the year. Both TSI work and boundary-line maintenance fit readily into such a program; you can probably pay the year's ad valorem taxes in late December; you can speed up charitable contributions. If your income has been unusually small up to September, you can reverse the process, speeding up income and slowing down expenses.

Flexibility of timber sales is even more helpful. You can prepare the sale in October or November and have bids returned in time to close during the last few days of December. When you know the exact amount of the consideration, you can make it fall into either year by hurrying the close or dragging your feet, or you can spread the income over several years by an installment sale or a deferred-payment arrangement. Selling timber at the best price takes 30 or more days, however, so you need to plan ahead if you want to take advantage of these opportunities. Getting the job done by December 1 is a good idea, for there is always a crowd of sellers in the last week. When big changes in the tax laws are forthcoming, there are even enough sellers to knock the price down. Would you believe that some persons hate to pay taxes so much that they will sell into a falling market?

## ACCOUNTING RECORDS

Since normal operation of a timber tract does not include frequent transactions, your accounting records can be quite simple, but some things are essential. Foremost is the cost or depletion basis of each component. No matter how or when you acquire the property, you must assign some value to trees and some to land. You can make these assignments merely by a pencil memorandum on your ledger sheet or check stub, but the record should be permanent, for you will often refer to it in later years. If you have failed to do this, any consulting forester can make a formal appraisal of the value of your property when you acquired it. His records extend for many years and cover many sales, and his report, when properly done, will be acceptable to the IRS.

Also important are records to substantiate operating expenses. Here again, they may be only pencil memoranda, for example, of trips you took on certain days to inspect the tract, showing mileage and other expenses. Check stubs for other expenses will be sufficient. You will find that memory is not good enough for either your purposes or those of the IRS; a poor memory costs money in excess taxes. Pencil memoranda may be sufficient as long as they are permanent, but I strongly recommend more formal records. In accounting, as well as in law and forestry, you must make your record as you go or run the risk of trouble. IRS agents are reasonable but thorough individuals. You can help your tax adviser help you if you keep proper records.

Your tax adviser and the IRS will insist that your records be detailed enough to show what profits you make from your property, but good records serve other purposes too. Your return on invested capital is of great importance, and your tract must perform well in comparison with other possible investments, or you should sell it. Your tax adviser and consulting forester can help you set up a simple means of measuring this performance for your own use. Such a record might be valuable if you ever have to sell it. Rates of return are important to all investors, and records of profitable operations are powerful sales weapons.

## SELECTION AND USE OF YOUR TAX ADVISER

Tax laws applicable to timberland investments were complicated enough for most laymen when I first wrote this book in 1964. Major complications were added in 1976, 1981, 1985, and 1986, and more will surely follow as Congress struggles to raise the money that it spends with ease. On the other hand, income taxes are a major problem only at times of timber sales, perhaps at intervals of 10 to 20 years. Therefore, it seems to me that professional tax help is a must at such times and that it is not essential to spend time worrying about every statement of legislators who are members of the tax-writing committees.

A well-known tax adviser is the certified public accountant, and other accountants and some lawyers may be equally competent in this field. You need one familiar with timberland operations; these are fairly numerous in timbered sections. Any adviser can read tax laws, but he must base his recommendations on records you furnish him and things you tell him. If he is familiar with timberland operations, he will remember to ask you for items that you forget, such as deductible expenses, and he will be much better at suggesting possible tax advantages in all timberland operations.

Discussions in this chapter are based mainly on the federal tax treatment of timberland income and expenses, and although states generally follow the same rules, there may be important differences.

State laws often require that you pay income taxes to the state in which the tract is located, even though you may live elsewhere; payment of such a tax usually allows a credit against the tax you owe the state of your residence, so double taxation rarely occurs. Therefore, it is wise to consult a tax adviser in the state where your land is located. This is especially important in case of death of nonresident landowners, since estates will probably have to be administered in both states.

# 10
# The Lawyer

Law reaches into the daily life of each of us, and a lawyer is more important in timberland investment than is generally realized. Many persons seek a lawyer only when they get into trouble, but a lawyer is most valuable in keeping you out of trouble. Timberland investment puts a high premium on the latter because of its long-term nature; mistakes may come to light many years after they happen and much too late to correct. A landowner without a lawyer is almost certainly headed for trouble.

The lawyer's services to you fall into two main divisions, those in connection with purchase and sale of properties and those in connection with their operation; we discuss the services in this order. The first division is a two-way street that you will travel in different ways at different times.

## IMPORTANCE IN PURCHASE AND SALE OF PROPERTIES

**Purchase and Sale Contracts.** Your lawyer helps you avoid trouble when you buy or sell property by making sure that you reach definite agreements on every aspect of the trade. A written contract may be necessary only when large amounts are involved or when there is likely to be a long time between the first agreement to buy and sell and actual closing of the trade. In any case, however, it is essential to decide on all details, and unless the sale is actually closed at the time of the first agreement, some written memorandum is mandatory. Enforcement of such an agreement by either party is virtually impossible without something in writing. Timing is most important because people are human. Both parties to a trade are in their most agreeable humor at the time of the original agreement, and it is easy to make these decisions then. As time passes, each assumes that unsettled matters will be settled in a manner favorable to him, and both parties may change their minds. These human propensities set the stage for disagreements, irritating and unnecessary at all times and sometimes costly. A lawyer is an expert in avoiding disagreements and eliminates the causes of many by asking the following questions.

What is the consideration, and how is it to be paid? Cash payment is relatively simple, but many sales are made on an installment basis. An installment sale requires, in addition to a deed, preparation of a note and a mortgage, deed of trust, or other security instrument.

What is to be conveyed? Do any reservations arise from this trade or from some earlier time? Mineral reservations are common, and timber, grazing rights, ROWs, and many other things may be reserved or excepted; reservations may be either permanent or temporary. What form of conveyance is to be used? Further discussion of quitclaim and warranty deeds appears later.

What kind of title information is needed, and who will furnish it? The next section deals with title work in detail, but you must agree first on what will be done and who will pay for it. Ordinarily, the seller furnishes evidence that he owns what he is selling, but this feature may be the subject of negotiation.

Who is to pay current ad valorem taxes? The seller often pays the portion that has accrued up to the date of sale, but the amount may be assumed by the buyer. If the taxes are prorated using the amounts for the previous year, the simplest solution is for seller to give buyer a check for his pro rata share of taxes at time of closing and recite in the deed that the buyer agrees to pay all ad valorem taxes for the year. There may be a problem here if the sale includes only part of seller's land; the tax collector may insist upon payment of all taxes or none.

Who pays for any state tax stamps that must be affixed to the deed? These are usually the responsibility of the seller, but they may become the obligation of the buyer if the seller fails to affix them. Many states require tax stamps of one form or another, particularly if some of the minerals are separated by the deed.

Is a commission to be paid? To whom and by whom? Commissions are usually paid by the seller, but they may be negotiated. An attempt by the responsible party to avoid paying a commission that has been earned may cause unpleasantness for both parties.

How and where is the trade to be closed? The two parties can meet anywhere and exchange the deed for money, but more indirect methods are usually selected. Often it is sufficient for the seller to deposit the deed with a bank, accompanying it with a letter stating to whom and under what conditions it is to be delivered. A real estate broker or lawyer may serve as escrow agent under a simple agreement when the transaction includes earnest money. As transactions increase in size and complexity, more formal arrangements are necessary.

What sort of recording is necessary, and who pays for it? The buyer usually records the deed at his own expense, since this is public notice of his purchase, but the seller may require recording to show his title to certain reservations and his fulfillment of requirements about tax stamps. Mortgages are usually recorded by the beneficiary. A more satisfactory arrangement may be to include recording of all instruments among the services of the closing attorney or agent. If a mortgage or deed of trust arises from the sale, this method is especially desirable, since the beneficiary must assure that the mortgage is a first lien.

Who prepares the necessary papers, and who pays for this? Although others may be willing, this is certainly a job for a lawyer, and the more experienced he is, the better. In few other activities does the do-it-yourself method bring such risks of disaster. Very few lawyers get rich from handling these details in an expert manner; some have gotten rich in extensive litigation to correct errors made at this point.

The questions raised above indicate the important parts of purchase and sale agreements; the many details may seem bothersome. In the normal transaction, however, they are not; they can often be answered in less time than it takes to describe them. They must all be answered, however, for there are at least two solutions to the problems each question raises. Although the law will solve those not solved by the parties, this solution may not be satisfactory to either, and everyone is usually happier over a complete agreement. The conference at which the first agreement to buy and sell is reached is a horse-trading session of the first degree, and the party with the most expert lawyer at hand often comes away with sizable benefits. Thorough preparation for such a conference pays handsome dividends. After agreement has been reached, the next step is to see what the seller owns and the buyer receives.

**Title Work.** Almost all your land was owned at one time by the United States. The federal government acquired it through the American Revolution, purchase, conquest, or treaty. It then passed it along either directly to individuals or indirectly by being conveyed to states, which later conveyed it to individuals. Original transfer of title from the United States and all subsequent transfers from one party to another are accomplished by legal documents that are, or should be, recorded in a public office set up for the purpose by the county or other legal subdivision in which the land is located. This recording is public notice that the owner has acquired the property. Transfers from one owner to another make up the chain of title, and under ideal conditions, each transfer from the United States down to the present owner is on record. Such a chain of title shows who is the record owner of, or has record title to, the property. Record title is a strong claim to ownership, and this is what a lawyer investigates in his title examination. The other type of claim to ownership is based upon possession and may be an even stronger claim.

After the lawyer finishes his title work, he reports what he has found and gives his opinion of the title and its merchantability together with the basis therefor. His opinion may be based on an abstract, a summary of the important provisions of every paper on record showing transactions that affect title to the tract. An abstract is bulky and expensive, and your lawyer can tell you whether one is necessary or desirable. Methods of making title examinations and types of public records vary from state to state.

The lawyer's opinion is what really matters, and you must read it carefully. He may say that the owner's title is virtually worthless. In the usual form, the lawyer states that he finds the owner has a good title subject to certain exceptions, and then he lists these exceptions. One exception almost always found is the ad valorem tax for the current year, which is not yet due and payable. Similarly excluded are facts that a survey of the property would reveal. He looks only at the public records and is unaware of adverse possession or boundary-line disputes that exist on the ground. (The inventory should reveal these.) He will also show the existence of reservations or easements, but will not normally give all their provisions. You should get a copy of these instruments and read them. The clerk of the office where they are recorded can provide one for a nominal fee. Study of these instruments is essential; fine print in one of them may eliminate your chance for profit. Other exceptions may arise from previous financial transactions not properly closed out. Some lawyers specialize in title work, and their ability to spot a title flaw is uncanny.

Once the flaws have been determined, discuss them with your lawyer to see how serious they are and what can be done to correct them. Many technical flaws may be so inconsequential that they are not worth the expense of correcting. Some serious ones may require expensive corrective action to eliminate entirely, but can be reduced greatly in importance by simple expedients. Others may render the title worthless. The discussion should also cover those facts revealed by the timberland inventory or other work done on the ground. The time to explore these matters is before you buy the property, not after.

To continue this discussion, I must digress to consider the statute of limitations and a few differences between quitclaim and warranty deeds.

As an illustration of the statute of limitations, suppose that you punch John Jones in the nose. You will make him angry and may send him to the hospital for repairs on his nose. He may stay angry forever which is his right. He may also want to sue you for injury to his dignity and to recover the cost of repairing the damage you did. He probably has the right to sue you, but must do so within a limited period of time. Length of this period is set by a statute of limitations and varies with the type of action and the state laws governing the action. In everyday language, the statute of limitations begins to run the day you punch him. He must sue you within the specified period or lose his right of action against you. This kind of law makes it impossible for Jones to keep you in permanent jeopardy because of this one event.

Statutes of limitation are important to timberland investors because they apply to such things as timber theft, adverse possession, and damage of all kinds. Most persons hate arguments and disputes and, for this reason, often delay action when they catch a timber thief or suffer a loss from fire caused by a neighbor. Postponement of a decision is a decision in itself. You must either do something about these things promptly or lose your right. In many cases of poor management, loss is not even discovered until the time limit set by statute has already expired. Existence of these laws is one more strong argument for good timberland management.

A quitclaim deed conveys whatever interest the signer, or grantor, owns. A grantor may own everything or nothing, and he makes no guarantees to the buyer, or grantee. In a warranty deed, the grantor conveys whatever interest he owns, but also guarantees, among other things, that his title is good. This does not mean that the title is good; it merely means that grantor guarantees it is. Obviously, the guarantee is no better than the individual who makes it, and ordinarily his liability is limited to the amount of the purchase price. But suppose that, unknown to the grantor, a flaw that later causes title failure existed at the time of conveyance so that he could not have conveyed a good title. The statute of limitations, in some instances, begins to run on the date of conveyance, and the warranty may be barred before title failure is known. These facts may render a title worthless, so a quitclaim deed to a good title may be better than a warranty deed to a bad one. This brief discussion barely touches a complicated subject, but does point up the advantages of title insurance.

Title insurance is issued by many private companies and provides compensation up to the face amount of the policy for loss sustained by title failure. You pay the premium only once and are covered as long as you own the property. You must consult your lawyer for all details of title insurance; I recommend it for many reasons. First, the statute of limitations does not run on its coverage. Second, it protects you from loss from factors that title examination cannot reveal, such as insane persons or forgeries in the chain of title. Third, the insurer agrees to defend your title against all lawsuits, even those of a nuisance nature only. Fourth, some policies protect you against loss from lack of a right of access to and from the land; this can be very important to you. Cost of title insurance is usually less than one-third of 1% of the insured value, and the premium must be capitalized, not deducted. Decision to obtain title insurance is the buyer's, but responsibility for its cost is a matter for negotiation. Title insurance covers conditions when the policy is issued; consequences of your later actions are your responsibility.

Three other points are worth mentioning in connection with your record title. First, it is always possible that public records will be destroyed by fire or some other disaster. In such a case, your record title can vanish in a moment. Therefore, you must keep all title documents in a safe place. They will support your claim if something happens to the public records, and they may have to be recorded again at a later date. Title insurance is helpful in such an event.

Second, possession will eventually cure almost any record-title defect, but is not effective against any government. The document transferring title from the United States directly to an individual is commonly called a "patent," and it or a certified copy of it should be obtained and recorded. It is usually an impressive document complete with ribbons and seal and can be obtained at nominal cost from the Bureau of Land Management of the Department of the Interior in Washington, DC. If title to your land passed through a state, you should obtain and record a document of similar nature from the state agency in charge of land records. Obtaining these patents often requires three to four weeks and may be essential if you have to sell your property. It is also possible that some government still owns your land. Therefore, it is a good idea to take care of this detail now.

Third, you may have acquired your tract by inheritance, gift, or other means that made title examination unnecessary; if so, I recommend that you examine your title now. Although some flaws are removed by the passage of time, many are not. Flaws are most easily corrected when there is no urgency, such as there might be when you agree to sell the property or when the statute of limitations is about to run against you. Mineral discoveries likewise make good titles invaluable. Future events are impossible to predict. You can be ready for anything if your title is clear.

## IMPORTANCE IN OPERATION OF PROPERTY

**Timber-Sale Contracts.**  Sale of timber is perhaps the most frequent activity. Sale contracts must convey the timber to be sold in a legal and workable manner and contain specific penalties for violations such as cutting of trees not included in the sale. They must also contain language that clearly indicates that the persons harvesting the timber are not your employees, unless you fully understand the consequences and are willing to accept them.

Some agencies, governmental and otherwise, have published sample conveyances that might be used in selling timber, and you may be tempted to use them by filling in the blanks and changing words here and there. Do not fill them out, except with help from your lawyer. Terms and conditions vary widely from sale to sale, and each is important. Sales may be complete liquidations or partial cuts governed by marking, species, or diameter limits. Lump-sum sales usually provide for cash payment in advance; pay-as-you-go sales require that the conveyance specify exactly the method, rate, and time of payment. All sales have a time limit, but there is often a provision allowing the buyer to purchase additional time for more money (or a higher rate per piece in pay-as-you-go sales). Clauses to cover damage to fences, buildings, roads, livestock, and so on, are common, and responsibilities of the parties in the event of a forest fire may vary widely. Either the seller or the buyer may be an individual, partnership, or corporation, and there are small but important differences in state laws applicable to timber sales. These factors make use of sample conveyances dangerous and use of a lawyer very desirable or mandatory.

Occasionally you will find a buyer who insists upon using a conveyance drawn by his company or lawyer. It may be quite satisfactory, and you should make every effort to please your customers. Nevertheless, you must never sign such a conveyance until it has been reviewed by your lawyer. This review usually takes only a few minutes and may reveal significant omissions. The buyer may not intend to mislead you; he may just be unfamiliar with your particular situation and is not concerned with your interests or problems.

**Right-of-Way Agreements.** This is such a big field and such an important source of income for you that I have covered ROWs in great detail in Chapter 4. Study of that chapter shows that agreements of this kind are infinitely varied and may have serious consequences for you. You must never sign even the most-innocent-looking instrument until it has been reviewed by your lawyer. The time to spot pitfalls is before you sign the agreement, not after; your signature may wipe out a valuable trading position. It is hard for me to overemphasize the importance of ROW agreements. You may receive only one request in your lifetime; you will not have a later opportunity to correct any mistakes you make. The information presented in the first part of Chapter 4 was obtained by long and sometimes costly experience.

**Public Liability.** Since a timber tract is not as busy as a city street, you are not exposed to many risks from a public-liability standpoint; your exposure usually depends on the status of the persons who use your land. If you invite a friend to hunt or fish on it, he becomes an invitee. If he asks and receives your permission or if he enters without permission, he is either a licensee or trespasser, respectively. You may have certain responsibilities to invitees and entirely different responsibilities to the others. Therefore, it pays to be careful about what you say, and signs that read, "Hunters Welcome," for example, may change your exposure greatly. The growth in outdoor recreation will continue to entail greater use of the forests, and you should determine what risks are involved before use starts on your land.

A good solution to this greater use of forests and other related problems is to paint your boundary lines and put up signs that read, "Posted, No Trespassing" at intervals along the lines. Doing this helps to establish the status of persons using your land. It is also a strong indication of possession and may be the only overt kind of possession you can exert until your trees are large enough to cut. Your lawyer can tell you about the proper wording and spacing of these signs.

Many cultural operations such as TSI work or controlled burning are performed by your employees or independent contractors. You have certain responsibilities for their actions, depending on their relationship to you. Use of your employees may make it necessary to carry workmen's compensation insurance, and your public-liability exposure may be much greater, in addition to your expanded accounting burdens. Although many of these problems are removed by use of independent contractors, there is usually a remainder of exposure to liability; certain risks are so hazardous by their nature that they cannot be delegated. You can usually obtain adequate protection by requiring the contractor to carry insurance that covers you and him. Your lawyer can list the risks that should be covered, and the contractor's insurance agent will certify that the contractor carries the necessary insurance.

**Other Operating Considerations.**   Your lawyer can help you get a good title when you buy a tract. You will also need his help in maintaining it. Many apparently insignificant actions can affect your title. As purchaser, you can often correct adverse possession before acquisition, but it may start during your ownership. Boundary-line disputes and adverse possession are intermingled problems, and neither is solved by the passage of time. Certain easements can be acquired by adverse possession. On a well-managed property, the owner carries out many different activities from time to time, and these may have legal importance as evidence of possession. Some may be necessary for legal reasons alone. There is always the risk that your tract will be damaged by fire or other acts caused by someone else; the proper action to take is almost entirely governed by legal considerations. In case of fire, you should move rapidly to investigate the cause and origin of the damage. Many lawsuits over fire damages have collapsed in the middle of the trial because the landowner could not prove how and where the fire started. These difficult problems require individual solutions and expert legal advice.

## SELECTION OF THE LAWYER

The foregoing discussion indicates some of the complexities of your problems. Even apparently insignificant actions may become important because of the long-term nature of your business. Therefore, you need the best lawyer you can find, and you should consult him about the legal aspects of all actions. Many persons are familiar with some legal principles; you can usually get free legal advice from everyone you know. Do not take it. Law is a vast field, and every problem requires an individual solution. In this book, I cannot solve and do not attempt to solve the legal problems that face you; I can merely call your attention to the importance of your lawyer.

Finding a lawyer should be no problem. You need a specialist in issues connected with timberland and one with the widest possible experience. It is helpful if the lawyer is a timberland investor himself; any consulting forester can give you the names of several such lawyers. Nearly every law or legal principle mentioned in this book varies from state to state, so you need a lawyer familiar with laws of the state in which your land is located. If you live in another state, your local lawyer can help you locate one.

Lawyers have much the same fee arrangement as consulting foresters; it is wise to discuss this early. They usually charge in proportion to what they do and how long it takes. You will find that the lawyer is worth much more than he costs. You can afford the best professional help obtainable, but not the serious mistakes of ignorance or inexperience.

# 11
# Sale of Timberland

Timberland investments must often be sold to raise cash, to take advantage of price rises that appear to be temporary, or to change the form of assets so that they may be more easily managed. Many principles discussed in Chapter 3 apply to the sale of the entire investment, but the sale of land is an art in itself and requires considerable study. Whether you are a buyer or a seller, you will benefit from a thorough knowledge of this part of the business.

## PRICING

Things sell for what they are worth, and the sooner you get the money the better. You must never forget these rules when selling. Although sellers commonly disregard them, they do so at their own expense and invariably encounter costly disappointment.

The greatest mistake you can make is to offer your property for 50% more than it is worth and more than you will sell it for. You may think that this will give you a chance to come back with a counteroffer when you receive an offer from a prospect. You are dead wrong. Prospects reconnoiter the property, recognize the substantial overpricing immediately, and vanish without making any kind of offer. Their interest was aroused by the initial offering, but killed by the first investigation; since the work they must do to evaluate the tract costs money and time, most of them go quickly on to something else if their preliminary appraisal is not somewhere near the offering price. An experienced buyer told me that counteroffers more than 10% below the offering price are a waste of time, so he never goes to the expense of preparing one. All the initial overpricing does is destroy your first impact on the market. All experienced real estate salespeople know how important it is to move a property on the wave of interest generated by the first offering. Setting the proper price in the beginning enables you to do this and accomplish the other main objective at the same time.

This objective is to get the money now, and the importance of doing so can be seen by referring to the example discussed in Chapter 8. That property was worth $175,000 the day it was offered for sale and the day it finally sold one year later. Failure to set a realistic price cost the lumber company $12,250 in real interest (probably equivalent to $17,500 in nominal interest) and about $1360 in ad valorem taxes and management expenses. It is impossible to raise the price of a property on the market to compensate the owner for timber growth that might be taking place or expenses he might be incurring during the sales effort, for the usual reason that the property does not sell is that it was overpriced in the first place. Other expenses are hidden, for the seller does not usually make allowance for the time he spends negotiating with prospects. These considerations place a high premium on a quick sale.

The first essential step toward this goal is a timberland inventory that is as up-to-date as possible and prepared by a competent, independent authority. Such an inventory enables the seller to set a realistic price and is a powerful tool in selling. Buyers know its utility, and it is effective in arousing their confidence. Exaggerated and unsupported statements about timber volumes and values are quickly recognized for what they are and often create enough suspicion to scare off persons who might otherwise be excellent prospects. Most timberland is bought as an investment, and if its price has the right relationship to its income, the buyer without any help will supply all the desire necessary to consummate the sale.

Chapter 8 discusses an investor's approach to timberland purchases on the wholesale market; you should use that investor's approach to set the price in most cases. There is a ready market for properly priced tracts and almost no market at inflated prices. Chapter 8 also mentions the role of dreams and pleasure in the retail market for timber tracts. Your local real estate broker can help you assess how important they are. You must realize which market applies to your property; retail prices are a waste of time in the wholesale market.

## CURB APPEAL IN TIMBERLAND

Curb appeal is a term used by residential real estate brokers to describe traits that make a house especially appealing when you see it from the curb on your first visit. It includes such things as a well-tended lawn, attractive flowers, impressive trees, a recent paint job, and an obvious state of near-perfect maintenance—anything that shows the owners to be persons with good taste and pride of ownership. These brokers say that curb appeal is a powerful factor in helping them make a sale. Surprisingly enough, curb appeal exerts the same effect on timberland even when many buyers are primarily concerned with return on assets. Described below are several actions that add far more value than they cost.

1. *Get trash off and keep it off.* Nothing reduces the value of a tract so much as an informal trash dump. Once dumping starts and the owner does nothing about it, the neighbors decide that dumping is permissible, and the eyesore grows at an accelerated rate. From time to time, our clients have rejected otherwise desirable purchases because of trash dumps that occupied only a small area, but ruined many acres of lovely scenery. They now haul trash dumped on their lands back to the person who dumped it, or they bury it because, when the time comes to sell, they do not intend to be rejected for this reason.

2. *Brush out and paint boundary lines.* You want to make it easy for potential buyers to find the tract, and the work is some assurance that there is no adverse possession.

3. *Remove useless trees.* By useless I mean not only crooked, diseased, or defective trees, but also overtopped or very crowded trees in merchantable stands and unwanted hardwoods in pine plantations. Buyers who pay top prices want a tract that is operating at 100%; they do not want to be required to tinker with it after the purchase.

4. *Plant idle acres,* everyone of them. It is worth the trouble to carry a bucket of seedlings to old loading grounds of one acre or less and to plantation failures large enough to notice. These areas are unimportant in themselves, but your purpose is to demonstrate that every square foot of the tract is productive.

## MARKETS

The most obvious market is a big timber company that owns land nearby or adjacent to yours. Such a company is often willing to pay a high price if the tract meets the needs of the timber-procurement manager, and is easy to deal with once you understand its requirements. Although the company will insist on checking it, your timber inventory will reduce the time required for field examination. The company will be wary of adverse possession and require that it be corrected or that affected portions be excluded from the sale. It will make a thorough examination of the title and perhaps require that you furnish title insurance or other satisfactory evidence of ownership. Big-company land purchases must be approved by several departments or echelons of management, and large transactions often must be approved by the board of directors. The company representative will be glad to describe its procedure to you. It will need an option for the time necessary to complete this procedure and will be unwilling to pay more than a nominal amount for it. It will usually make a reconnaissance and will perhaps complete some of the field examination without an option. It will generally not take an option unless it intends to purchase the property.

The most profitable market is that made up of your neighbors. Every person is naturally interested in buying land that adjoins his and will make a special effort to do so if he can get the money. Neighbors represent a chance to sell the property at retail and will often pay a premium because of the location or because they intend to convert at least part of it to another use.

The largest market is investors. Price is all-important, and the only difficulty is reaching them. Most of them say that they will buy a property anywhere, but they rarely buy tracts that do not join theirs or are not located in a certain county. Newspaper ads will reach some of them; others may be located by searching the county tax rolls or by diligent inquiry among local foresters and timber buyers. Through years of publishing a newsletter, my firm has gradually accumulated a list of investors coded by the county they are interested in; this list enables us to send announcements of a typical sale to 250 timber buyers and 300 timberland investors. Other foresters and real estate brokers may have similar lists.

## SELLING PROCEDURE

Your offer to sell should be presented in a letter or brochure that can be easily mailed. It should cover every detail of interest to a purchaser; by listing all the facts (and facts only), your presentation will make it easy for each prospect to see how desirable the property is for his purposes. A summary of the timber inventory and a letter describing terms and conditions are an excellent way to present it. A thorough written offer to sell will both interest the serious prospect and discourage the idle curious. You want to do both, since sightseers waste valuable time.

The offer must state price and terms. Cash is always desirable, and usually scarce. If the sale is for cash, you should investigate possible sources of credit in order to make helpful suggestions to prospects. If you plan an installment sale, you should state the terms available to prospects and the financial data needed from them.

Every serious prospect will want to make a ground reconnaissance of the property before attempting a detailed appraisal; you should allow the prospect time to do this. The amount of free time needed varies widely, but you should be cautious in giving it. You must avoid those who profess great interest, ask for and obtain a 30-day option at little cost, and then peddle the property all over the world at an increased price. You must offer the property subject to prior sale and refuse to grant special privileges for longer than a few days to any prospect unless you receive adequate compensation.

You can obtain adequate compensation by selling an option to buy. An option grants an exclusive right to buy on certain conditions for a definite period and should be drawn up with the help of your lawyer. For the protection of both parties, an option should cover all important points in an unmistakable manner. The consideration is a matter for negotiation, but is often 0.5% for each 30-day period and may or may not apply on the purchase price.

You can also get adequate compensation by entering into a purchase and sale contract. The purchaser agrees to buy the property on certain terms and conditions and offers earnest money in an amount sufficient to guarantee performance or compensate seller for failure. The seller agrees to sell the property on the same terms and conditions and agrees that earnest money will be held by an escrow agent. The amount of earnest money is negotiated also, but is usually less than 5% and applies on the purchase price. Banks and real estate brokers often serve as escrow agents and will insist that the contract provide definite instructions about how and when to disburse the earnest money. Failure of purchaser to fulfill the contract causes him to lose the earnest money; failure of seller may cause a lawsuit. Although the contract has a time limit, the time period usually is not fixed as in an option, but varies according to the time schedule set up for the different activities of purchaser and seller.

## METHODS

Many sellers try the do-it-yourself method first, since it has the apparent advantage of eliminating a commission, an advantage more apparent than real. In selling a timber property, it takes time to prepare the offering letter, show the property to prospects, answer many questions that arise, conduct negotiations before the contract is executed, and complete closing activities. If your time is valuable, you will usually find that the attempt to save the cost of a commission is false economy in time alone. Moreover, the sale of timberland is a very technical business, and there is also a psychological advantage in negotiating through a representative.

For many reasons, use of a sales agent is the best way to sell a timber tract. First, the agent does everything necessary to bring about the sale at his own expense and suffers the loss if he fails to earn a commission by selling the property. Second, an experienced agent creates an atmosphere of urgency that brings buyers to a decision quickly. Third, he is expert at translating favorable decisions into action. A verbal agreement to buy timberland is of doubtful value and must be followed quickly by written contracts and considerations. Fourth, an agent knows the intricate details involved in closing a sale and makes an excellent supervisor to expedite these matters. Fifth, an agent is an expert on human nature and senses characteristics that make your property attractive to each prospect. He often sees things that you do not. A wise old lawyer once said that a lawyer who represents himself has a fool for a client; the principle involved in this saying usually applies to the sale of timber properties.

You should use care in selecting the agent; he must be experienced, ethical, and capable in order to represent you properly. As a general rule, real estate agents specialize in properties of a certain kind, and you need a specialist in timberland investments. The business is technical, and prospective investors want facts, not fiction or high pressure. To interest serious prospects, particularly timber companies, your agent must be able to present these facts from a background of personal experience. Many states require that real estate agents be licensed; you should investigate this, since the law may penalize you for dealing with an unlicensed agent.

Once you select the agent, you should deal with all prospects through him alone, even though this seems an unnecessarily complicated procedure at times. If you negotiate directly with prospects, you invariably cause confusion, delay, and unnecessary expense, and you may cause failure. Remember that you have retained a professional, and leave the selling job to him. You should insist, however, that neither he nor any cooperating broker ever quote the property at a price *above* the listed price. This practice is common and is a sure sign of an amateur. It is done in order to allow price concessions in the future, is never successful, and actually hinders the sale, since it discourages many prospects. You will have no trouble with your agent if you select him with care, but he may cooperate with agents in other places who are not personally known to him. You should have a clear understanding about this cooperation.

Auctions are seldom successful for selling timberland for several reasons. First, the major element of value is merchantable timber, and very few auction companies understand how to present timber volumes properly or realize the importance of the timber estimator, his reputation, or his methods. Second, most buyers are professionals for whom each tract is just another investment, so there is not the excitement or emotion that is often generated at auctions of art treasures. Third, auctions require the bidder to be present, and this is burdensome for a buyer who usually has to bid on four or five tracts every business day. Finally, it is difficult to predict the results of an auction; you will incur much of the expense of conducting the sale whether the property sells or not. You should think hard before choosing this method.

Sale agreements with real estate brokers are usually covered by agency contracts. These are often drawn by filling in the blanks of a printed form, and they cover such details as price, terms, legal description, commission, length of agency, division of option or escrow funds, and so forth. Your lawyer should review it before you sign; if the agreement is drawn by the broker, it may take better care of him than of you.

## EXPENSES

The biggest expense is the commission. It varies from almost a nominal amount to as high as 15%, depending on size of the transaction, merchantability of the property, and services that the agent is required to perform. Ten percent is common up to prices of $100,000, and smaller percentages may apply as the size increases. Much of the agent's work is done when an option or sale contract is signed, and such a contract reduces his chances to sell the property if it is not exercised or fulfilled. He may also have to do a great amount of work shortly after the contract is signed. Therefore, he is entitled to a much larger percentage of option or earnest money if buyer fails to fulfill the contract.

Whether seller provides a certificate of title, an abstract, or title insurance is a matter of choice, but an offer to sell that includes some provision for showing good title to the property greatly increases its merchantability. Title insurance offers a good solution; your lawyer can tell you about its cost and that of other types of title information.

Some deeds may require tax stamps in proportion to the amount of consideration. The seller normally pays for them, but the buyer may agree to do so. They do not have to be affixed to the deed before it is recorded, but must be affixed eventually. Minerals are often separated from the surface at time of sale and retained by the seller. They may then be subject to ad valorem taxes, and many states allow the mineral owner to buy mineral stamps in lieu of all future ad valorem taxes. Such stamps must be affixed to the deed and should be paid for by the party who retains the minerals. Recording of the deed is usually the responsibility of the buyer, since it is public notice of his purchase.

## PIECEMEAL SALES

You can sometimes get a better price for a timber tract by breaking it into smaller parcels or by dividing it into its components. The number of buyers with $40,000 is much larger than the number with $400,000. Proper subdivision may enable you to interest buyers whose desires vary widely; one part of a tract may be good for a small farm, while another may be ideal for a country retreat. Many timber buyers cannot buy land because of lack of capital, but will pay top prices for timber that can be cut now, so a separate sale of timber will give them an interest in the property.

When dividing the tract into parcels or components is feasible, you can usually hold a sealed-bid sale. You must furnish very detailed information on all parcels and then ask for bids on the timber or the land or both on each parcel. Such a procedure eliminates the need for setting the right price in advance; the mechanics of holding such a sale are discussed in Chapter 3.

The piecemeal approach has disadvantages. First, it is slow and requires much negotiation. Loss of interest on money and the amount of time necessary to deal with many prospects may more than offset any premium prices obtained. Second, sale of certain parcels or components may reduce value of the remainder. Separation of minerals, for instance, often seriously reduces value of the surface. Sale of timber means that you must allow sufficient time to cut and remove it, and there are few buyers for the surface during the period of timber reservation. Sale of certain parcels may reduce access to the remainder, and the effect of this on prospective buyers is hard to estimate in advance. You should consult an experienced real estate broker and your consulting forester before starting such a program.

## VALUE OF TRACT FOR RESIDENTIAL OR INDUSTRIAL DEVELOPMENT

Conversion of a timber tract into higher uses can be very profitable, and knowing whether this is possible is necessary to set a realistic price. To investigate this, I interviewed Stewart Wight, Senior Vice President, Landauer Associates, International Real Estate Consultants, and published the following excerpts in our newsletter:

JMV:  Many landowners and foresters have been fooled by the market value of timberland near towns and cities. They expected prices much higher than timberland prices, but the bids contained no premiums. Isn't such land worth more for future development?

SW:  Some of it is; some of it isn't. It depends on many things, and one is what you mean by "near." Distance out from the city is important because of geometry. Area of a circle depends on the square of its radius. Therefore, a tract four miles out is only 33% farther than one three miles out, but the area of the fourth-mile circle is 140% of the area of the third-mile circle. As you go out, supply of land increases rapidly, and its market price falls just as rapidly.

JMV:  The last time we were disappointed, the tract was only one mile from a subdivision being developed. Wouldn't that lead you to expect a premium?

SW:  Nearby development is a good sign, but your tract may still be a long way from residential property. How far was it from the nearest utilities such as electricity, gas, water, and telephone? The distance to a sewer system is especially important, since having to depend on septic tanks would greatly reduce the number of homes that would be built. Although the nearby homes may seem close to you, the cost of bringing utilities to your tract may be very high.

JMV:  Any other considerations?

SW:  Investors and appraisers consider many other factors, but one is well-known to almost everyone: the direction in which a town or city is growing. Towns don't grow equally around the circumference as trees do; there is usually fast growth in one direction, often to the north or northeast, and slow growth in other directions. Timberland in the growth path will bring premiums much sooner.

JMV: How fast do towns and cities grow? If you own a tract on the fringe, how long will it be before development runs the price up?

SW: Well, every situation is unique, and if the size of the tract and the amount of money involved are large, you really ought to call on a professional appraiser. In general, however, the diversion of land to urban uses is slow. A recent U. S. Forest Service survey on central Florida, the boom area that contains Tampa, Orlando, and Disney World, revealed that only 5% of the commercial forest area was diverted during the entire decade of the 1970s.

## TRADING TALK

From participants in the real estate market, you will hear statements and questions that illustrate several important facts about the sale of timber properties. They are repeated over and over again, though they amount to little more than nonsense.

"I will not sell for less than $_____, if I have to keep it forever." This remark is made by someone who does not realize the power of interest. He does not understand that $10,000 today is usually better than $10,700 a year from now, because ownership of money enables him to earn interest, whereas ownership of land makes him liable for ad valorem taxes. If economics does not crush the speaker, timber growth may eventually make his land worth the price.

"Would you sell for a lower price?" Nobody would dare say to a lady, "If I asked you to marry me, would you?" but the first question is common. The way to get an answer is to make a firm offer and watch what happens.

"Although your property is an excellent buy at the price, I don't want it now." Assuming that the speaker can afford your price, this really means that the property is not an excellent buy, or he would want it. The speaker does not want to hurt your feelings.

"I'll have my offer in next week. Can you give me until then?" This is a request for a free option, and you should reply that the property is offered subject to prior sale and that you hope you will be able to consider his offer when it arrives.

"Several persons are anxious to buy my property, but I will let you have it if you will hurry." This obvious attempt to create a sense of urgency usually fails and often means that the speaker has no other prospects. Proper pricing will normally create interest among buyers.

"Timberland around here is selling for $_____ to $_____ per acre, and there is very little on the market. You ought to get at least that much for yours." The speaker is usually repeating gossip current in the local business community and probably has no personal knowledge of your property or others that have recently been sold. You should ask him if he will make you a firm offer at these prices.

# 12
# Loans

Timberland investors need credit like all businesspeople, but they have special problems along this line because they need credit in large amounts and for long terms. Long-term credit is harder to get than short-term credit, as you can see by the bond quotations in the daily news. Timberland investment is new to most lenders; it came into its own as a business only since World War II, and some lenders still remember disasters that accompanied timber bonds of the early 1900s. Nevertheless, money-lending is competitive, and the supply of credit for timberland is expanding. Let us discuss some sources available now.

## FARM CREDIT SERVICES

Farm Credit Services (FCS) is the name of the organization under which the field operations of the Federal Land Bank Association and the Production Credit Association have been consolidated. A full merger of the two groups may eventually occur. Farm Credit Services offer timberland loans, and the help you can get from them can be explained by describing the situation to a loan officer. The Jackson Farm Credit Services office makes loans on timberland in Alabama, Mississippi, and Louisiana. It serves every county in the three-state area and has branch and satellite offices for the convenience of farmers in its territory. Any office can provide applications for loans and detailed information about the loans.

Any person, partnership, or farming or timber-growing corporation (one that derives at least half of its income from these sources) now engaged or soon to be engaged in timberland investments may be eligible. Owners of properties under lease to big timber companies are eligible if the lease terms are acceptable.

Eligibility for a loan depends on several basic credit factors, for example, value of the land, value of the timber (including rate of growth), other sources of income available to repay debt, a sound financial position, a good credit rating, demonstrated ability to manage a timber property (either with or without help of a professional), and a sound management and development plan.

Loans are made on stands of both pine and hardwood timber with sufficient volume of merchantable timber. There should be enough annual growth to provide a substantial yield for the term of the loan. Loans are also made on young pine timber smaller than merchantable size, provided the trees will reach merchantable size in less than five years. Proceeds of loans may be used for a wide variety of purposes.

Each property offered as security is appraised to determine its loan value. FCS appraisers arrive at loan value by using normal stumpage prices, giving consideration to present volume of timber that may be merchantable under usual conditions. Loan value is also based on the appraised value of the tract for continued production of timber.

As with other lenders, there are application, appraisal, and other fees connected with obtaining loans. Recent, reliable timber inventories may be acceptable and thus reduce the appraisal fee. Since these fees change frequently, applicants should call the local FCS office for exact information about them.

Amount of the loan depends on the appraised value of land and timber. It usually varies from 50% to 85% of the appraised value of the property, which is near the market value at today's prices. Larger loans may be obtained if the borrower is able to assign additional collateral. Loan-approval authority varies with each loan officer, and the average time for closing loans under normal conditions varies from 30 to 60 days.

Terms of loans range from 5 to 40 years. The principal can be repaid quarterly, semiannually, or annually, and can be paid in full at any time without large penalties. Under certain conditions principal payments can be deferred during periods of development of timber; you might be able to pay interest each year and make principal payments every five years.

A range of interest rates is available on FCS loans—the rates depend on the aforementioned credit factors and the cost of money. Recent legislation has provided for federal assistance to FCS on its old loans, but money for new loans comes from the sale of bonds to the investing public.

Since the FCS is owned by its members, all borrowers purchase 5% to 10% of the loan in stock. When the loan is paid in full, the stock is retired at face value, assuming viability of FCS. Dividends are paid on the stock when earnings permit, but none have been paid for several years. In late 1987 the Federal Land Bank stock became impaired and could not be refunded; now (1988) its safety has been guaranteed by the federal government, but money for refunding is still not available. All of this could have the effect of increasing the interest rate on the loan and should be investigated.

Annual growth or its accumulation, as established by the appraisal, may be released without payment on the principal of the loan. For release of more timber, principal payments in proportion to the value will be required, although there may be exceptions to this rule.

Farm Credit Services has several advantages for its borrowers. Through its predecessors it has been a dependable source of credit for more than 75 years. Its interest rates are consistent with the cost of money. There are few prepayment penalties. Credit life insurance is available if the borrower is in good health and under 66 years old.

In August 1976, the Federal Land Bank of Jackson started a rural appraisal service available to farmers and timberland investors. The service offers three types of appraisals:

1. Letter appraisal. This brief report gives the estimated value of the property and is not intended as a basis for a credit decision by the FCS.
2. Form appraisal. This more detailed report is intended for use by the FCS or other lenders as a basis for a loan and is made on forms approved for that purpose.
3. Comprehensive appraisal report. This detailed report includes information on soil classes, uses of property, building values, and so on. It may also be used by the FCS or other lenders as a basis for a loan.

The service charges fees for these appraisals, depending on the type needed. Its appraisers offer no technical advice or assistance.

## COMMERCIAL BANKS

Commercial banks also lend money on timber properties. Regulations governing these loans are issued by the Federal Reserve Board and the Comptroller of the Currency, and each bank has a copy of the latest regulations. As a general rule, they can lend 40% of the value of merchantable timber for a maximum of 10 years. This term is acceptable only if 10% of the principal is amortized annually; otherwise the maximum term is two years. Since the value of most properties includes some consideration for land and reproduction, this regulation reduces the utility of commercial bank credit.

Additional funds may be available from commercial banks to borrowers who have already established satisfactory financial relationships with them. Essentially, however, banks are sources of short-term credit with the terms of loans measured more in months than in years. They depart from this practice only with reluctance and for good fiscal reasons; therefore, they are not active in timberland loans.

## INSURANCE COMPANIES

The most active and satisfactory lenders are insurance companies. Most larger companies have some experience in the field, and the extent of their interest in loans of this kind is growing. Most companies have graduate foresters as timberland-loan managers, and all have access to competent professional help.

These loans carry an interest rate of about 11% at present, and although the maximum term is usually 10 years for fixed-rate loans, later refinancing is easy if experience has been satisfactory. Principal repayments may be postponed for the first few years. Prepayment privileges vary by company; one allows prepayment without penalty, provided that not more than 20% of the principal is retired in any one year. As a general rule, insurance companies are not interested in loans of less than $1,000,000.

Insurance companies are restricted by law to loans of less than 75% of appraised or market value, whichever is less, and they prefer to restrict loans to 65% or less. This is substantial help, however, since the investor can borrow $2 to $3 for every $1 of equity capital he contributes. The companies require financial statements from the borrower, showing that his net worth has the proper relationship to the amount of the loan. They expect the borrower to show some financial strength, since they do not want to acquire the property by foreclosure. Few timberland loans stand on their own bottoms; therefore, the lender often requires personal endorsement of the note.

Mortgage-loan departments are organized in echelons, each echelon being limited in the amount of loan on which it can give a definite commitment. Most timberland loans are so large that they require extensive appraisal work by lower echelons and final approval at the home office. Therefore, most companies require a standby fee of approximately 1% with the application. If the application is approved and the loan is not accepted by the applicant, he forfeits the standby fee to compensate the company for work done by its employees. Otherwise, the fee is refunded.

Appraisals include some value for merchantable timber, reproduction, land, minerals, and other features producing income. Companies usually require a recent timber inventory by a qualified authority, even though the amount of the loan is limited by the price of the property. Here again the company must assure itself that value of the property is sufficient to retire interest and principal of the loan. Some companies require that the timber inventory be quite detailed; you should investigate these requirements if you plan an inventory to be used for loan purposes. Appraisal values for merchantable timber are close to current market values. Occasionally, an investor uses a loan to purchase a property covered by a cutting contract providing for specific annual payments in cash. If the party agreeing to make payments is obviously well able to fulfill this contract, the lender may not require a timber inventory, but will require its employees to make a thorough inspection of the property on the ground. Contracts of this kind make obtaining a loan much easier in most cases. Time required from date of application to date of final loan commitment is from 30 to 60 days when the amount is near $1 million, assuming full and intelligent cooperation from the applicant; faster action is possible on smaller amounts.

Some companies obtain loans through exclusive brokers, and others deal directly with the borrower. Although either method is satisfactory from the borrower's standpoint, you should ask for a detailed statement of charges connected with obtaining the loan. During preliminary stages, you should shop around for the best terms, but you will have to pick the company before filing an application. Most require title insurance on the property to be mortgaged. Since all companies are subject to the same fluctuations in the money market, you will find almost no difference in the rates quoted by each company. Borrowers with exceptional financial resources may be able to shave the rate by 0.5%. These companies are experienced and competitive, and they can tailor a loan to fit almost any conditions. Mortgage-loan managers continually study businesses of all kinds and can give you valuable advice.

You will notice that insurance companies and the Federal Land

Bank use component-parts appraisals in establishing timberland loan values, although I said earlier that this practice is a mistake unless great care is used in assigning values to various parts. They correct any mistakes that might be made by requiring the borrower to show how the loan will be repaid. This means that they are concerned mainly with the return the property will produce.

## SELLERS

Credit in large amounts is provided by owners of timberlands who are willing to sell them on terms. Potential purchasers should explore this possibility. A seller sells something because he needs money, and he may be willing to make concessions to get it. Since many sellers are individuals and can seldom obtain a return on capital more than the interest on savings accounts, they will often agree to an interest rate about equal to the prime rate. They usually think in terms of much less than 10 years, but may be willing to postpone principal payments until late in the life of the loan. A variation on this theme calls for modest payments in the first two or three years followed by a balloon note at the end. You run the risk of not being able to refinance the final portion, but this is less of a danger if the period of small payments is long enough.

Sellers also extend credit to take advantage of tax laws. Many have a substantial profit in the property to be sold and are anxious to spread the tax on this profit over many years. In general, a seller can spread his profit, and therefore his tax, over several years if he receives less than 30% of the sale price in each year. This provision works to the advantage of both buyer and seller. Changes in tax laws are made constantly, however, and you should consult with your tax adviser when considering such a trade.

## SUMMARY

The institutions described in this chapter are the present sources of timberland loans. Although there appear to be adequate funds for timberland loans, these loans are not as common as might be expected. One reason for this is the low return earned by many properties; loans are unsatisfactory when the enterprise earns *less* than the interest rate. Timberland investors can remove this obstacle by increasing yields and profits. Another reason is that there are few sources of loans less than $100,000, since small loans are costly to negotiate and service. A solution to this problem may arise as these investments grow more popular.

Some charitable foundations are moving into the timberland business, and many provide quite flexible loans. Investment policies of these foundations are often solely in the hands of their directors and trustees; they may be willing to provide funds in a combination of equity and debt that permits low interest rates in anticipation of large future profits. Some state governments offer loans to certain classes, particularly veterans, on lenient terms. Real estate brokers and consulting foresters can help you with information about these loans.

If none of these agencies meets your needs, please remember that timberland investment is a relatively new business and cannot attract a large volume of credit until lenders have a long and happy experience. They are watching your progress with keen interest. You can help yourself and all other investors by succeeding.

# 13
# The Big Timber Companies

Big timber companies are worth very serious study. Most of them have owned land and practiced some sort of forestry for 60 or so years. They have concentrated skill, energy, brainpower, and large amounts of capital on the problems of growing trees and have learned many things that can be applied on your land. In the process, they have also made almost every mistake imaginable. But before you begin your study, you need to understand certain things about these companies so that you will know how to evaluate what you learn.

## DIFFERENCES BETWEEN THEM AND YOU

Perhaps the biggest difference between these companies and you is that they are bureaucracies and you are a principal, an owner, an entrepreneur. The company foresters whom you encounter are actually skilled specialists who concentrate on a tiny part of the business, for example, land management, timber procurement, public relations, research, and so on, and rarely see the big picture unless they reach the level of vice president. By that time they are so busy with big administrative jobs that they have little time to advise you, and they have been immersed for so long in the affairs of a single company that much of their outlook is one-sided. A superb policy for a particular company may be a very bad one for you.

Another very big difference is that these companies originally bought their land to ensure supplies of raw material and still look upon it to some extent as a necessary evil. Selling timber on the open market has never been their main business (indeed, most of them would regard doing so as a sign of failure); they make their main profits converting trees into paper, lumber, plywood, and other products. Although raw-material costs are important, their big investments and main expertise are in manufacturing facilities. In 1987 for instance, less than 16% of the assets of one well-known company were in timber and timberlands. Since these assets are only a minor part of the total but provide essential security for all the other assets, the companies in one way or another accept a slightly lower rate of return on them and, consequently, pay more than ordinary investors would for tracts that are well-located for their mills and approve regeneration costs that would be terrible investments for you.

Insulated from the investment world by his bureaucracy, a company forester rarely knows the risks and rewards in investment alternatives. He knows only what "good forest-management" means in his company, and he often thinks it is good just because it qualifies under this limited definition. Consequently, he may in all sincerity recommend steps that will eventually eliminate chances for suitable profits.

Most company foresters spend money, but do not generate income, so they rarely know how much annual income is consumed by costs and how little remains as net return to the investor. That is, they rarely know what this book is all about. In one huge company I mentioned elsewhere, management costs (not including regeneration) ate up 33% of annual income. You can imagine what sort of advice you would get from foresters who believe in such expensive management.

They are always on the opposite side of the trade from you. It is obvious that no procurement forester can give unbiased advice to a landowner about selling timber and then buy it from him. But the land-management foresters in the same company have been accustomed to growing what their own procurement foresters want to buy, and they may sincerely believe that these are the most profitable products for you. In an interview published in my company newsletter, the chief executive of a big plywood producer reported that his foresters thought that the most profitable crop was trees large enough for plywood, whereas in a large area around many of its mills by far the most profitable crop is a mixture of big pulpwood and small sawmill trees. This man was not trying to mislead anyone (he would not even if he could); he was just speaking as the head of a big company that is nevertheless only a small fraction of the total market for timber.

Finally, they cannot give great attention to detail. A company forester in charge of 50,000 acres or more does not know about or have time to correct all obvious errors in spacing of plantations, painting of boundary lines, or thinning of pulpwood stands. Consequently, some visible big-company results should not be imitated because they are actually the kind of mistakes that could harm you.


## SIMILARITIES BETWEEN THEM AND YOU

The biggest similarity is that big companies are really excited about and very heavily involved in growing trees. Their timber-procurement and land-management foresters often chose forestry careers because they love to see trees grow, and they are fascinated by what they do and see every day. As they serve year after year in the same area, these persons absorb an enormous amount of information about the biology of tree growth, the physical and economic conditions of doing business, and the personalities and characters of other persons active in forestry. Although they may not be good advisers on what forest-management plan you should adopt, their knowledge can be very helpful in executing the plan you choose.

Big timber companies need an economic and social climate favorable to timber-growing for profit. This climate must include many things: an adequate fire-control organization, reasonable ad valorem taxes, income taxes that fit the realities of the business, a good system of public roads, regulations that protect the environment without making manufacturing operations impossible, workmen's compensation rules and highway safety regulations that allow loggers to compete with those nearby, and perhaps other factors that will become important later. Without these conditions, they cannot operate, and you will have no market for your crops.

Big companies have a vital interest in understanding how trees grow and in increasing this growth in size or quality or both. Consequently, they do a great deal of research in their own facilities and support additional programs in universities or cooperatives (the cooperative led by Harold Burkhart is a prime example). Results of all this research is often available to the general public; I urge you not to wait until a company forester tells you about it, but to go directly to the agency conducting the research and ask questions. As I stated above, these companies are bureaucracies, and it is hard to get them to change their ways enough to apply the research results they have paid for. Perhaps it is not surprising that alert individual investors, because they are entrepreneurs, are the first beneficiaries of company-financed research on tree growth.

Since their main business is converting trees into useful products, these companies have an even stronger interest in what their customers want and in how to supply these wants at a profit. They strive constantly to increase the yield from individual logs and to reduce logging costs, both efforts that eventually raise stumpage prices. Technological advances in making softwood plywood indicate how large these changes can be. In 1973 one large company produced 2500 square feet of plywood from a pile of logs containing 1000 board feet Doyle scale; in 1987 the same company produced 4000 square feet from a pile the same size. Another example is the development of tree-length logging with big machines that reduced handling costs; over the years this raised pulpwood stumpage prices in some areas by 150%. You can imagine how these changes altered demand for timber. Such changes do not occur overnight, so if you keep abreast of them through contacts with big timber companies, you will have plenty of time to react.

Big companies are very concerned about whether timber will become scarce. Ever since the virgin timber began to disappear 100 or so years ago, there has been one prediction of timber famine after another, and none of them has occurred. But since there are limits on how many trees we can grow and no apparent limits on human reproduction, a timber famine is possible. Correctly guessing whether or not one will happen in the next 10 years will enable you to make a better estimate of future earnings from your tract. I think you will get the most reliable information concerning a timber famine from top executives of big timber companies. In addition to receiving frequent reports about current supplies from their procurement foresters, they are in constant contact with demands from their customers and new technology being developed by their manufacturing organizations.

## CONFLICTS BETWEEN THEM AND YOU

Occasionally some of their policy goals are in conflict with yours, especially their efforts to increase the supply of timber. You will see some of them trying to increase the allowable cut from national forests; it should be plain that the availability of this government timber will decrease the market for yours. Some of them also support government subsidies for practices such as tree-planting and TSI work. Unless you participate, the effect of these programs is to use your tax money to increase the supply so that the price of your timber will go down or remain the same.

Related to these efforts are others designed to reduce the cost of timber supplies by eliminating the need to compete for them. The vehicles are programs in which the company provides forestry assistance at little or no cost to timberland owners and in return receives the right of first refusal on timber from the property; nearly every big timber company has such a program and calls it by a different name. As I have shown elsewhere, no single company has ever been able or willing to pay top dollar every time, so timberland owners participating in the programs are sure to suffer loss of income in the long run.

Reducing your income is exactly the wrong move if the company really wants you to increase your efforts to produce timber. In my talks with top executives of these companies, I have found none who believes that a timber shortage is likely, so increasing timber supplies is not the prime motive. The strategy is clearly that of reducing the cost of raw material while denying the same cheap timber to competing companies.

Additional confirmation of this strategy comes from the fact that the programs are run by the timber-procurement departments. Procurement foresters are rated on their ability to buy enough timber to run the mills at prices cheap enough to allow profitable operations; they would be delighted to see an unbroken forest extending to the horizon in every direction with themselves as the only buyers.

There is nothing illegal or unethical about these efforts. They are merely normal operations in the free market, and if you were the president of such a company, you would be pushing them too. My only point is that, if you participate in such a program, you believe that there *is* a free lunch (not a belief that many persons boast about). The problem is not that the company charges for its management, but that you do not know how big the charge is.


## CONFUSING SIGNALS FROM BIG TIMBER COMPANIES

Most big timber companies believe and state publicly that growing trees for sale on the open market is good business; then they make investments that seem to be the epitome of bad business. Two outstanding researchers recently investigated the reasons behind these actions.

Clair H. Redmond of the U. S. Forest Service and Frederick W. Cubbage of the University of Georgia surveyed big timber companies to discover their capital-budgeting practices and received completed questionnaires from 41, a response large enough to be representative. Their findings were published in *Capital Budgeting in the Forest*

*Products Industry: A Survey and Analysis,* Research Bulletin 333, by the University of Georgia Agricultural Experiment Stations.

The first surprising answer concerned variation in discount rates according to length of investment: "Firms consistently replied that no adjustment in discount rates was made according to length. . . . Ninety percent of the responding firms stated that rotation ages and interest rates are not directly related." In other words, these companies do not expect any more return from money that will be tied up for 35 years than from money that will be tied up for 35 days. In the world where other investors operate, long-term rates are higher than short-term rates, long-term bonds yield a higher return, and few lenders will make 30-year, fixed-rate loans.

There was another surprise: "Reported 1984 real stumpage-price appreciation rates used by companies in the survey ranged from 0 to 5 percent. . . . Average real rates were 2.9 percent and 2.8 percent for sawtimber and pulpwood respectively." Since the physical growth of timber rarely exceeds 8% annually, anyone using in his investment analysis an additional real price appreciation of 2.8% would be willing to pay 35% more for a given property or site preparation treatment than an investor not using such assumptions. So far as I know, no other timberland investors in 1984 tacked on a real-price-appreciation kicker of any size; indeed, most thought, and correctly as it turned out, that timber prices were likely to fall, not rise.

Other answers revealed that most companies (58%) considered growing timber to be *less* risky than other investments, that 60% of the firms treated woodland investments differently from other firm investments, and that most firms in 1984 were actually using a real, after-tax discount rate of 5.9%. Essence of the findings is that most big timber companies deploy the capital sunk in timberlands according to quite different, and much less stringent, standards than those used by the vast majority of other investors.

Not long after I made the calculations in Chapter 17 showing that real returns of more than 8% annually from tree growth alone are nearly impossible, I attended the presentation for investors made by one company before security analysts in New York. The chairman and the chief financial officer stated that the company's average cost of capital was 14% and that they did not commit it to ventures that did not promise to pay more. Under later questionning by different analysts, the chairman stated that they applied the same test to investments in timberland, that they did not include a big amount of inflation in their forecasts, and that they are continuing to buy large areas of timberlands. They obviously know more than you and I and are using different numbers, for I have told you all I know and your comments to me reveal that you are still confused about how they stretch 8% to equal 14%.

The most confusing big timber company investments are the big sums sunk in site preparation and planting of cutovers. These are surely $150 per acre, and as you can see from the calculations in Chapter 17, this amount is about equal to the present value of land and planted trees combined at a real discount rate of 7%. If the chairman's company is doing any of this, how can he achieve an annual return of more than 14%? If he were to tell his secret to all investors, they would rush to grow all the timber his company would ever need.

## BIG TIMBER COMPANY ATTITUDE TOWARD TIMBERLAND OWNERSHIP

The strongest argument for timberland ownership arises from the timber-procurement department. Even a company owning large areas of timberland must buy two-thirds of its raw material on the open market and then get all of it cut and delivered to the mills. The size of this job is staggering. A medium-size company, one of my clients, buys each year an average of 265 tracts scattered over 29 counties and conducts logging on these tracts plus 160 parcels of its own land. In the mountain of legal, financial, personnel, equipment, and weather factors involved in this operation, the number of things that can go wrong is unlimited, and each of them raises the chance that a mill will run out of logs, have to shut down, and then start up again at great cost. In trying to avoid this ultimate disaster, the wood-procurement manager can buy several years' supply of timber with a time limit on each tract or carry an enormous pile of logs on the yard, which will eventually spoil or decay; both alternatives tie up very large amounts of capital. An attractive solution to his problem is to buy a permanent, growing, readily accessible, living inventory, that is, land with a moderate stand of merchantable timber which is located on a good road close to the mill and can be logged in wet weather. If the manager selects these tracts wisely, a relatively small area of them will enable him to cope with short-term emergencies at irregular intervals when the normal procurement process fails. Such investments should be outstanding successes.

After 45 years of watching big timber companies do well with their manufacturing investments and poorly with their timberland investments, I have often wondered why they did not sell their timberlands and concentrate on the profitable part of their business. One of them is now trying to do this. It realizes that a superior timber-procurement organization is the equivalent of a large land base and that paying an occasional premium for timber is far less costly than tying up capital at low returns. I think its initial success will continue.

I have finally decided (guessed may be a better word) that, beyond the minor needs of the timber-procurement manager, big companies have three reasons for owning timberland: fear, stragtetic moves against equally fearful competitors, and diversification.

Intellectually, it seems easy to believe that timber is plentiful, to accept that no mill has shut down since World War II because there was no timber to be bought, and to realize that a good procurement department may be equivalent in safety to owning 250,000 acres, but practically, it seems to be impossible. When the nightmare of running out of timber wakes the chief executive in the dark, when most things seem far worse than they really are, the intellectual concepts are cold comfort and not enough to let him go back to sleep. He yearns for the tangible security of owning land. Soon the company begins annual appropriations to buy it, and its bankers, underwriters, and foresters all applaud this move toward security. Since these asset purchases are capitalized and not expensed, they produce no immediate effect on earnings. Eventually, however, the company's return on total capital is dragged down by this low-return deployment, Wall Street analysts and stockholders grumble about low earnings and stock prices, and the upheavals caused directly or indirectly by raiders in the early 1980s cure the earlier investment mistakes. Then the staying power that seemed so formidable reveals its true weakness and disappears. Many acres that many thought were permanently locked up in company ownerships are suddenly for sale.

Fear can be a good thing, however, when it exists in the hearts and minds of competitors. If their leaders have the same nightmares, they become more fearful when they see one company buying up land. Therefore, the land buyer's strategy may not improve its return on capital, but may reduce its potential competition.

Some company chiefs aver that they own land for protection against rises in timber prices, stating that they will cut their own if open-market timber becomes too expensive. This is hard to believe. They would not be prudent if they failed to sell any product for less than its market price, but instead took a licking on it just to make other operations look better. In such a situation, they might be better off to sell the other operations. The fact is that timberland ownership is a diversification for them and should be judged on whether diversification increases total earnings or gets them into businesses outside their true expertise.

## WHY IS THEIR RETURN SO LOW?

One reason for the low return is the high cost of management; almost everything a big timber company does can be done cheaper by an individual. The salary level of its foresters is not unusually high, but there is a sizable package of fringe benefits. It is hard to give these foresters a sense of urgency about costs, because they are several steps removed from the actual money-making process. They are bureaucrats, think like bureaucrats, and are measured like bureaucrats, and the fact that they happen to work for a company in private enterprise makes no difference. They do not compete against anybody, except indirectly, and it is hard to measure efficiency of their work. (I do not consider bureaucrat to be a term of disgrace, infamy, or contempt, for our whole society would collapse without their labors. But by definition they always work on tiny fractions of the total effort, and they are never financially responsible for results of the whole.) The company is the constant target of nuisance lawsuits, restrictive legislation, ad valorem tax discrimination, union organizers, and empire-building bureaucrats within its own ranks, and although these disadvantages are common to all large-scale enterprises, the nature of the business does not permit offsetting advantages that usually accompany large size. Unless ownership is very consolidated, unit cost of management does not fall as total area increases. Need for brainpower to direct manpower poses a perplexing problem for the company. Until total land area becomes very large, it is hard to justify the cost of a capable person who does nothing but think about problems and policies. Since the foresters are preoccupied with day-to-day administration and training, this kind of brainpower is essential.

Another reason is the inflexibility of the operation. The company owns lands to produce raw material for its mills and must channel the productivity of each acre toward this product insofar as possible. A pulpmill must grow pulpwood and allow trees to be used for other purposes only when it appears unlikely that they will be needed at the mill. Of course, it is possible to make money by growing nothing but pulpwood in certain markets, but the stand tables in other chapters show that individual trees do not grow at the same rate and that production of some sawtimber is inevitable. When the company fails to sell these trees at higher sawtimber prices and takes them to its pulpmill, it is missing the main chance. Finally, no company forestry department can benefit from the procurement mistakes of other companies, as individual landowners often do. You have already seen that a timberland investor needs every possible chance for profit, and greatest success depends on complete freedom of management.

Another type of inflexibility makes it almost impossible to sell certain parcels of land for conversion to higher uses. Sales of this kind are very profitable, but the administrative difficulties of selling any company land are numerous. Every sale must be reviewed by the district forester, chief forester, woodlands vice president, and several officers at headquarters, and what began as a handsome profit is soon entirely consumed by administrative costs.

## THE UNIQUE RESOURCE IN BIG TIMBER COMPANIES

As I have tried to explain, every forester employed by a big timber company has some information that is valuable to you once you know how to separate the wheat from the chaff, but the same can be said about other foresters. The unique resources in a big company are the chairman and two or three other top executives who see and understand the whole picture. Such persons must comprehend and be responsible for the economic journey from a seed or seedling just planted to the ultimate consumer. Once you identify these persons in several companies (and there must be several because each knows well only his own company), you should grasp every opportunity to read their writings or hear them talk. They are extremely valuable resources. They are the experts on the *whole* business, whereas others are experts only in details.

# 14

# Guesses About the Future

Accurate predictions of even one second of the future are impossible, but a timberland investor must make some guesses about it and hope that he is right. Timber-growth predictions have a fair degree of accuracy, but trends of a more general nature are usually more important. One major attraction of timberland investments is the steady rise in the price of all land; everybody knows this, but few can predict exactly where and when it will occur. Anything that helps you guess right contributes to your success as an investor, so I shall try my hand at it and switch to forecasting weather or interest rates if my guesses turn out to be bad.

## NO SHORTAGE OF TIMBER

There will be no shortage of timber. I feel completely confident of this. We have heard cries of timber famine for 75 years and yet have much more now than we did in the 1930s. I am sure for several reasons that those who cry famine are wrong.

First, they underestimate the private landowner because they do not understand him. When they see timberland producing at only half its apparent capacity, they assume that its owner will not invest in growing more trees because he does not have enough capital or will not get involved in a long-term venture. Almost as a knee-jerk reaction, the famine criers call for more government subsidies.

The private landowner is a lot smarter than they are. He can calculate return on investment as well as anybody. The reason he has not invested to increase production in the past is that prospective returns did not match obvious risks. (If all landowners had planted trees 40 or 50 years ago, as they were then urged to do by many foresters, we would have a timber glut of huge proportions, and you can imagine what prices would be.) If you could calculate the efficiency of his investments, I think that you would find him the equal of other asset managers. By following his own wisdom, he has made a profit and produced all the timber we can use and then some.

Second, the scarcity-mongers must base their case on a very long-range prediction. Since there is plenty of timber for the time being, we will not be in any danger until 30 years from now, and as I pointed out in Chapter 8, most investors know that predictions of conditions even 20 years off are worthless. An editorial in *FORBES* magazine put it another way: "Anyone who says businessmen deal in facts not fiction has never read old five-year predictions." All predictions of timber famine for the last 75 years have been wrong because other predictions of the predictors did not work out. Are present predictions likely to be better?

Third, they underestimate the impact of scientific and technological developments. In Chapter 13 I mentioned a company that, in a 14-year period beginning in 1973, increased the yield of plywood from typical pine timber by 60%; in the 10-year period just before 1973, the company's yield had increased less than 9%. Who could have anticipated that the improvement in yield would switch from gradual to dramatic? Are not similar improvements surely ahead of us? No one can yet assess the true impact of discoveries in tree genetics and herbicides, for instance, but they are certain to increase timber supplies.

Fourth, the tools needed for sharp increases in timber supplies are described in this book. No new discoveries are needed. All that landowners need to do both to make money and to increase timber supplies is apply what we already know. I am confident that they will do so when the time comes.

Finally (and the reason for my confidence), the price will undoubtedly rise as timber becomes less abundant. Such a rise will increase the supply because it will pay to log timber that is now too inaccessible for profitable exploitation. It will also decrease the demand and make substitutes more desirable. There will always be as much timber as the world is willing to pay for.

## NO SHORTAGE OF PREDICTIONS OF SHORTAGES

There will continue to be predictions of timber shortages. Capable bureaucrats have a vested interest in the subsidy programs that they helped to set up in the first place and have been administering for years. Furthermore, some of them really believe that they are saving us from timber famine.

Others justify subsidy programs because they keep the price of timber products from rising and hurting the consumer. My wife and I are consumers just like everyone else. We think that we can take care of ourselves and certainly do not need help from a bureaucrat who loves to spend our money on his fancies.

If timberland investment is as good a business as I believe it is, it does not need a subsidy. It certainly needs to avoid the grotesque distortions that litter the farm economy. If the subsidy boosters really want to improve the economic climate for timberland investors, they should urge tax reductions so that the investors could spend the money more wisely than the subsidy boosters.

## INCREASING IMPORTANCE OF THE INDIVIDUAL
## TIMBERLAND INVESTOR

The individual timberland investor will become much more important. Although he owns only 60% of the commercial forest land in the United States, he is the only owner directly responsive to the market, and by market I mean all demands of all citizens of this country and its world trading partners. Industrial ownerships are managed to produce the products most wanted by the individual manufacturer. Public forests are more and more managed to suit the desires of small but vociferous pressure groups who often want only a narrow range of benefits. Both industrial and public ownerships, therefore, lack flexibility and cannot respond quickly to change. This may be a good thing, and if I were the managers of these ownerships, I would probably do what they are doing. But the wisdom of all these managers can never match the collective wisdom of the people as expressed in their market actions. Since the individual timberland investor pays close attention to this market and does his best to satisfy its demands, he is the one who will provide, in both the short and the long run, what the American people want.

The individual investor will become more important because there is coming into being a body of consulting foresters organized to serve his needs. For years there has been no one on his side; now there is. You cannot expect an investor to commit large sums to investments when the only help he can obtain comes from government foresters with built-in restrictions on their competence and range of services, or from timber-company foresters with a built-in conflict of interest because their employers are timber buyers. Now that the number of consulting foresters is growing every day, the individual investor will make more money from his lands and will increase his investment in them.

The investor will become more important because of his enormous staying power. The biggest timber company in the country has to sell timber every day to stay alive; the smallest timberland investor in the country can sit on his timber for years until the price is right, all because his income from other sources is enough for him to live on and then some.

The increased role of the individual investor will be a good thing in many ways. As he has already demonstrated, he will grow whatever timber is needed, but not an overabundance. He examines each expenditure and constantly appraises the entire investment. Since he is spending his own money, he makes his dollars work hard and efficiently. His independence guarantees flexibility; he can change forest-management plans in minutes to take advantage of fleeting market opportunities or special tax situations. As Ludwig Erhard of Germany said, "Turn the people and the money loose, and they will make the country strong."

## CONTINUED RISE OF THE SOUTH AS THE BEST AREA FOR TIMBERLAND INVESTMENT

The South, already important as the country's wood supplier, will become more so. It is undoubtedly one of the most profitable tree-growing regions of the world. It has adequate to abundant rainfall, fast-growing species suitable for many products and easy to regenerate, and terrain and a road network that permit cheap movement of trees to market. It manufactures over 60% of the nation's paper and provides excellent markets for pulpwood, the first merchantable product from a timber stand; its markets for other forest products are very good. It is close to large population centers where forest products are used in great quantities. Its foresters have 50 years of experience in growing trees for the market and stand ready to apply their knowledge and skill to meet new challenges. These characteristics decrease costs, increase profits, and will speed the flow of capital into southern timberlands.

Perhaps more advantageous than all these features (but surely less obvious) are the investors themselves and the brainpower they focus on the business. Things they learn by owning and managing their tracts soon become known to all others through the informal but effective network connecting them. No other area of the world contains so many minds working on how to employ wisely so much capital in growing so much timber.

I think that all of this put together is grounds for almost unbridled optimism if you own southern timberland. Closer attention to the financial aspects of timberland management can only result in increased appeciation of the advantages of the South and corresponding increased interest in its timberlands by investors. At the same time, application of what is in this book will enable investors to increase their profits without increasing their prices and thus enable the region to maintain its position as the low-cost supplier of wood to all world markets. Speedy but well-thought-out action to put your southern properties into efficient production should pay handsome dividends.

## EXPANSION IN MARKETS

There will be a steady improvement in markets for products from timberland. Total timbered area of the United States is decreasing. Two hundred million people need room to live, highways to travel, farms to cultivate, utilities for service, and water to drink. Interstate highway ROWs require about 45 acres per mile, and much of this land comes from timber properties. Uneconomical small farms in timbered sections have long since been abandoned and have reverted to trees, so there is no new supply of land. Where farming is profitable, however, land-clearing is proceeding at a rapid pace and is apt to be permanent. The tremendous growth of this country creates an insatiable demand for pipelines and powerlines, and much of this area comes from timberland. Every major city needs water supplies, and a reservoir covering 25,000 acres is becoming a common sight. These big lakes have a greater impact than their areas indicate, for the land flooded is often the most productive tree-growing portion of the vicinity.

Increasing demand and decreasing supplies usually mean rising prices; there will surely be some of these and corresponding happy days for timberland owners when they occur. But rising prices usually mean falling demand, and there will surely be some of this and bad times for timberland owners when mills lose their markets to substitutes. These forces always keep things in a state of flux, but I think that timber products will manage to hold onto a real price increase of 1% a year. Although such an increase may not seem dramatic, it is enough to increase the income stream from a typical timber tract from 7% to 8% and thereby increase its value by 15%.

**TABLE 14-1**
**Real Rates of Change for Selected Periods**

| Period | Real Rates of Annual Price Change | |
|---|---|---|
| | Sawtimber | Pulpwood |
| 1955–1963 | −7.4% | −2.0% |
| 1963–1973 | +11.4% | +2.6% |
| 1973–1975 | −30.4% | −14.9% |
| 1975–1979 | +17.7% | +4.6% |
| 1979–1983 | −10.6% | −1.1% |

I feel comfortable with this prediction if you will allow enough time for it to work out, but there will surely be some big ups and downs in the meantime. Studies done by Professor Russell B. Milliken of the University of Georgia reveal the real rates of change in prices for selected periods shown in Table 14.1.

Over the 28-year period 1955–1983, the average annual real price change was +0.8% for sawtimber and about 0% for pulpwood, which means that the two products more or less kept up with inflation. The big swings listed mean that investors should be prepared to hold on through several years of downs and to sell heavily after several years of ups.

## TREND TOWARD MANUFACTURING PLANTS WITHOUT LAND BASES

There will be a continuing trend toward manufacturing plants that depend on private timberland investors to grow needed raw material. I believe this is a beneficial trend.

First, it is efficient use of capital for the industrial concern. Its expertise is the manufacture and sale of useful products from wood, and concentration on the area of expertise always increases profits. Its income does not suffer the drag of carrying timberlands that produce a low return for an owner with a high-cost structure. Its capital requirements are smaller, since that required to grow raw material is supplied by individual investors. It can invest these savings in research on new products and processes, thereby increasing its profit and the market for timber products at the same time.

Second, smaller capital requirements mean that more mills will be built, assuming that markets develop as everyone expects. Money is always hard to find for new ventures, and it is easier to find small amounts than large amounts. Timberlands are particularly difficult to finance because the business is new and the properties do not often produce the regular annual incomes that make financing easier. An adequate supply of raw material offered on the open market by timberland investors eliminates one major problem of a board of directors planning construction of a manufacturing plant.

## REAPPRAISAL OF EXISTING FORESTRY PROGRAMS

Some existing forestry programs will be discontinued because they were a waste of time in the first place or because they are not needed.

Foresters have been continually preoccupied with the problems of small landowners, whose timberlands are supposedly unproductive because of bad management and small amounts of capital. Educational programs were inaugurated to convince these persons of the advantages of good forestry. This approach was supposed to cure the problem; however, this was always an impossibility. You cannot make a capitalist by education alone, and you cannot expect "good forest management" from an individual with six children trying to scratch out a living from a 200-acre farm and outside work. The market will correct this situation, since more capable and experienced investors will soon acquire these lands by continuing to make a profit every year. Trying to educate persons who are financially unable to use the knowledge is pouring money down the drain. (And as I have shown elsewhere, the "problem" was not bad management and small capital; it was that many of these owners were too "smart" to follow the foresters' advice.)

Many industries and some governments hired foresters to teach good forestry by performing various forest-management services for little or no cost. Such programs were successful at the beginning, as a review of the old Southern Pulpwood Conservation Association activities shows, but once the capable investors have learned the lesson, they do not want unnecessary services. In fact, they are suspicious of free programs, for worthwhile services are worth paying for. Timberland investors know that, one way or another, they are paying for such assistance, and they are afraid because the price tag is not clearly visible. Industries in general have been quick to recognize that selling forestry by free services is no longer needed, so they have converted these programs to the timber-procurement mechanisms described earlier. Governments are generally still trying to educate landowners, but increasing demands on tax revenues will force them to shift their efforts into services that are more needed, such as better fire control.

## LESS COMPETITION FROM U.S. FOREST SERVICE TIMBER

Private landowners will encounter less timber-selling competition from the U.S. Forest Service. More restrictions on USFS sales will come from the success of single-use pressure groups who seem to want to stop all timber sales from national forests, and from the strong tendency of the Congress to pass laws requiring economic enterprises to meet noneconomic criteria.

Furthermore, the USFS is moving away from its customers. It seems to believe that timber is scarce and that the market is dominated by sellers. It is not acting like a good merchant and is limiting its markets in ways besides those I discussed in Chapter 3.

In at least one forest the USFS no longer uses form classes for calculating sale volumes, but instead uses one local volume table for the same species throughout the forest. This procedure is undoubtedly accurate so far as each year's total cut is concerned, for it is applying average volumes obtained from hundreds of thousands of trees to other hundreds of thousands. But the forest is scattered over 25 or so counties and contains very variable conditions, so estimated volumes on each small sale can vary quite a bit from the average. Since timber buyers bid on these sales one at a time, the USFS makes life harder for them when it publishes inventories that are obviously wrong. This same forest plans to distance itself even farther away from its customers; in the near future, it intends to publish in sale prospectuses no volume data except cubic feet of wood and number of trees by DBH classes.

USFS sales are also getting bigger. Most contain well over one million board feet, and some more than ten million. When the sale price is $1,000,000 or more, many potential buyers are eliminated. Even though the required down payment is only 10%, the liability of being forced to carry out the contract is a formidable matter for most buyers.

## NO SHORTAGE OF BIG PROBLEMS

There will be enough big problems to worry you. This is a safe prediction because there are always big problems. In 1985, for example, all forestry publications and seminars on timberland were crowded with discussions of, and usually diatribes against, the Reagan tax-reform proposals, the imports of Canadian lumber, and the very strong dollar that was giving foreign producers an edge in the markets for many forest products. No matter when you read or reread these words, the same problems or acceptable substitutes will be present. All are very complicated, changing every day, and completely beyond an individual's ability to solve or reduce.

If they worry you a great deal, sell your property, and invest in other things. Most owners believe that such problems will not be as bad as forecast or that they are nimble enough to zig when these powerful forces zag. Those who think that a new and permanent degree of uncertainty has arrived merely raise their discount rate to compensate for the change.

## WORLD MARKETS TO SET OUR PRICES

Those who suffered through the early 1980s know what a very strong dollar can do to us. Whenever our prices are raised to a very high level for any reason, supplies that were previously uneconomical to produce move into the market. Our high prices of the 1970s and a fall in their dollar enabled the Canadians to put in the infrastructure, build the mills, and eventually grab a big fraction of our market for lumber. The same thing happened to market pulp; at one time it was cheaper to haul wood pulp from Brazil to New England mills than to make it from trees within sight of them. Now that our dollar has fallen about 50%, we have the upper hand, but this ebb and flow will never cease.

Wood is a commodity, and commodities hold their markets only by being the cheapest (all things considered) solutions to the problems of consumers. In our case, the key to being a low-cost supplier is management and more management. Our infrastructure is already in place, and our mills are already the most efficient in the world. The missing link is more brainpower applied to timberland investments.

## BETTER NEAR-TERM PREDICTIONS OF TIMBER PRICES

I have emphasized that predicting the future price of timber is impossible. But as we all now know from bitter experience, one organization can always *knock down* prices, and this is the Federal Reserve Board, which is usually referred to as the Fed. It may not be able to raise them, but it can always knock them down in a short time and maybe for several years. Being able to spot the approach of such a disaster is at least a help in making correct guesses about the future. Therefore, I want to show why the Fed deserves careful study and constant watching by all timber owners.

Throughout the course of history in every society, there has always been a tug of war between two economic classes: the few who have accumulated financial wealth and the many who are trying to accumulate it. The wealth-owners are cautious and want stable money, steady or falling prices, deflation or at least no inflation, and investments such as bonds that offer safety and a reasonable return. The wealth-seekers are optimistic and want "easy money," rising prices of physical assets, some inflation or at least no deflation, and investments such as homes, farms, small businesses, timberlands, and oil wells, the kind of investments needed to develop the country. The wealth-owners want sound financial conditions; the wealth-seekers want strong economic growth. Since both are parts of the same society, each needs the other to accomplish its goals, so money flows constantly between the two via the different financial markets.

The Fed is the regulator of this flow. It does its work by raising or lowering the price of money, the interest rate. The methods it uses are mysterious to most of us, but no one who witnessed the 20% prime rate of 1980 can doubt the Fed's power over interest rates.

When rates are low, money flows away from bonds and into physical assets, so wealth-owners lose and wealth-seekers win. When rates are high, the reverse is true. Nothing reveals this flow better than the business of growing trees for profit. Under good management, the physical growth of trees into the most profitable products produces a compound annual return of about 8%; such a real return makes timberland very competitive with other investments. If the interest rate is 6%, the economic-growth crowd owning timberlands has the edge over the sound-money crowd owning bonds. If interest rates stay at the same low level, the pendulum swings even farther in the same direction. More and more people buy houses, demand for lumber increases, stumpage prices rise, and timber owners score a bigger win. Conditions like those in 1979 prevail.

While this is going on, the Fed hears an ever-louder chorus of criticism from the banks and bondholders, the people whom it deals with every day and feels most comfortable with. They warn of the dangers of inflation and emphasize the need for sound money. Eventually the Fed decides that the sound-money crowd has lost enough. It jacks up interest rates, perhaps to 20% as it did in the spring of 1980, and the advantage flows strongly in the opposite direction. There is a scramble to get out of timber and into bonds, so the supply of timber on the market increases and its price falls. Then the price falls even more because new families cannot afford a home at such rates, so demand for timber products falls.

These changes do not happen overnight, but they still seem surprisingly fast and large to most of us who enjoyed record prosperity in 1979. When interest rates hit a peak in April 1980, timber buyers pulled completely out of the market and did not return in force until prices in some areas had dropped nearly 50%.

The Fed's swings from easy money to tight money and back again do not have an automatic effect on timber prices and the general economy. During the Great Depression of the 1930s, everyone was so scared and demand was so low that very low interest rates did not generate increased economic activity. The evidence suggests to me that the Fed's swings toward easy money will not guarantee higher prices, but its swings toward tight money will guarantee lower prices.

The Fed's actions are determined by its board of governors, seven intelligent, well-meaning persons experienced in financial affairs. To guide their decisions these governors have available an unequaled amount of information about economic conditions in the United States and the world. Nevertheless, there is often disagreement among them about whether the country needs lower or higher interest rates. (Most of us see evidence each day that 25 different economists looking at the same data often arrive at 25 different interpretations.) And even when they are in unanimous agreement, they are still human and, like other humans, make mistakes. They were raising interest rates just before the stock market crash of October 1987 and had to change course abruptly.

Finally, the Fed deals only in averages and is not concerned with the impact of its actions on particular commodities. For instance, the zero inflation rate it achieves may be the result of a 50% drop in oil prices while the price of lumber is rising 50%. Since its only weapon is the interest rate, it can only knock down the price of most commodities by raising the price of a single one, money. Therefore, those concerned only with timber prices should give little weight to what is happening to the cost of living and very great weight to the level of interest rates.

Because of its great power, the Fed attempts to conduct its operations in secrecy. In their public remarks, its governors try to avoid giving clues to the actions they intend to take, and former chairman Paul Volcker was famous for long, disjointed, rambling comments on the economy that confused almost everyone. Sometimes by design or mistake the board does the opposite of what its members say. Therefore, timber owners should disregard what the Fed says and pay attention only to what it does.

The key to what it does is the Fed Funds rate. This is the rate that banks pay on funds borrowed overnight or for short periods to bring their reserves into proper balance with increases in their loans. The Fed Funds rate reacts immediately to the slightest changes in supply and demand; it shows exactly what the Fed is doing and reveals the direction in which all interest rates are headed. Fortunately, it is reported often during the day by every source of business news that I know about. Fortunately, no agency can exercise enormous power without giving signals to all investors.

How long does it take the Fed to knock down timber prices? I think that the lead time is several months. Paul Volcker took office in August 1979 and immediately started raising interest rates, but these rates did not get high enough to stop timber buyers cold until April 1980. The first Volcker rise was large and rapid, and a more gradual rise may have taken longer to produce the same results. I do not know; nobody knows. But I feel safe in saying that timber owners will have several months to react, plenty of time to convert large volumes to cash.

The Fed swings have an additional impact on timber. When U.S. interest rates rise, investors all over the world want part of the action, so the dollar rises in relation to other currencies. Therefore, prices of U.S. timber products such as wood pulp, paper, plywood, lumber, and logs rise, and all our overseas customers take their business elsewhere. They take with them all the frosting on our cake. Although most timber, perhaps 90%, produced in North America is consumed here, industry's ability to sell the remainder overseas usually means the difference between a good market for timber owners and a routine one.

So, how important is the Fed to owners of 40 to 400 acres of timberland, the owners who can choose the timing of major timber sales? Very important. These owners will profit a great deal by learning everything possible about the Fed, not only about the technical ways in which it manipulates interest rates, but also about the individuals on its board and the political pressures on them. In my opinion, there is no better book on this subject than *Secrets of the Temple: How the Federal Reserve Runs the Country* by William Greider (Simon & Schuster). And we should all recognize the truths in these words from Mr. Greider:

Money is, above all, a political question—a matter of deliberate choices made by the state. Like all political questions decided by fallible human beings, money is subject to the variables of political action—understanding and intent, influence and error. Money is an everyday argument among competing interests, in which some benefit and some lose, depending on the outcome. Money is a social plan that rewards or punishes, stimulates or restrains. Money may encourage democratic aspirations or thwart them.

Now that we know what the Fed can do, we have one clue about the course of timber prices over the near term.

# 15

# Case History of a Successful Timberland Investor: Charting a Course

In preceding chapters, I have discussed the important aspects of timberland investment. Now let me summarize first by listing in order the steps you should take, and then by presenting a hypothetical case history of the operations of Robert Bryant.

Bryant's grandfather, an independent oil operator, purchased minerals, royalty, and leases all over his state beginning in the 1930s and, when the price appeared to be cheap, bought the surface also. In this manner, he acquired in 1952 a tract of 2130 acres 120 miles southeast of his headquarters. At the time of purchase, he gave only minor consideration to its possibilities as timberland. Rentals from mineral leases produced an adequate return on his investment; ad valorem taxes were low; most merchantable timber had recently been removed. Bryant's father continued the emphasis on minerals, but occasionally sold timber in pay-as-you-go sales or by informal bidding between two buyers whom he knew personally. By 1977, however, when Bryant takes over the management, values have increased a great deal, and sound money management makes it necessary to explore other possibilities. What steps does he take?

## STEP 1: CHOOSE FORESTRY ADVISER

Unfamiliar with the services available to timberland owners, Bryant calls on the state forestry department, discovers that its services to private landowners are mainly educational, and receives a list of consulting foresters practicing in the state. Using criteria described in Chapter 2, he selects one and invites him to discuss his business problems. After a brief explanation of what he owns and what he wants, he asks the forester to suggest a solution and to discuss his customary fee schedule and working arrangements. The forester states that his firm offers a complete line of services to timberland investors, that his fees vary with the type of work, and that he prefers to undertake work one step at a time, without a long-term forest-management contract. This gradual approach pleases Bryant; he knows little about timberland and consulting foresters, but realizes how important the relationship can be. After an hour of discussion, Bryant is satisfied with the forester's competence and commonsense and chooses him as a forestry adviser. If the relationship proves to be satisfactory for both, this decision is probably Bryant's most important one, for he has an asset of large size and relies heavily on his forester's advice when making decisions of long-term consequence.

## STEP 2: TAKE TIMBERLAND INVENTORY

To begin with, the forester suggests an inventory of Bryant's tract. It may have no or very dim possibilities for timber operations (and this will end their association); at any rate, they cannot make sound plans until they know what Bryant has. The forester recommends a 10% inventory, describes what data will be gathered, and quotes a fee on a per-acre basis. On being assured that the fee also covers the time necessary for a planning conference after the report is submitted, Bryant tells him to proceed. Ten days later, the forester submits the following report:

HOWARD, STEPHENS AND DOUGLASS
*Consulting Foresters* COURT SQUARE SOUTH BUILDING
ANYTOWN, STATE

14 April 1977

Mr. Robert Bryant
P.O. Box 187
Anytown, State

Dear Mr. Bryant:

We have just completed a timberland inventory of your property described as SW¼, W½ of NW¼, Section 26; Entire less NW¼ of NW¼, Section 27; S½ of NE¼,

SE¼, Section 28; E½, Section 33; W½, NE¼, E½ of SE¼, Section 34; W½ of NW¼, W½ of NE¼ of NW¼, SW¼ of SW¼, Section 35, all in Township 5 North, Range 10 West, and NW¼ of NW¼ less West 10 acres, Section 2, Township 4 North, Range 10 West, containing 2130 acres. Our report is presented below and on the attached map (page 198).

### Specifications and Sampling Procedure

We tallied as sawtimber all pine trees 9.0 in. and up DBH and all hardwood trees 11.0 in. and up DBH and as pulpwood all trees over 5.0 in. DBH but smaller than sawtimber. We divided the trees into 2 in. DBH classes and estimated volumes to the following top diameters inside bark: pine sawtimber 6 in., hardwood sawtimber 10 in., pulpwood 4 in. Pulpwood volumes include standing trees only; we made no estimate of pulpwood volume in tops of sawtimber trees. We tallied all pine species as pine, all gums as gum, all oaks as oak, and yellow poplar as poplar.

Sawtimber inventory is based on a 10% strip sample; we passed twice through each 40-acre block and, on each pass, tallied the sawtimber trees on a strip 66 ft. wide. Pulpwood inventory is based on a 2% plot sample; we tallied trees of this size on 1/10-acre plots spaced five chains apart on the cruise line. Number of pine trees in the 4 in. DBH class were tallied on the pulpwood plots. Growth data were obtained by taking an increment core from the tree nearest the center of each pulpwood plot.

### Timber Inventory

Our estimate of the total number and volume of trees by DBH class, species, and product is as follows (see page 190):

Pulpwood volumes are given in unpeeled cords of 128 cubic feet each, and sawtimber volumes are given in thousands of board feet, Doyle scale. Four-in. trees are listed under pulpwood although they are below merchantable size. Hardwood trees occur on the tract only in scattered strips of pine-hardwood type (see map); therefore, we do not believe we took a sufficient sample of them to produce a reliable estimate. Because of their small volumes and low values, this is not a serious error.

Trees smaller than the 4 in. DBH class are present in considerable numbers under stands of larger trees; most of them became established at the same time as the larger trees and are small now because they are overcrowded or overtopped. They will not make a significant contribution to future growth. Your problem is either too many trees per acre or none at all. Average volume per acre is low because trees are small and because many acres are idle or used for other purposes. We divided the tract arbitrarily into seven blocks during inventory, and volumes for each block are given on sheets following the map. (See pages 191–197.)

Scattered all over the tract are patches of old pine stumps suitable for distillate wood. We think their volume is between 500 and 1000 tons; they are concentrated enough to be merchantable.

## Forest Types

The map shows the location of the two main forest types on your tract. One is pine and is almost a pure stand of longleaf pine. The other is pine-hardwood made up of 50% pine and 50% hardwood. In this type the pine species is loblolly, and the hardwood species groups are those shown under timber inventory.

## Growth Study

In calculating timber growth on your property, we ignored the hardwood component; it contains only about 5% of the volume and less of the value. We estimate annual growth of pine to be 173,000 board feet of sawtimber and 302 cords of pulpwood, and we believe you can remove this volume each year without dipping into timber capital. This very high *percentage* rate comes about because many pulpwood trees are growing into sawtimber and because all present sawtimber trees are relatively small. It will gradually drop if you do not remove each year's growth.

Growth rates vary widely by DBH classes; 12-in. trees grow better than 8%, 20-in. trees less than 3.5%. There is also a great difference within DBH classes depending on condition of individual trees. Well-spaced, vigorous trees grow rapidly; suppressed trees grow hardly at all.

## Soil Analysis

We did not make a thorough study of the soils, but information available from the U.S. Soil Conservation Service indicates that the site index for your pine areas is 80 and that for the pine-hardwood areas is 90. This is a very general statement, but indicates that you have no serious problems here and will do for the time being. At present, your major concern is making the best possible use of existing stands, and measurements of growth in the field will provide all necessary guides. We recommend more thorough study of your soils when markets and financial resources make possible more intensive forest management.

## Markets and Market Prices

Markets for all forest products are excellent. Within 30 miles of the tract, there are 10 sawmills, 5 pulpwood dealers, 3 plywood mills, 1 pulp mill, and 2 pole buyers, and competition among them is spirited. We estimate stumpage values for pine pulpwood to be $25.00 per cord and for sawtimber per MBF to be as follows: pine $175.00, gum and oak $50.00, and poplar $55.00. Stumpage value of distillate wood is $2.00 per ton. There is an insignificant volume of hardwood pulpwood—so small that we did not include it in the inventory—which has a market value of $6.00 per cord and can be expected to double or triple within the next 10 years. Unfortunately, it can never contribute substantially to income.

Fire
---

Except for pine-hardwood areas too wet to burn, the entire tract burned over this past winter, and there are signs that this is a common occurrence. Since almost every tree is a longleaf pine, there is little loss from death of merchantable trees. On the other hand, there is a definite growth loss each year because many trees are defoliated by fire, and constant burning prohibits establishment of young pines in many areas that are now idle. These idle acres, inherently productive, are scattered all over the tract in irregular strips and patches which show on aerial photographs but are much too complicated to show on the map. We believe they can be made productive quickly and cheaply by planting, but no planting should be done until the fire problem is solved. The fires appear to be of incendiary origin to provide early spring grazing for numerous cattle in the area, and although your county is under the state fire control program, several determined firebugs completely overpower all fire suppression organizations. This is a major problem; we estimate your timbered land is at least 30% idle because of fire.

Development Work
---

Planting is needed on about 600 acres, but should not be undertaken until you can control fire. No TSI work is needed now or in the near future; constant burning has eliminated all pine reproduction and almost all hardwood from pine areas. Thinning is desirable on 480 acres as shown on the map. We estimate that a thinning from them will produce about three cords of pulpwood per acre now.

Trespass
---

All merchantable timber has been removed within the last year from about 35 acres in the southwest corner of SW¼ of SE¼, Section 33. This appears to be trespass; we found no evidence of an established boundary line either south or west of cut area. Mr. Rice, mentioned below, knew nothing about cutting.

Adverse Possession and Other Use
---

The gravel pit in NE¼ of SW¼, Section 26, occupies five acres, is abandoned, and is being recaptured by pine seedlings.

The pasture north of Highway 42 occupies forty acres, is heavily grazed, but receives no cultivation. These conditions also apply to the 15-acre pasture on east side of NE¼ of SE¼, Section 34.

The cultivated fields in the southeast portion of tract occupy 80 acres and have been prepared for planting this year. The two barns are in use. All four houses on the tract are occupied, and Julius Rice, General Delivery, Anytown, lives in the one in the southeast corner of SE¼ of SE¼, Section 34. Mr. Rice told us that he leases the pastures, fields, and houses from you and subleases some facilities to others. He said that all fences shown are yours and necessary for his operations; if not, they may be evidence of adverse possession.

Rights of Way

The map shows rights of way we found and measured on the ground. The largest is that of ABC Power Company; it is 100 ft wide, about 8000 ft long, and contains 18.6 acres. The DEF Pipeline Company ROW is 25 ft. wide, about 3000 ft. long, and contains 1.7 acres; there is also a telephone or telegraph line down its center. There are three ROWs of the local electric power association, they are 20 ft wide, a total of 16,380 ft long, and contain 7.7 acres. The ROW for State Highway 42 is 60 ft wide, about 10,560 ft long, and contains 14.5 acres. The only other road ROWs that reduce timber-growing area are those in the extreme southeastern portion and a short stretch just south of the highway; they are 30 ft wide, about 4500 ft long, and contain 3.1 acres. The total area used for all ROWs is 45.6 acres; there may be additional areas affected if any powerline ROW agreement permits cutting of danger trees.

Boundary Lines

Some boundary lines are established by fences shown on map; these fences appear to be accepted by adjoining owners. In the northern portion, you have at least one mile of common boundary line with XYZ Paper Company; these two strips of line are painted white and maintained by the company. Although we investigated at several points, we found no evidence of established lines on the west side of the land in Sections 28 and 33 or the south side of the land in Sections 33 and 34; this situation may have led to the cutting, and we believe these must be surveyed.

Please call on us if we can give you any further information or assistance. After you have a chance to study these data, we will be happy to help you plan and execute those programs you select.

Respectfully submitted,

Howard, Stephens, and Douglas
CALVIN R. DOUGLAS

CRD:bn
Attachments

Bryant now has the information needed to evaluate his asset and plan for the future. Of course, each property is different, and so is each owner, but this gives you an illustration of what a timberland inventory should contain. You probably have some data on your property, but they may be incomplete or out of date. You should resist the temptation to economize by using such data; even under optimum conditions, you must make many assumptions and plan about the future; plans based on a shaky foundation lead to trouble.

## STEP 3: MAKE FINANCIAL FORECAST

Bryant and his forester now sit down with pencil and paper to see what returns can be had, now and later, from operation of the property as a timberland investment and to determine whether the money that can be realized from its sale could be better utilized in another way.

First, they look at income. Annual growth is 173 MBF of sawtimber and 302 cords of pulpwood, which, at the values in the report, can be sold for $37,825. The forester states that he will mark the trees for cutting, sell them, and inspect logging operations for a fee of 9.5% ($3593), leaving a net of $34,232. Rental from the lease to Mr. Rice is $800 per year, bringing total net income to $35,032.

Next, they look at expenses. Last year's taxes were $2600, and although these are likely to increase gradually, they use this figure. The tract has 10 miles of boundary, but 1 mile is already maintained by XYZ Paper Company. The forester estimates that it will cost $375 per mile ($3375) to brush out and repaint these and that this work should be done every nine years; average cost per year is thus $375. No other expenses seem necessary at present; Mr. Rice leases and lives on part of the tract, and the forester, in marking timber or inspecting cutting, will be on the remainder frequently. Therefore, total annual expense is $2975, and net annual income is $32,057.

The forester estimates that the tract, without minerals, can be sold for $225 per acre ($479,250), and at this value, a net income of $32,057 produces an annual return of 6.7%. Bryant thinks that land values will rise, and this consideration makes him content with the 6.7% return for the time being.

There are two possibilities for increased income. Rice pays $800 per year for the use of four houses, 137 acres of cultivable land, and 240 acres of fenced woods pasture; this seems a low price and may be increased. Substantial increases in timber growth will be possible when elimination of uncontrolled fire permits intensive forest management; the forester states that the tract is capable of producing a net annual timber harvest of $60,000. Therefore, Bryant has a fair return and good prospects. Without them, he would sell the tract at this point; with them, he proceeds to the next step.

## STEP 4: CHOOSE TAX ADVISER

Bryant, who well understands the importance of taxes, chose his tax adviser, a certified public accountant, many years ago and consults

# TABLE 15-1
## Estimate of Total Number of Trees by DBH Class, Species, and Product

### Pulpwood

| DBH | Pine Trees | Pine Vol. | Soft Hardwood Trees | Soft Hardwood Vol. | Hard Hardwood Trees | Hard Hardwood Vol. | Misc. Hardwood Trees | Misc. Hardwood Vol. | Total Trees | Total Vol. |
|---|---|---|---|---|---|---|---|---|---|---|
| 4 | 58,860 |  |  |  |  |  |  |  | 58,860 |  |
| 6 | 33,950 | 1,256 |  |  |  |  |  |  | 33,950 | 1,256 |
| 8 | 27,750 | 2,553 |  |  |  |  |  |  | 27,750 | 2,553 |
|  |  | 3,809 |  |  |  |  |  |  |  | 3,809 |

### Sawtimber (number of trees by class)

| DBH | Pine 2 | Pine 3 | Pine 4 | Oak 1 | Oak 2 | Gum 1 | Gum 2 | Poplar 1 | Poplar 2 |
|---|---|---|---|---|---|---|---|---|---|
| 10 | 5,710 | 7,350 |  |  |  |  |  |  |  |
| 12 | 1,280 | 2,650 | 1,700 | 90 | 40 | 130 | 140 | 30 | 40 |
| 14 | 300 | 710 | 450 | 80 | 50 | 50 | 110 | 20 | 50 |
| 16 | 160 | 380 | 230 | 20 | 60 |  | 40 |  | 30 |
| 18 | 40 | 180 | 210 |  |  |  |  |  | 10 |
| 20 | 10 | 20 | 10 |  |  |  |  |  |  |

### Sawtimber (totals by species)

| DBH | Pine Trees | Pine Vol. | Oak Trees | Oak Vol. | Gum Trees | Gum Vol. | Poplar Trees | Poplar Vol. | Misc. Trees | Misc. Vol. | Total Trees | Total Vol. |
|---|---|---|---|---|---|---|---|---|---|---|---|---|
| 10 | 13,060 | 378.8 |  |  |  |  |  |  |  |  | 13,060 | 378.8 |
| 12 | 5,630 | 322.5 | 130 | 4.7 | 270 | 10.6 | 70 | 2.8 |  |  | 6,100 | 340.6 |
| 14 | 1,460 | 144.1 | 130 | 8.3 | 160 | 11.6 | 70 | 5.1 |  |  | 1,820 | 169.1 |
| 16 | 770 | 109.7 | 80 | 9.0 | 40 | 5.0 | 30 | 3.8 |  |  | 920 | 127.5 |
| 18 | 430 | 95.2 |  |  |  |  | 10 | 1.8 |  |  | 440 | 97.0 |
| 20 | 40 | 10.2 |  |  |  |  |  |  |  |  | 40 | 10.2 |
|  | 21,390 | 1,060.5 | 340 | 22.0 | 470 | 27.2 | 180 | 13.5 | 0 | 0.0 | 22,380 | 1,123.2 |

# TABLE 15-2

**Block 1:** W½ of NW¼, Section 26; NE¼, NE¼, E½ of NW¼, Section 27

320 Acres

## NUMBER OF MERCHANTABLE TREES BY DBH AND LOG LENGTHS

### Pulpwood

| DBH | Pine Trees | Pine Vol. | Soft Hardwood Trees | Soft Hardwood Vol. | Hard Hardwood Trees | Hard Hardwood Vol. | Total Trees | Total Vol. |
|-----|-----------|-----------|---------------------|--------------------|---------------------|--------------------|-------------|------------|
| 4 | 10,240 | | | | | | 10,240 | |
| 6 | 5,600 | 207 | | | | | 5,600 | 207 |
| 8 | 4,250 | 391 | | | | | 4,250 | 391 |
| | | 598 | | | | | | 598 |

### Sawtimber

| DBH | Pine 1 | Pine 2 | Pine 3 | Pine 4 | Pine 5 | Oak 1 | Oak 2 | Oak 3 | Gum 1 | Gum 2 | Gum 3 | Poplar 1 | Poplar 2 | Poplar 3 | Misc. Hardwood 1 | Misc. Hardwood 2 | Misc. Hardwood 3 |
|-----|--------|--------|--------|--------|--------|-------|-------|-------|-------|-------|-------|----------|----------|----------|------------------|------------------|------------------|
| 10 | 750 | 830 | | | | | | | | | | | | | | | |
| 12 | 250 | 450 | 300 | | | | | | 30 | 10 | | | | | | | |
| 14 | 60 | 130 | 80 | | | | | | | 20 | | | | | | | |
| 16 | 50 | 120 | 70 | | | | | | | 20 | | | | | | | |
| 18 | 40 | 70 | 70 | | | | | | | | | | | | | | |

### Total

| DBH | Pine Trees | Pine Vol. | Oak Trees | Oak Vol. | Gum Trees | Gum Vol. | Poplar Trees | Poplar Vol. | Misc. Trees | Misc. Vol. | Total Trees | Total Vol. |
|-----|-----------|-----------|-----------|----------|-----------|----------|--------------|-------------|-------------|------------|-------------|------------|
| 10 | 1,580 | 44.9 | | | | | | | | | 1,580 | 44.9 |
| 12 | 1,000 | 56.8 | | | 40 | 1.4 | | | | | 1,040 | 58.2 |
| 14 | 270 | 26.4 | | | 20 | 1.6 | | | | | 290 | 28.0 |
| 16 | 240 | 34.1 | | | 20 | 2.5 | | | | | 260 | 36.6 |
| 18 | 110 | 26.2 | | | | | | | | | 110 | 26.2 |
| | 3,200 | 188.4 | 0 | 0.0 | 80 | 5.5 | 0 | 0.0 | 0 | 0.0 | 3,280 | 193.9 |

# TABLE 15-3

**Block 2: E½, Section 33**

**320 Acres**

## NUMBER OF MERCHANTABLE TREES BY DBH AND LOG LENGTHS

### Pulpwood

| DBH | Pine Trees | Pine Vol. | Soft Hardwood Trees | Soft Hardwood Vol. | Hard Hardwood Trees | Hard Hardwood Vol. | Total Trees | Total Vol. |
|---|---|---|---|---|---|---|---|---|
| 4 | 10,020 | | | | | | 10,020 | |
| 6 | 5,600 | 207 | | | | | 5,600 | 207 |
| 8 | 3,100 | 285 | | | | | 3,100 | 285 |
| | | 492 | | | | | | 492 |

### Sawtimber — Number of trees by log length

| DBH | Pine 1 | Pine 2 | Pine 3 | Oak 1 | Oak 2 | Oak 3 | Gum 1 | Gum 2 | Gum 3 | Poplar 1 | Poplar 2 | Poplar 3 | Misc. Hardwood 1 | 2 | 3 |
|---|---|---|---|---|---|---|---|---|---|---|---|---|---|---|---|
| 10 | 500 | 570 | | 30 | | | 30 | 30 | | | | | | | |
| 12 | 140 | 340 | 200 | 20 | | | | 20 | | | 30 | | | | |
| 14 | 50 | 130 | 80 | | 20 | | | 10 | | | | | | | |
| 16 | 30 | 60 | 40 | | | | | | | | | | | | |
| 18 | 10 | 60 | 60 | | | | | | | | | | | | |

### Sawtimber — Trees and Volume

| DBH | Pine Trees | Pine Vol. | Oak Trees | Oak Vol. | Gum Trees | Gum Vol. | Poplar Trees | Poplar Vol. | Misc. Trees | Misc. Vol. | Total Trees | Total Vol. |
|---|---|---|---|---|---|---|---|---|---|---|---|---|
| 10 | 1,070 | 30.5 | 30 | 0.9 | 60 | 2.3 | | | | | 1,070 | 30.5 |
| 12 | 680 | 39.2 | 20 | 1.0 | 20 | 1.6 | 30 | 2.5 | | | 770 | 42.4 |
| 14 | 260 | 25.8 | 20 | 2.5 | 10 | 1.3 | | | | | 330 | 30.9 |
| 16 | 130 | 18.4 | | | | | | | | | 160 | 22.2 |
| 18 | 130 | 28.7 | | | | | | | | | 130 | 28.7 |
| | 2,270 | 142.6 | 70 | 4.4 | 90 | 5.2 | 30 | 2.5 | 0 | 0.0 | 2,460 | 154.7 |

# TABLE 15-4

## Block 3: SE¼, E½ of SW¼, Section 27
### 240 Acres

## NUMBER OF MERCHANTABLE TREES BY DBH AND LOG LENGTHS

### *Pulpwood*

| DBH | Pine Trees | Pine Vol. | Soft Hardwood Trees | Soft Hardwood Vol. | Hard Hardwood Trees | Hard Hardwood Vol. | Total Trees | Total Vol. |
|---|---|---|---|---|---|---|---|---|
| 4 | 5,940 | | | | | | 5,940 | |
| 6 | 3,300 | 122 | | | | | 3,300 | 122 |
| 8 | 3,750 | 345 | | | | | 3,750 | 345 |
| | | 467 | | | | | | 467 |

### *Sawtimber*

| DBH | Pine 1 | Pine 2 | Pine 3 | Pine 4 | Pine 5 | Oak 1 | Oak 2 | Oak 3 | Gum 1 | Gum 2 | Gum 3 | Poplar 1 | Poplar 2 | Poplar 3 | Hard Hardwood 1 | Misc. Hardwood 1 | Misc. Hardwood 2 | Misc. Hardwood 3 |
|---|---|---|---|---|---|---|---|---|---|---|---|---|---|---|---|---|---|---|
| 10 | 680 | 1,000 | | | | | | | | | | | | | | | | |
| 12 | 160 | 330 | 200 | | | 10 | | | 10 | | | 20 | | | | | | |
| 14 | 10 | 40 | 20 | | | 10 | | | | | | 10 | | | | | | |
| 16 | | | 30 | | | | | | | | | | | | | | | |
| 18 | | | 10 | 10 | | | | | | | | | | | | | | |

| DBH | Pine Trees | Pine Vol. | Oak Trees | Oak Vol. | Gum Trees | Gum Vol. | Poplar Trees | Poplar Vol. | Misc. Trees | Misc. Vol. | Total Trees | Total Vol. |
|---|---|---|---|---|---|---|---|---|---|---|---|---|
| 10 | 1,680 | 49.6 | | | | | | | | | 1,680 | 49.6 |
| 12 | 690 | 39.3 | 10 | 0.3 | 10 | 0.3 | 20 | 0.6 | | | 730 | 40.5 |
| 14 | 70 | 7.0 | 10 | 0.5 | | | 10 | 0.5 | | | 90 | 8.0 |
| 16 | 30 | 4.2 | | | | | | | | | 30 | 4.2 |
| 18 | 20 | 4.6 | | | | | | | | | 20 | 4.6 |
| | 2,490 | 104.7 | 20 | 0.8 | 10 | 0.3 | 30 | 1.1 | 0 | 0.0 | 2,550 | 106.9 |

## TABLE 15-5

**Block 4: W½, Section 34**

**320 Acres**

### NUMBER OF MERCHANTABLE TREES BY DBH AND LOG LENGTHS

#### Pulpwood

| DBH | Pine Trees | Pine Vol. | Soft Hardwood Trees | Soft Hardwood Vol. | Hard Hardwood Trees | Hard Hardwood Vol. | Total Trees | Total Vol. |
|---|---|---|---|---|---|---|---|---|
| 4 | 14,260 | | | | | | 14,260 | |
| 6 | 8,050 | 298 | | | | | 8,050 | 298 |
| 8 | 6,600 | 607 | | | | | 6,600 | 607 |
| | | 905 | | | | | | 905 |

#### Sawtimper

| DBH | Pine 1 | Pine 2 | Pine 3 | Pine 4 | Pine 5 | Oak 1 | Oak 2 | Oak 3 | Gum 1 | Gum 2 | Gum 3 | Poplar 1 | Poplar 2 | Poplar 3 | Misc. Hardwood 1 | Misc. Hardwood 2 | Misc. Hardwood 3 |
|---|---|---|---|---|---|---|---|---|---|---|---|---|---|---|---|---|---|
| 10 | 1,000 | 1,320 | | | | | | | | 20 | | | | | | | |
| 12 | 100 | 210 | 130 | | | | | | | 10 | | | | | | | |
| 14 | 20 | 40 | 10 | | | | | | | | | | | | | | |
| 16 | | 20 | | | | | | | | | | | | | | | |
| 18 | | | 10 | | | | | | | | | | | | | | |

| DBH | Pine Trees | Pine Vol. | Oak Trees | Oak Vol. | Gum Trees | Gum Vol. | Poplar Trees | Poplar Vol. | Misc. Trees | Misc. Vol. | Total Trees | Total Vol. |
|---|---|---|---|---|---|---|---|---|---|---|---|---|
| 10 | 2,320 | 67.5 | | | 20 | 0.9 | | | | | 2,320 | 67.5 |
| 12 | 330 | 25.2 | | | 10 | 0.8 | | | | | 460 | 26.1 |
| 14 | 70 | 6.4 | | | | | | | | | 80 | 7.2 |
| 16 | 20 | 2.8 | | | | | | | | | 10 | 2.6 |
| | 2,860 | 104.5 | 0 | 0.0 | 30 | 1.7 | 0 | 0.0 | 0 | 0.0 | 2,890 | 106.2 |

# TABLE 15-6

**Block 5:** NE¼, E½ of SE¼, Section 34; SW¼ of SW¼, Section 35; NW¼ of NW¼ less West 10 Acres, Section 2

310 Acres

## NUMBER OF MERCHANTABLE TREES BY DBH AND LOG LENGTHS

### Pulpwood

| DBH | Pine Trees | Pine Vol. | Soft Hardwood Trees | Soft Hardwood Vol. | Hard Hardwood Trees | Hard Hardwood Vol. | Total Trees | Total Vol. |
|-----|-----------|-----------|---------------------|--------------------|---------------------|--------------------|-------------|------------|
| 4 | 4,100 | | | | | | 4,100 | |
| 6 | 2,800 | 104 | | | | | 2,800 | 104 |
| 8 | 2,600 | 239 | | | | | 2,600 | 239 |
| | | 343 | | | | | | 343 |

### Sawtimber

| DBH | Pine 1 | Pine 2 | Pine 3 | Oak 1 | Oak 2 | Oak 3 | Gum 1 | Gum 2 | Gum 3 | Poplar 1 | Poplar 2 | Poplar 3 | Misc. Hardwood 1 | Misc. Hardwood 2 | Misc. Hardwood 3 |
|-----|--------|--------|--------|-------|-------|-------|-------|-------|-------|----------|----------|----------|------|------|------|
| 10 | 350 | 1,080 | | | | | | | | | | | | | |
| 12 | 130 | 270 | 200 | 40 | 40 | | 60 | 80 | | 10 | 30 | | | | |
| 14 | 50 | 140 | 100 | 40 | 40 | | 50 | 60 | | 10 | | | | | |
| 16 | 40 | 70 | 60 | 20 | 40 | | | 10 | | | | 10 | | | |
| 18 | 10 | 30 | 40 | | | | | | | | | 10 | | | |

### Total (Sawtimber)

| DBH | Pine Trees | Pine Vol. | Oak Trees | Oak Vol. | Gum Trees | Gum Vol. | Poplar Trees | Poplar Vol. | Misc. Trees | Misc. Vol. | Total Trees | Total Vol. |
|-----|-----------|-----------|-----------|----------|-----------|----------|--------------|-------------|-------------|------------|-------------|------------|
| 10 | 1,430 | 45.9 | | | | | | | | | 1,430 | 45.9 |
| 12 | 600 | 34.8 | 80 | 3.1 | 140 | 5.6 | 40 | 1.7 | | | 860 | 45.2 |
| 14 | 290 | 29.3 | 80 | 5.4 | 110 | 7.5 | 10 | 0.5 | | | 490 | 42.7 |
| 16 | 170 | 24.4 | 60 | 6.5 | 10 | 1.3 | 10 | 1.3 | | | 250 | 33.5 |
| 18 | 80 | 17.6 | | | | | 10 | 1.8 | | | 90 | 19.4 |
| | 2,570 | 152.0 | 220 | 15.0 | 260 | 14.4 | 70 | 5.3 | 0 | 0.0 | 3,120 | 186.7 |

# TABLE 15-7

**Block 6: SW¼, Section 26; W½ of NW¼, W½ of NW¼ of NE¼, Section 35**

**260 Acres**

## NUMBER OF MERCHANTABLE TREES BY DBH AND LOG LENGTHS

### Pulpwood

| DBH | Pine Trees | Pine Vol. | Soft Hardwood Trees | Soft Hardwood Vol. | Hard Hardwood Trees | Hard Hardwood Vol. | Total Trees | Total Vol. |
|---|---|---|---|---|---|---|---|---|
| 4 | 4,200 |  |  |  |  |  | 4,200 |  |
| 6 | 2,600 | 96 |  |  |  |  | 2,600 | 96 |
| 8 | 2,400 | 221 |  |  |  |  | 2,400 | 221 |
|  |  | 317 |  |  |  |  |  | 317 |

### Sawtimber

Number of trees by number of logs

| DBH | Pine 1 | Pine 2 | Pine 3 | Pine 4 | Pine 5 | Oak 1 | Oak 2 | Oak 3 | Gum 2 | Gum 3 | Poplar 1 | Poplar 2 | Poplar 3 | Misc. Hardwood 1 | Misc. Hardwood 2 | Misc. Hardwood 3 |
|---|---|---|---|---|---|---|---|---|---|---|---|---|---|---|---|---|
| 10 | 950 | 1,030 |  |  |  |  |  |  |  |  | 10 |  |  |  |  |  |
| 12 | 200 | 500 | 320 |  |  |  |  |  |  |  | 10 |  |  |  |  |  |
| 14 | 60 | 140 | 100 |  |  | 10 |  |  |  |  | 10 |  |  |  |  |  |
| 16 | 20 | 40 | 30 | 10 | 0.5 |  |  |  |  |  |  |  |  |  |  |  |
| 18 | 10 | 30 | 20 |  |  |  |  |  |  |  |  |  |  |  |  |  |
| 20 |  | 10 | 10 |  |  |  |  |  |  |  |  |  |  |  |  |  |

Volume summary

| DBH | Pine Trees | Pine Vol. | Oak Trees | Oak Vol. | Gum Trees | Gum Vol. | Poplar Trees | Poplar Vol. | Misc. Trees | Misc. Vol. | Total Trees | Total Vol. |
|---|---|---|---|---|---|---|---|---|---|---|---|---|
| 10 | 1,980 | 56.1 |  |  |  |  | 10 | 0.5 |  |  | 1,960 | 56.1 |
| 12 | 1,020 | 59.3 |  |  |  |  | 10 | 0.8 |  |  | 1,030 | 59.8 |
| 14 | 300 | 29.9 | 10 | 0.5 |  |  | 10 | 1.3 |  |  | 320 | 31.2 |
| 16 | 90 | 12.9 |  |  |  |  |  |  |  |  | 100 | 14.2 |
| 18 | 60 | 12.4 |  |  |  |  |  |  |  |  | 60 | 12.4 |
| 20 | 20 | 6.1 |  |  |  |  |  |  |  |  | 20 | 6.1 |
|  | 3,470 | 176.7 | 10 | 0.5 | 0 | 0.0 | 30 | 2.6 | 0 | 0.0 | 3,510 | 179.8 |

196

# TABLE 15-8

Block 7: SW¼ of NW¼, W½ of SW¼, Section 27; SE¼, S½ of NE¼, Section 28

360 Acres

## NUMBER OF MERCHANTABLE TREES BY DBH AND LOG LENGTHS

### Pulpwood

| DBH | Pine Trees | Pine Vol. | Soft Hardwood Trees | Soft Hardwood Vol. | Hard Hardwood Trees | Hard Hardwood Vol. | Total Trees | Total Vol. |
|---|---|---|---|---|---|---|---|---|
| 4 | 10,100 | | | | | | 10,100 | |
| 6 | 6,000 | 222 | | | | | 6,000 | 222 |
| 8 | 5,050 | 465 | | | | | 5,050 | 465 |
| | | 687 | | | | | | 687 |

### Sawtimber

Number of trees by log length (number of 16-ft. logs) — Pine

| DBH | 1 | 2 | 3 |
|---|---|---|---|
| 10 | 1,480 | 1,520 | |
| 12 | 300 | 550 | 350 |
| 14 | 50 | 90 | 60 |
| 16 | 20 | 40 | 30 |
| 18 | 10 | 10 | |
| 20 | 10 | 10 | |

Trees and Volume

| DBH | Pine Trees | Pine Vol. | Oak Trees | Oak Vol. | Gum Trees | Gum Vol. | Poplar Trees | Poplar Vol. | Misc. Trees | Misc. Vol. | Total Trees | Total Vol. |
|---|---|---|---|---|---|---|---|---|---|---|---|---|
| 10 | 3,000 | 84.3 | | | | | | | | | 3,000 | 84.3 |
| 12 | 1,200 | 68.0 | 10 | 0.3 | | | | | | | 1,210 | 68.3 |
| 14 | 200 | 19.4 | 10 | 0.8 | 10 | 0.8 | | | | | 220 | 21.0 |
| 16 | 90 | 12.9 | | | 10 | 1.3 | | | | | 100 | 14.2 |
| 18 | 20 | 3.2 | | | | | | | | | 20 | 3.2 |
| 20 | 20 | 4.1 | | | | | | | | | 20 | 4.1 |
| | 4,530 | 191.9 | 20 | 1.1 | 20 | 2.1 | 0 | 0.0 | 0 | 0.0 | 4,570 | 195.1 |

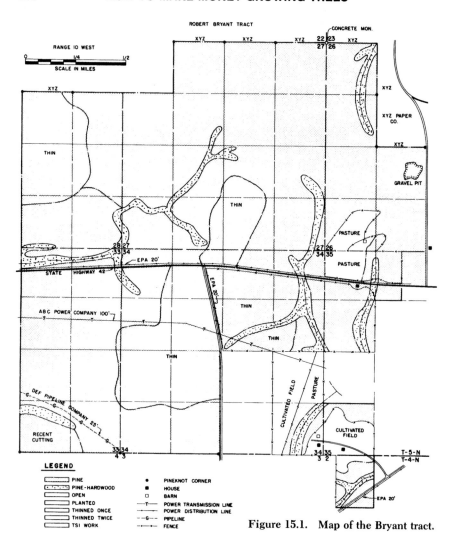

Figure 15.1.   Map of the Bryant tract.

him on all business operations. To continue his study, he asks his CPA to analyze projected income from a tax standpoint.

Total purchase price in 1952 was $31,950 ($15 per acre), and because of his grandfather's primary interest in minerals, the allocation per acre was $5 to minerals, $10 to land, and nothing to timber. Therefore, there is no depletion basis for timber, and timber sales will be all capital gains. The tract is located in a state that does not allow special treatment of capital gains, so Bryant's income is subject to federal taxes of 28% and state taxes of 5%.

The CPA calculates the annual remainder after taxes to be as follows:

| Income | | |
|---|---|---|
| Timber sales | $37,825 | |
| Less commission | 3,593 | |
| Less depletion basis | 0 | |
| 'Net income from timber sales | 34,232 | |
| Rental income | 800 | |
| Total income | | $35,032 |
| Expenses | | |
| Boundary-line maintenance | 375 | |
| Ad valorem taxes | 2,600 | |
| Total expenses | 2,975 | |
| Net taxable income | | $32,057 |
| Less federal tax at 28% | | 8,976 |
| Less state tax at 5% | | 1,603 |
| Net income after taxes | | 21,478 |

This seems a small return from an asset that can be sold for $479,250, so the CPA continues his investigation. Since the original cost of the land alone was $21,300, a sale at $479,250 will produce a gain of $457,950. Subtracting federal taxes of 28% = $128,226 and state taxes of 5% = $22,898 leaves a remainder of $328,126, so his after-tax income equals 6.5% on his after-tax principal. (You have probably heard some landowners say, "I don't want to sell timber now, because I don't want to pay taxes." The fact is that, after a timberland investor gets his original investment back, the tax man automatically acquires the government's share of the property.) Bryant has two alternate investments for this sum. One is a tax-free municipal bond paying 7%, and the other is a certificate of deposit paying 8%, which yields 5.4% after taxes.

An investment's value depends on how much money it produces after taxes in the long run; consequently, Bryant's timberland has more merit for him than appears at first glance. His return is better than or about equal to those from other media, and possibilities for much great future profits are good. Now convinced that he has an attractive property, he proceeds to the next step.

## STEP 5: CHOOSE LAWYER

In 1952 Bryant's grandfather thought the price of the land was cheap, and since he knew the previous owner was a careful businessman and income from minerals was high, he made only a hasty examination of the title, concentrating on minerals. Now the value has appreciated a great deal, timber operations seem likely to produce large incomes now and later, and the timberland inventory shows the existence and importance of many items formerly ignored. Obviously, more legal investigation is needed, so Bryant chooses a lawyer known for expertise in timberland. With a copy of the timberland inventory in hand, the lawyer makes a thorough search of the title and, in his opinion, lists and discusses the exceptions.

First is the ROW conveyance to ABC Power Company on 5 July 1928, by which the company acquired the following:

. . . the right to construct, operate, and maintain electric transmission lines and all telegraph and telephone lines, towers, poles, and appliances necessary or convenient in connection therewith from time to time upon a strip of land 100 feet in width, as said strip is now located by the final location survey thereof heretofore made by said Company, over and across the lands of which it is hereinafter described as being a part, together with all rights and privileges necessary and convenient for the full enjoyment of use thereof for the purpose herein described, including *the right of ingress and egress to and from said strip* and the right to cut and keep clear all trees and undergrowth and other obstructions on said strip *and danger trees adjacent thereto where necessary.*

Said strip is a part of a tract of land described as follows: S½ of NE¼, Section 33, and S½ of NW¼, SW¼ of NE¼, NE¼ of SE¼, Section 34, all in Township 5 North, Range 10 West. Said strip is substantially described as follows: Fifty feet on each side of a line beginning at a point on the east line, said point being north 2120 feet from the southeast corner of Section 34, thence N73°13′W 1730.0 feet to a point on south boundary of SW¼ of NE¼, Section 34, thence N73°13′W 1761.7 feet more or less to an angle point, thence N83°49′W 4,627.3 feet, more or less, to a point on west boundary line of S½ of NE¼, Section 33.

The lawyer points out the importance of the provision italicized above. The right of ingress and egress applies to all land described, not the ROW strip only, and may have some minor undesirable effect in the future; such all-inclusive access rights cannot be acquired by eminent-domain proceedings and should have been limited to the 100-ft strip. The danger-tree provision is necessary for the company, but it should have required the company to pay for trees cut. In addition, the agreement contains no reversion clause. It is too late to correct these errors. The agreement includes the exact location of the line, coinciding with that shown in the timberland inventory, a requirement that Bryant should follow in future conveyances.

The ROW agreement with DEF Pipeline Company on 20 June 1930 is much simpler and has much more serious consequences. The former owner conveyed the following:

. . . a right of way to lay, construct, maintain, and operate a pipe line or lines, consisting of one or more pipes, and appurtenances thereto, including telephone or telegraph lines in connection therewith, and the free right of ingress and egress to and from said right of way for the purpose of laying, constructing, maintaining, repairing, replacing, operating, or removing at will said pipe line and appurtenances thereto, and across the following described land: $E\frac{1}{2}$, Section 33, and $W\frac{1}{2}$, $NE\frac{1}{4}$, Section 34, all in Township 5 North, Range 10 West.

Although the agreement provides that the rights conveyed shall revert to the surface owner if they cease to be used, no location is stated, nor is there any mention of width. The company now uses only a 25-ft strip containing less than 2 acres in the southwest portion of the tract; nevertheless, it has the right to operate more or less at will on all land described above, a total of 800 acres. This seriously limits Bryant's ability to make trades in the future and may hinder use of the land for residential or other development. Note here that the rights were sold in 1930. Bryant did not realize the existence or importance of this conveyance until 47 years later, and the ultimate importance may not be evident until 47 more years have passed. The lawyer states that there may be some remedy, so Bryant instructs him to proceed with it. (I shall omit further details of this because of the legal technicalities involved.)

The public records contain no highway or road ROWs, no easements for electric-power association lines, and no lease to Rice. In response to an inquiry from the lawyer, the state highway department reports that its files contain no ROW conveyances across the Bryant tract. This being true, the lawyer states that the highway department, by adverse possession, has acquired at least an easement on the area involved. Therefore, Bryant cannot cut and use trees on the highway or road ROWs, but he may be entitled to be paid for them if the highway department sells them; the lawyer asks the forester to report any cutting on the road ROWs.

The electric power association provides copies of its easements, and the lawyer records them in the public records as additional evidence of Bryant's possession. He finds that they contain no serious defects and do not allow cutting of danger trees, so he asks the forester to report cutting of this type, since it would be unauthorized.

The lawyer thinks that the arrangement with Rice is too informal, that Rice or another tenant may possibly bring about a case of adverse possession, and that a lease is desirable as evidence of possession. Furthermore, Rice's annual rental is low because he is supposed to supervise the entire tract; since he did not prevent or know about the 35-acre trespass in Section 33, a more definite expression of this responsibility may be wise. The lawyer prepares the following lease to be executed and recorded:

---

STATE OF _____
COUNTY OF _____

### AGRICULTURAL LEASE

---

This lease entered into on this date by and between Robert Bryant, hereinafter referred to as Lessor, and Julius Rice, hereinafter referred to as Lessee. Lessor does hereby lease and let unto Lessee the following described lands, together with any and all improvements situated thereon:

South half of Southwest Quarter, Section 26; East half of Northwest Quarter east of road, Northeast Quarter south of highway, East half of Southeast Quarter, Section 34; West half of Northwest Quarter, West half of Northeast Quarter of Northwest Quarter, Southwest Quarter of Southwest Quarter, Section 35, all in Township 5 North, Range 10 West, and Northwest Quarter of Northwest Quarter less West 10 acres, Section 2, Township 4 North, Range 10 West.

The term of this lease shall be for a period of one year from the first day of January 1977 to the 31st day of December 1977 and shall automatically be extended each year for an additional term of one year unless either party shall give notice to the other party on or before the first day of December of his desire to terminate same.

The annual rental, in addition to the other considerations hereinafter set forth, shall be Eight Hundred Dollars ($800), payable on or before the 30th day of September.

It is mutually agreed between Lessor and Lessee:

1. Lessee will not use leased lands for other than agricultural and residential purposes.

2. Any three of the four houses located on the leased premises may be sublet in the discretion of Lessee; however, Lessee must make his residence on the leased premises and all agricultural operations on the leased premises shall be carried on by Lessee.

3. Lessee shall not cut or deaden any trees of merchantable species, regardless of size. Lessor reserves unto himself, his successors and assigns the right of ingress and egress to and across the leased premises for the purpose of his timberland and/or mineral operations on the leased premises and on lands adjoining the leased premises owned by Lessor.

4. Lessee agrees to maintain without expense to Lessor the buildings, fences, and other improvements located on the premises in at least as good condition as when received by him.

5. The parties recognize that Lessor owns approximately 1800 acres of land adjoining the leased premises and as a part of the consideration for the execution of this lease by Lessor, Lessee agrees to make periodic inspections of these other lands as often and to the extent circumstances may indicate warranted, but in any event at least semiannually Lessee shall walk the perimeter thereof and report to Lessor any irregularities noted.

6. Lessee recognizes the title of Lessor to the leased premises and to the lands adjoining owned by Lessor and makes no claim to any of the said lands, adverse or otherwise, other than under the terms of this lease agreement.

7. Should Lessee fail to perform any of the covenants and agreements contained herein, including specifically but not limited to payment of the prescribed rental, Lessor may at his option cancel and terminate this lease and remove Lessee from the premises. In the event of termination of this lease for any breach by Lessee of any covenant or agreement contained herein, Lessee shall not be entitled to any rebate or adjustment or any unearned portion of rent accrued or paid to Lessor.

EXECUTED IN DUPLICATE ORIGINAL on this, the _____ day of

_____, 1977

_____

Lessor

_____

Lessee

(Acknowledgment forms omitted for brevity.)

---

There are no other title flaws, and since those discussed can be either corrected or reduced in importance by adapting forest-management programs to them, Bryant proceeds to the next step.

## STEP 6: CHOOSE AND IMPLEMENT
## FOREST-MANAGEMENT PLAN

Here is the meat in the coconut. As I said earlier, a management plan is premature as part of timberland inventory; now is the time. A well-considered plan is essential to keep Bryant from running off in all directions. He now has enough data and professional advisers to make a wise one.

He decides that a regular annual income is not desirable; he wants his timberland to work as part of his investments, and to provide income when other assets do not and opportunities for deductible expenses when other assets produce bountifully. Therefore, he chooses to do now those things that are obviously desirable and schedule future actions as they fit his needs. His forester suggests four steps:

1. Sale of all old pine stumps suitable for distillate wood.
2. Sale of all sawtimber growing at a compound rate of less than 6% and other sawtimber trees that are diseased, crooked, or otherwise defective. (The forester states and the inventory indicates that this timber is located in the pine–hardwood areas and at their borders and that the sale will produce about $25,000.)
3. Sale of all pulpwood that should be removed from the thinning areas, which will produce about $30,000 and must be coordinated with sawtimber sales to prevent disputes between loggers.
4. A survey of 2¾ miles of unestablished boundary line on the south and west sides of the tract at an estimated cost of $1600.

The CPA states that Bryant can make either lump-sum or pay-as-you-go sales without jeopardizing capital gains treatment of his income. On the advice of the forester, he elects to sell sawtimber on a lump-sum basis and other products on a pay-as-you-go basis. The lawyer suggests that potential danger trees near the ABC Power Company ROW be cut regardless of growth rate, since they might be cut by maintenance crews without Bryant's knowledge.

Bryant chooses a well-known surveyor to establish the line and, after determining that his fee is the usual one, selects the forester to carry out timber and stump sales. The forester states that he will study the fire problem and suggest what might be done in the Fall of 1977 to alleviate it. Bryant writes a memorandum confirming these decisions, and the management plan is complete. Chapter 16 discusses at length how it is executed and how such a scheme might be applied to your property. Except in unusual cases, more elaborate plans are not necessary; the important thing is to consider all possible programs with emphasis on the financial aspects of each. Doing so makes success likely. Timberland investment does not require magic or genius—merely hard work and careful thought. As time passes, Bryant will be ready for the next two steps.

## STEP 7: CHOOSE OTHER PROFESSIONAL ADVISERS

Additional advisers will be needed only when the occasion arises, and Bryant's present advisers may be helpful in choosing others. Bryant is an expert on minerals, but you are likely to need a minerals adviser if you own minerals that are valuable or are about to become valuable. You may need a real estate broker if the locality becomes more heavily populated or the tract becomes more desirable for purposes other than timber-growing. In certain cases, you will need a specialist in recreational developments.

Bryant has some cultivable land now, and there may be other parts that can be made suitable for farming. He will need advice from someone familiar with soils, their value for agriculture, and the cost of conversion. This advice may be valuable in renegotiating the lease with Rice, but he postpones action on this, since he is already committed for 1977.

## STEP 8: REAPPRAISE THE TIMBERLAND INVESTMENT AT LEAST ANNUALLY

Substantial new developments make reappraisal necessary whenever they occur, but an annual review of the timberland investment, including progress of the past year and plans for the next year, is an excellent idea. Few assets produce properly when you buy them and forget them. Trees grow, market prices change, new species become salable, population pressures on land vary, and personal finances are altered. September is a good month for the annual review, since growth for the year is complete. At that time, income from other sources may be estimated accurately, and yet there remains enough time in the calendar year to make timberland operations fit more closely into your total investment program.

## PROGRAM FOR WOULD-BE TIMBERLAND INVESTORS

Bryant's course (with suitable variations) can well be followed by all timberland owners, but other factors must be considered if you want to invest in timberland for the first time. You should follow the program outlined below.

First, you need to have a property, preferably several, offered to you. Do not choose one that suits your fancy and then try to buy it. Enticing an owner to part with his property invariably means that you will pay or offer to pay him more than he thinks it is worth, and he is right much more often than you are. You should look for those who want to sell and are looking for you. A good means of locating them is a small advertisement in the classified section of a newspaper of wide circulation. You will often be surprised at the number of replies. You should also inform local real estate brokers and foresters of your desires; the first group will earn commissions by pleasing you, and the second group is often in touch with landowners anxious to sell.

Once you begin to receive offers, carry out Step 1 above. A good forestry adviser can help you greatly in investigating offers. Some tracts will be obviously worthless for your purposes; some can be culled on cursory examination; a few may be worth inventory; finally, one will be worth buying. Your adviser can save you much time and expense at this stage.

Eventually, a property will appear so desirable that you will carry out Step 2. Do not be discouraged if data gathered in inventory condemn it as an investment. You will be out the cost of the inventory, but this is a lot cheaper than getting rid of a bad buy, and the knowledge you gain by a thorough investigation will be valuable later and will improve your efficiency in appraising other offers. Under no circumstances should you buy a property without a thorough investigation. All sellers try to create the impression that buyers are standing in line to get their properties. Do not be stampeded; if you miss one good deal, another will be along soon. Fast action may be essential at rare times, but wise tortoises win more races than foolish hares. During the time you are looking, your capital can be earning some return in other assets, whereas losses caused by hasty purchases can be recovered only with difficulty. Perseverance will soon enable you to buy a tract that meets your requirements, and you can follow the entire program.

One great advantage of timberland investment is that you can do nothing—or at least nothing except pay taxes and prevent trespass and adverse possession, actions essential to maintain your ownership.

Nature abhors a vacuum, and your timberland will produce something no matter what you do. The advantage in this is twofold. First, timberland requires only the minimum of management by the investor; even when the investor does nothing, it will grow more timber. Second, a forest-management program started in prosperity can be postponed, reduced, or eliminated in adversity. Hard times always come eventually, so everyone hesitates to begin a program of capital investment from which there is no escape. Timberlands, being dynamic, lend themselves well to variation in available investment funds; cultivation this year makes them more valuable, even if the program must be discontinued next year. Moreover, values added by expenditures today may be realized in future times of need. Although maximum benefits come from continued cultivation of the crop, nature responds to the smallest amount of help. Now is the time to begin.

# 16

# Case History of a Successful Timberland Investor: Executing the Plan

Bryant's plan, detailed enough for the present, is made; now let us follow its execution. No two tracts or investors are alike, but perhaps his methods can be adapted to solve your problems. We shall examine his actions in detail as they occur.

First, into an ordinary file folder Bryant puts all his records: deed, early reports and correspondence, timberland inventory, title opinion, memorandum of forest-management plan, and so on. He will insist upon written reports of all future actions; all advisers urge that he make his record as he goes, and he will soon see the value of this advice. Next, he obtains another print of the inventory map, without shading this time, and affixes it to the inside cover of the file folder, facing the main body of the material. He will use this to record as much data as possible and will hereafter be able to see a picture of his operations merely by opening the file. We shall look at this map (Figure 16.1) from time to time to note his progress.

## SURVEYOR'S REPORT

The surveyor selected to establish $2\frac{3}{4}$ miles of southern and western boundary line submits a written report on 15 May 1977 plus a sketch of his fieldwork. He states that he was able to prove the location of the southwest corner of $E\frac{1}{2}$, Section 28, and the southeast corner of Section 33 by the original government field notes and that he established pine-knot corners at these points and at the southwest corner of $E\frac{1}{2}$, Section 33. He found no other items of interest except the cutting already reported in the inventory. Bryant files the report and sketch and marks on his status map (Figure 16.1) the corners established and the year the work was done.

## LUMP-SUM SALE OF SAWTIMBER

The first major activity is the lump-sum sale of sawtimber. Bryant selects his forester to carry out this sale. The forester states that he will handle all parts of the sale for a 9.5% commission, that strong competition in the area is likely to produce a suitable bid, but that he must charge Bryant a fee of $7/MBF for his work if no acceptable bid is received. Bryant agrees, and the forester marks and estimates trees to be cut and sends the following sale announcement to 250 potential bidders located within a 75-mile radius:

HOWARD, STEPHENS AND DOUGLASS
*Consulting Foresters* COURT SQUARE SOUTH BUILDING
ANYTOWN, STATE
22 May 1977

Dear Sir:

Acting as agent for Robert Bryant, we solicit sealed bids on the timber marked for cutting on about 80 acres of his land in Sections 26, 27, 28, 33, 34, and 35, Township 5 North, Range 10 West, Any County, State. We have marked trees to be cut with yellow paint, and our estimate of their volume in board feet, Doyle scale, is as follows:

| | |
|---|---:|
| Pine | 168,700 |
| Gum | 10,700 |
| Oak | 7,400 |
| Poplar | 12,500 |
| Total | 199,300 |

Since our reputation is at stake, we tallied the number of trees with utmost care and estimated their volume in accordance with the most prevalent scaling practice in the area. We cannot guarantee them, however, because utilization practices vary too widely. Bidders should assume that they will pay any severance or documentary taxes due. The sale agreement will provide penalties to cover cutting or damage of unmarked trees, and a period of time until 30 June 1978 will be allowed to cut and remove the timber. Attached are a sheet showing the kind and size of trees marked (page 212) and a sample for the conveyance to be used (pages 210–211).

Only sealed bids will be accepted, and owner reserves the right to reject any or all bids. Bids should be mailed to Mr. Robert Bryant, c/o Howard, Stephens and Douglass, P.O. Box 902, Anytown, State. Bids must be made on a lump-sum basis and must be received at the above address not later than 12:00 noon on 5 June 1977.

We will be at the traffic light at the intersection of State Highways 42 and 15 at 9:00 a.m. on 29 May 1977 to show interested parties over the area. The timber is located about four miles west of this point. Please feel free to call on us for further information or assistance.

Sincerely,

Howard, Stephens and Douglass
CALVIN R. DOUGLASS

CRD:bn
Attachments

---

STATE OF _____
COUNTY OF _____

### TIMBER DEED

For and in consideration of the sum of One Hundred Dollars ($100.00), cash in hand paid, and other good and valuable considerations, the receipt and sufficiency of all of which are hereby acknowledged, ROBERT BRYANT, hereinafter called "SELLER," does hereby convey and warrant unto _____, hereinafter called "PURCHASER," all timber marked by Howard, Stephens and Douglass for cutting, as hereinafter indicated, on the following described lands:

West half of Northwest Quarter, Section twenty-six; South half, Section twenty-seven; South half of Southeast Quarter, Section twenty-eight; North half of Northeast Quarter, Section thirty-three; Northeast Quarter, East half of Southeast Quarter, Section thirty-four; and West half of Northwest Quarter, West half of Northeast Quarter of Northwest Quarter, Southwest Quarter of Southwest Quarter, Section thirty-five, all in Township Five North, Range Ten West, Any County, State.

All timber sold under this agreement has been marked with yellow paint spots below stump height and on the body of the trees. For any unmarked trees containing merchantable timber which are cut by Purchaser, his employees, contractors, or employees of contractors. Purchaser shall pay Seller at double the current price of stumpage for the class of material said trees contain.

No unnecessary damage shall be done to young growth or to trees left standing. Purchaser shall have the right of ingress and egress on, across and over the lands owned by Seller, except cultivated fields and open pasture lands, for the purpose of logging the timber conveyed herein; fences required to be cut for access shall be kept in place at all times and permanently repaired when such access is no longer needed. Purchaser may cut and use such small hardwood timber as may be necessary for bridging, roadbuilding, and logging.

Unless extension of time is granted in writing by Seller, the timber sold under this agreement shall be cut and removed from the above-described lands by June 30, 1978; title to any timber sold under this agreement and remaining on the lands described above after such deadline or any extension thereof shall revert to Seller.

Purchaser agrees and warrants that it will at all times indemnify and save harmless Seller against any and all claims, demands, actions or causes of action, for injury or death of any person or persons, or damage to the property of any third person or persons, which may be due in any manner to operations of Purchaser upon these lands.

WITNESS MY SIGNATURE on this, the _____ day of June 1977.

_____

Robert Bryant

(Acknowledgment forms, omitted here for brevity, are necessary to complete conveyance.)

_____

On June 5, Bryant receives five bids ranging from $23,382 to $30,366 and accepts the highest. A sixth bid arrives two hours late and is returned unopened. Bryant's lawyer prepares the conveyance that afternoon; it is executed by both parties; the sale is closed before the end of the day. Bryant makes sure that the conveyance is recorded and keeps a copy in his file; both actions add to his record of possession.

Unless they are extended, rights of purchaser under this conveyance expire on 30 June 1978. The vast majority of purchasers complete their work well before the expiration date, but sometimes unusual weather, bad management, poor supervision of loggers, or drops in prices of finished products delay logging too long. Most purchasers expect to pay for extensions; if they do not, title to the remaining timber reverts to the seller, and he can sell it again.

He now plots this action on his status map (Figure 16.1); although the sale is both harvest and thinning, it is sufficient to show a partial cutting in 1977. In addition, while marking timber near the northeast corner of the tract, the forester discovered an additional mile of common boundary line with XYZ Paper Company. It begins at the northeast corner of N¼S of N¼S, Section 26, and runs due west 1 mile; except for a concrete monument at the section corner, there is a pine knot at each quarter-mile. Bryant plots this information also.

# TABLE 16-1

**Robert Bryant Tract**

Sections 26, 27, 28, 33, 34, and 35, T5N, R10W, Any County

## NUMBER OF MARKED TREES BY DBH, SPECIES, AND 16-FT LOG LENGTHS [a]

| DBH | Pine | | | | Oak | | | Gum | | | Poplar | | | Misc. Hardwood | | |
|---|---|---|---|---|---|---|---|---|---|---|---|---|---|---|---|---|
| | 1 | 2 | 3 | 4 | 1 | 2 | 3 | 1 | 2 | 3 | 1 | 2 | 3 | 1 | 2 | 3 |
| 10 | 28 | 31 | | | | | | | | | | | | | | |
| 12 | 31 | 63 | 13 | | 60 | | | 43 | 13 | | 8 | 7 | | | | |
| 14 | 32 | 137 | 133 | 13 | 42 | 3 | | 19 | 27 | 1 | 5 | 20 | 7 | | | |
| 16 | 18 | 137 | 165 | 20 | 11 | 4 | | 9 | 19 | 3 | | 14 | 9 | | | |
| 18 | 3 | 81 | 102 | 10 | 8 | 1 | | | 6 | 3 | 1 | 8 | 9 | | | |
| 20 | 2 | 28 | 28 | | 2 | 1 | | 1 | | | | 1 | 3 | | | |
| 22 | | 10 | 6 | | | 1 | | | | | | | 2 | | | |
| 24 | 1 | 3 | 2 | | | | | | | | | | 1 | | | |

| DBH | Pine | | Oak | | Gum | | Poplar | | Misc. | | Total | |
|---|---|---|---|---|---|---|---|---|---|---|---|---|
| | Trees | Vol. [b] | Trees | Vol. [b] | Trees | Vol. [b] | Trees | Vol. [b] | Trees | Vol. [b] | Trees | Vol. [b] |
| 10 | 59 | 1.7 | | | | | | | | | 59 | 1.7 |
| 12 | 107 | 5.7 | 60 | 1.9 | 56 | 1.9 | 15 | 0.6 | | | 238 | 10.1 |
| 14 | 315 | 33.8 | 45 | 2.4 | 47 | 3.3 | 32 | 2.6 | | | 439 | 42.1 |
| 16 | 340 | 55.5 | 15 | 1.3 | 31 | 3.5 | 23 | 3.2 | | | 409 | 63.5 |
| 18 | 196 | 46.1 | 9 | 1.0 | 9 | 1.8 | 18 | 3.6 | | | 232 | 52.5 |
| 20 | 58 | 17.2 | 3 | 0.5 | 1 | 0.2 | 4 | 1.2 | | | 65 | 18.9 |
| 22 | 16 | 6.0 | 1 | 0.3 | | | 2 | 0.8 | | | 20 | 7.3 |
| 24 | 6 | 2.7 | | | | | 1 | 0.5 | | | 7 | 3.2 |
| | 1097 | 168.7 | 133 | 7.4 | 144 | 10.7 | 95 | 12.5 | 0 | 0.0 | 1469 | 199.3 |

[a] Volume is shown in thousands of board feet, Doyle Scale.

[b] Explanation: figures under "DBH" show size of tree; line of figures directly opposite "DBH" shows merchantable height of trees in number of 16-ft logs. Figures in main body of table give number of marked trees of each size, height, and species. Thus the numeral 133 in row 3 opposite 14 indicates that the marked timber includes 133 pine trees that are 14 in. DBH and contain three 16-ft logs.

## STUMP SALE

The sale of stumps for distillate wood is a simple matter. There are only three buyers, and a letter from the forester asking for bids per ton as harvested produces a high bid of $4.08. The lawyer prepares the conveyance. Because of the small sum involved, no deposit is required to ensure completion, and the sale proceeds simultaneously with that of sawtimber because the two crews are not likely to interfere with each other. Since the sale is small and will never be repeated, Bryant does not plot it on his status map.

## PULPWOOD SALE

The pulpwood sale is postponed until the sawtimber loggers vacate the area so as to avoid any disputes about cutting of unmarked trees. Because of the delay, its advisability is reconsidered and approved again in July 1978 by Bryant, the CPA, and the forester. The forester marks trees to be cut and sends the following sale announcement to 25 pulpwood buyers in the area:

HOWARD, STEPHENS AND DOUGLASS
*Consulting Foresters* COURT SQUARE SOUTH BUILDING
ANYTOWN, STATE
10 July 1978

Dear Sir:

Acting as agent for Robert Bryant, we solicit sealed bids on the timber marked for cutting on his property in Sections 26, 27, 28, 33, 34, and 35. Township 5 North, Range 10 West. Trees to be cut are marked with blue paint; the area of marked timber contains about 480 acres; we estimate the volume to be 1350 unpeeled standard cords.

Bidders should assume they will pay any severance or documentary taxes due. At time of closing, owner will require a deposit of $500.00 to insure that all marked trees are cut and removed. Sale agreement will provide penalties to cover cutting or damage of unmarked trees, and a period of time until 30 June 1979 will be allowed to cut and remove the timber. Attached is a sample of the conveyance to be used [below].

Only sealed bids will be accepted, and owner reserves the right to reject any or all bids. The timber is suitable for pine pulpwood only and will be paid for weekly as harvested. Bids must be made on a per cord basis. They should be mailed to Mr. Robert Bryant, c/o Howard, Stephens and Douglass, P.O. Box 902, Anytown, State, and must be received at this address not later than 12:00 noon on 24 July 1978.

We will be at the traffic light at the intersection of State Highways 42 and 15 at 9:00 a.m. on 17 July 1978 to show interested parties over the area. The timber is located about four miles west of this point. Please feel free to call on us for further information or assistance.

Sincerely yours,

Howard, Stephens and Douglass
CALVIN R. DOUGLASS

CRD:bn
Attachments

---

STATE OF _____
COUNTY OF _____

### PULPWOOD DEED

For and in consideration of the sum of One Hundred Dollars ($100.00), cash in hand paid, and other good and valuable considerations, the receipt of all of which is hereby acknowledged, ROBERT BRYANT, hereinafter called "SELLER," does hereby convey and warrant unto _____, hereinafter called "PURCHASER," all timber marked by Howard, Stephens and Douglass, for cutting as hereinafter indicated, on the following described lands:

South half, Section twenty-seven; South half of Northeast Quarter, Southeast Quarter, Section twenty-eight; East half of East half, Section thirty-three; West half, Northeast Quarter, Section thirty-four, all in Township Five North, Range Ten West, Any County, State.

All timber sold under this agreement has been marked with blue paint spots below stump height and on the body of the trees. For any unmarked trees containing merchantable material which are cut by Purchaser, his employees, contractors, or employees of contractors, Purchaser shall pay Seller at double the current price of stumpage for the class of material said trees contained.

No unnecessary damage shall be done to young growth or to trees left standing. Purchaser shall have the right of ingress and egress on, across and over the lands owned by Seller, except cultivated fields and open pasture lands, for the purpose of cutting and removing the timber conveyed herein; fences required to be cut for access shall be kept in place at all times and permanently repaired when such access is no longer needed. Purchaser may cut and use such small hardwood timber as may be necessary for bridging, roadbuilding and logging.

Unless an extension of time is granted in writing by Seller, the timber sold under this agreement shall be cut and removed from the above-described lands by June 30, 1979, title to any timber sold under this agreement and remaining on the lands described above after such deadline or any extension thereof shall revert to Seller.

Seller acknowledges receipt from Purchaser of the sum of Five Hundred

Dollars ($500.00), to be returned to Purchaser when all marked trees have been cut and removed, or forfeited to Seller as liquidated damages should Purchaser fail to cut and remove all marked trees within the allotted time.

At the end of each week Purchaser shall pay to Seller for all material removed during that week at the rate of _____ per standard cord. No material shall be cut or removed during any time that such payments are in arrears without the written consent of Seller.

Purchaser agrees and warrants that it will at all times indemnify and save harmless Seller against any and all claims, demands, actions, or causes of action, for injury or death of any person or persons, or damage to the property of any third person or persons, which may be due in any manner to operations of Purchaser upon these lands.

WITNESS MY SIGNATURE on this, the _____ day of July 1978

Robert Bryant

(Acknowledgment forms, omitted here for brevity, are necessary to complete conveyance.)

---

Of the three bids received, Bryant accepts the high one of $26 per cord submitted by Stephens Timber Company. The lawyer prepares the conveyance, Stephens puts up the deposit, the sale is closed the following day, and cutting begins immediately.

Because of good weather and steady orders from the pulp mill, Stephens finishes cutting by the end of November; Bryant returns the deposit and enters the thinning on his status map. He also notes that Stephens owns SE¼ of NW¼, Section 28, and E½ of SW¼, Section 33.

At the annual review conference in September 1978, the forester states that there are no pressing problems in forestry or related matters. Bryant and the CPA decide that no revenue other than that being produced by the pulpwood sale is desirable. Therefore, no action is scheduled until the meeting next year. Timberlands and people are living things, however, and two unforeseen problems arise almost simultaneously, both emphasizing the importance of good records.

## BOUNDARY-LINE DISPUTES

In May 1979 Rice, the tenant, and John Smith, owner of W½ of SE¼, Section 34, disagree about location of the line between Smith's land and the cultivated field northwest of Rice's house, Smith contending that the proper location is 80 ft east of the existing fence. At the same time, H. E. Jones, owner of NW¼ of SW¼, Section 35, states that his western line is 10 ft west of the existing fence, that 12 trees included in the 1977 sawtimber sale actually belonged to him, and that he wants to be paid for them.

Bryant searches his file and finds nothing bearing on either issue. His forester reports that both fences appear to be 15 or more years old, but he can suggest no way to prove this conclusively. His lawyer recommends that both disputes be settled by agreement and that all future acts of possession be carried out right up to the lines. Finally, Bryant, Smith, and Jones select a surveyor and agree to accept the lines he establishes and to share his cost proportionately. The survey is made in the presence of Jones, Smith, and Bryant's forester and proves that Smith is wrong and Jones is right. Bryant pays Jones for the trees cut through error and puts all correspondence with Jones and Smith and the surveyor's report and sketch in his file. The surveyor paints the lines established, and Bryant promptly enters as much of this information as possible on the status map (Figure 16.1). Better management at earlier times could have prevented this expense, and Bryant resolves to practice it in the future.

## TSI WORK

In September 1979 Bryant is near the end of a year when his income from other sources is much higher than normal. He wants no additional income and desires to invest a small amount of money in the timberland if the expense is deductible and if the value added by the expenditure is sufficient to recommend the investment. His forester states that a fortunate absence of fire during the winters of 1977 and 1978 has allowed a good stand of loblolly pine reproduction to become established on about 80 acres north of the stream through N½ of NE¼, Section 33. These young seedlings are now three years old, but are completely overtopped by a stand of worthless hardwoods and are not likely to survive under such cover. He estimates the cost of TSI work to remove the hardwoods at $20 per acre ($1600) and also estimates that, five years after removal, the accelerated growth of young pines will increase the value of the area treated by $40 per acre. The treatment area is protected from fire on the south and east by the stream, and the other two sides can be protected cheaply if necessary. The CPA states that such an expenditure is deductible; Bryant orders the work done provided it is completed and paid for in 1979. With the help of the forester, he locates a contractor who does the work for $1700. He enters this work on the status map (Figure 16.1).

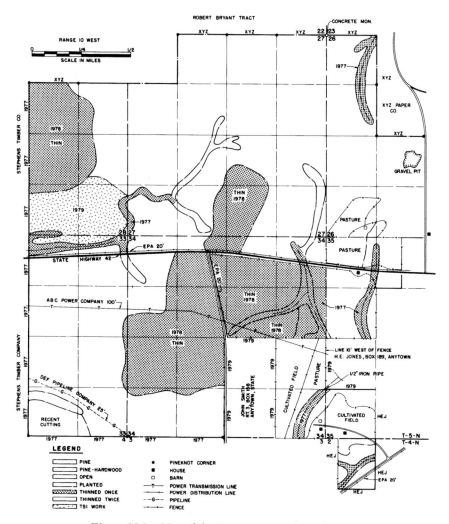

Figure 16.1. Map of the Bryant tract at the end of 1979.

## FOREST-MANAGEMENT RECORDS

Now let us pause and study Bryant's forest-management records through 1979. One of his first steps was to secure another print of the timberland inventory map; the print was made from the original tracing and showed everything except the shaded forest-type symbols.

After affixing it to one cover of the file, he devised another set of symbols for forest-management activities—including one each for planting, first thinning, second thinning, and TSI work—and added this new section to the legend at the bottom of the page. Using these symbols in conjunction with dates, he plotted on the map in as much detail as possible every action taken and every item of information obtained. At the end of 1979, his map looks like the Figure 16.1.

No one device is sufficient to show all needed information, but this map plus the file opposite it make a simple and effective tool. For example, if Bryant needs to know anything about the survey of his western line, a glance at the map shows that it was last done in 1977, and a quick turn in the file to the correspondence of that period reveals the action in detail.

Why is this necessary? First, Bryant is a busy man and cannot remember the myriad details of all his operations. His checkbook shows his bank account, his status map shows his timberland account, and both records permit a rapid review. His timberland is a sizable asset, and he makes important decisions about it each September. Therefore, he needs something to show the whole picture clearly and quickly, so that his decisions will be sound and cover all aspects. Second, although he seldom inspects the property on the ground, he wants a ready reference to carry with him when he does, so that his inspection trips will be efficient and thorough. The longer he manages the property, the more actions he takes and the harder it is to grasp the whole picture by thumbing through a file. Third, he realizes that the actual fieldwork is done by others, and that his experience is only secondhand. Since his relations with his advisers may be ended by death or disagreement, he wants a complete record to turn over to other agents or his heirs. Gathering these data again would be expensive and maybe impossible. All these considerations make the status map very important to him, and you should follow his example on your property regardless of its size. Now let us continue our study of his actions.

## TAXES AND MR. RICE

For several years after 1979, Bryant enjoys prosperous times and elects to do no cutting, allowing timber growth to accumulate for future use. Ad valorem taxes, originally nominal in amount, begin to rise sharply, however, and by 1984 reach 6.5% of assessed value annually. Bryant directs his attention to this matter and, for the first time, studies his assessment in detail.

He finds that uncultivable land is assessed at $19 per acre, cultivable land assessed at $40 per acre, and that he is assessed with 138 acres of cultivable land. He does not want to dispose of the cultivable land, but he can plant trees on it and reduce his assessment by changing the classification. He also notes that four houses and two barns have a total assessed value of $3000, about $500 each. These installations are leased to Rice, and Bryant calculates their cost to him in annual taxes as follows:

| | |
|---|---|
| Houses and barns | $3000 × 0.065 = $195.00 |
| Excess assessed value of cultivable land | 138 × $21 = 2898 × 0.065 = $\underline{188.37}$ |
| | 383.37 |

Since Rice pays rent of only $800.00, the facilities he uses produce an annual net income over that of timberland of only $416.63. Local inquiry reveals that the buildings can be sold for $1000; when this amount, less federal and state taxes, is invested in a savings account, it will produce $53.60 annually. Bryant thinks therefore that he can sell the buildings, invest the net proceeds, convert the fields to timber, obtain a reduction in ad valorem taxes, and end the year with $20.34 more net than he realizes from the Rice lease. In addition, he will be able to grow trees on 138 more acres. Further local inquiry reveals that the going rent for cultivated land is $10 per acre per year; the forester reports that Rice cultivates 70 acres and grazes the remainder.

Rice states that the two houses on the highway and the barn north of the highway are almost unusuable and that he can make little use of the pastures north of the highway. After much trading, Rice agrees to relinquish these three buildings and the northern pastures, to pay $700 per year for 70 acres of cultivated fields, and to pay $200 per year for use of the southern houses and barn and the right to graze all land south of Highway 42 and east of the road through the middle of Section 34. Revision of the lease confirms these changes. Bryant sells the relinquished buildings and applies for a reduction in assessment. He instructs the forester to submit a proposal to plant pine seedlings in the northern pastures, and he notes everything on the status map (Figure 16.2, p. 231).

This demonstrates the value of attention to details, especially the details of taxes that come up every year. Bryant increases his annual cash income from leases by $100; he decreases his annual tax bill by $152.10, or ($1500 × 0.065 = $97.50) + (40 acres × $21 = $840 × 0.065 = $54.60); he has the net proceeds from sale of the buildings for other investments; and he has 40 acres of old pastures for planting in pine seedlings. Similar results may be possible for you.

## SECOND PULPWOOD THINNING

At the review conference in September 1984, the forester reports that the area thinned for pulpwood in 1978 now needs another thinning of similar kind and extent. Bryant and his CPA study his income for the year and determine that additional revenue from timber sales is desirable, so Bryant approves the thinning, provided that all income is received in 1984. Since less than four months of the year remain, the forester suggests a lump-sum sale to satisfy this requirement. After it is approved, he follows the same woods procedure used in the first thinning, and Bryant enters the action on his map (Figure 16.2).

At the same conference, they discuss planting pine seedlings in the pastures relinquished by Rice. Money from the pulpwood thinning will be available, and they want to put all productive land into use. The forester reports, however, that there is still no effective control of forest fires and that the seedlings are likely to be burned up soon after planting. They postpone action on this.

## GRAZING LEASE

In 1985 a new state law requires cattlemen to prevent their cows from wandering onto state highways; this law, plus the steady development of the locality and the consequent shrinkage of available grazing land, offers Bryant an excellent opportunity. Local cattlemen request permission to erect fences on the north side of Highway 42 and on the south side west of the road in Section 34. The forester, convinced that the cattlemen have caused the fires, is enthusiastic about the possibilities offered by this request. He suggests that everything not leased to Rice be leased to the cattlemen, that the lease require them to prevent or control fires on the leased area (specifying that failure to do so would cancel the lease and require removal of the fences), that sufficient gates to allow access for timber operations be constructed, and that Bryant request an additional annual consideration of $1800, about $1.00 per acre on the leased area. The forester also states that the cattle population is neither large enough to cause browsing damage to seedlings nor likely to become so, and that the cows will reduce accumulation of fuel on the ground. After negotiation, the cattlemen agree to the fire-control provision and an annual rental of $900 and select one Edward Clark, one of their number, to receive the lease. After his lawyer prepares it, Bryant executes and delivers the following lease:

---

STATE OF _____
COUNTY OF _____

### GRAZING LEASE

This lease entered into on this date by and between Robert Bryant, hereinafter referred to as Lessor, and Edward Clark, hereinafter referred to as Lessee. Lessor does hereby lease and let unto Lessee the premises described as:

West half of Northwest Quarter, Southwest Quarter, Section 26; Entire less Northwest Quarter of Northwest Quarter, Section 27; South half of Northeast Quarter, Southeast Quarter, Section 28; East half, Section 33; West half less that part east of gravel road, Northeast Quarter north of Highway 42, Section 34; All north of Highway 42 in Northwest Quarter of Northwest Quarter and West half of Northeast Quarter of Northwest Quarter, Section 35, all in Township 5 North, Range 10 West.

The term of this lease shall be one year from January 1, 1985 to December 31, 1985. The annual rental shall be Nine Hundred Dollars ($900.00) in addition to the other considerations hereinafter set forth and shall be payable on or before the first day of the term. The lease shall automatically be extended for additional terms of one year each unless on or before the first day of December either party shall give notice to the other of his desire to cancel the same.

It is mutually agreed between Lessor and Lessee:

1. Lessee will not use said lands for any purpose other than livestock pasture. Lessee shall not cut, deaden, or remove any trees of merchantable species regardless of size.

2. Lessee may erect such fences as he may desire, but any fences erected shall be on and along the boundary line of the leased premises or rights of way of public roads. Fences erected along public roads shall contain at least two gates per mile at points to be designated by Lessor, and such gates shall be of a minimum width of ten feet.

3. Lessor reserves unto himself ingress and egress on and across the leased premises for the purpose of his timberland and/or mineral operations; in addition Lessor reserves unto himself the right to use and occupy the leased premises for any purpose or purposes not in conflict or inconsistent with the purposes of this lease.

4. Lessee will not himself nor will he allow any other person to burn any grass,

weeds, or other substance on said lands without prior consent of Lessor. It shall be the duty and obligation of Lessee to prevent and/or control all fires on the leased premises regardless of cause or source. In addition to all other rights and remedies of Lessor under this lease, if during any one year more than three hundred (300) acres are burned without prior consent of Lessor, Lessor may at his option cancel and terminate this lease and in such event it shall be the duty and obligation of Lessee to take down and remove all fences placed on the leased premises by Lessee.

5. Should Lessee fail to perform any of the covenants and agreements herein contained, including specifically but not limited to the payment of rent, Lessor may at his option cancel and terminate this lease and remove Lessee from the premises. In the event of the termination of this lease for any breach by Lessee of any covenant or agreement herein contained, Lessee shall not be entitled to any rebate or adjustment of any rental paid or accrued.

6. Lessee may at his option sublet or assign all or any part of the privileges acquired by him hereunder, but such assignment shall not operate to release or relieve Lessee of any of his obligations hereunder. It is further agreed that no more than two hundred (200) head of livestock shall be grazed on the leased premises at any one time.

EXECUTED IN DUPLICATE ORIGINAL on this, the _____ day of _____ 1985.

_____
Lessor

_____
Lessee

(Acknowledgment forms omitted for brevity.)

---

Bryant plots the new fences on his status map (Figure 16.2). He hopes that such multiple use of the land will provide extra income and solve a serious forest-management problem.

## OIL LEASE

In February 1987 Gilchrist Oil Company, in an effort to complete a drilling block, requests an oil lease on the 30 mineral acres owned by Bryant under the land in Section 2. Gilchrist offers a bonus of $1500 ($50 per acre) and annual rentals of $30 ($1.00 per acre) for a lease with a primary term of 10 years and tenders a 10-day draft for the bonus. Bryant, a mineral expert, realizes that the only sure consideration is the bonus, since Gilchrist can cancel the lease at its pleasure, and he succeeds in getting Gilchrist to reduce the term to five years. They reach tentative agreement on all points, but Bryant says that he must confer with his lawyer before signing, since some provisions may be objectionable.

Gilchrist submits the lease on the printed form commonly known as the "Producers 88," and Bryant and his lawyer read it carefully. (I shall not reproduce this form because of its great length. It contains many technical details of mineral operations and should be discussed with your minerals adviser. You can get a copy from any oil operator and many office-supply companies in oil country.) The lawyer points out that it contains the "Mother Hubbard" sentence (see page 60 for discussion) and recommends that this be removed. He also points out that it provides that "Lessee shall be responsible for all damages caused by Lessee's operations hereunder other than damages necessarily caused by the exercise of the rights herein granted." He recommends that Bryant put a period after "hereunder" and strike all following words. Bryant is willing to accept the draft, but the lawyer recommends that the lease and draft remain attached until the draft is paid.

Gilchrist agrees to these changes, and Bryant executes the lease and deposits it and the draft at his bank for collection. To add to his record of possession, he requires Gilchrist to record the lease. No additions to the status map are needed.


## MNO PIPELINE COMPANY

In mid-1987, MNO Pipeline Company approaches Bryant to acquire a ROW for a new pipeline through the northern portions of Sections 26 and 27. The buyer wants a 50-ft ROW through $NW\frac{1}{4}$ of $NW\frac{1}{4}$, Section 26, and $NE\frac{1}{4}$ of $NW\frac{1}{4}$, $N\frac{1}{2}$ of $NE\frac{1}{4}$, Section 27, and offers to pay $5.00 per rod for the ROW itself, plus whatever additional sums are necessary to compensate Bryant for timber on the ROW. The buyer states that he does not know the exact location of the ROW, because the location survey is not complete. Bryant delays decisions and asks the buyer to return when the survey is complete.

Bryant uses the delay to prepare for the coming trading session. When a call to his lawyer reveals that MNO has the power of eminent domain and can take the ROW from him, he resolves to accomplish his objectives by trading and without a lawsuit, if possible. He calculates that $5.00 per rod for a 50-ft ROW is equal to $264.55 per acre. His forester reports that, although the timber volume on the ROW cannot be accurately determined until the location is definite, the average value of merchantable timber on this part of the tract is $150 per acre. He also states that salvage of such a small volume is not economical. Since no minerals are to be conveyed, Bryant's depletion basis for the parcel is only $10 per acre, so almost the entire proceeds will be subject to combined federal and state taxes of 33%. (Your tax advisor can suggest other, perhaps more satisfactory, ways to handle depletion in ROW sales.) Furthermore, his annual ad valorem tax is $1.24 per acre, and he will be left with this burden on land that he cannot use. Considering all these things, he decides to calculate his position if he settles with MNO for $10 per rod or $529.10 per acre plus the timber value.

He will have a gain of $529.10 − $10.00 = $519.10, which will be subject to taxes of 33%, or $171.30, leaving a remainder of $357.80. An investment of $15.50 at 8% will yield $1.24 annually, about enough to pay ad valorem taxes forever, and since he will also be paid for the timber, he thinks that the compensation is adequate. Although he has spent time in calculation and negotiation and money on lawyers and foresters, he decides that he will sell for $10 per rod, or more if he can get it. When the buyer returns with the exact location, he and Bryant tentatively agree on $10 per rod plus the value of the timber. The buyer asks that this be divided into $4 per rod for the ROW and $6 per rod for damages. Bryant agrees and asks him to prepare the necessary papers for review by his lawyer.

For the ROW conveyance, the buyer fills in the blanks of the usual company form, and after checking the legal description and the consideration, Bryant hands it to his lawyer, who studies it, finds that it contains many undesirable conveyances and agreements, and underscores all words that should be removed. Here is the conveyance as he returns it to Bryant:

For and in consideration of the sum of $_____ the receipt of which is hereby acknowledged, Robert Bryant, hereinafter referred to as Grantors (whether one or more), does hereby grant, bargain, sell, and convey unto MNO PIPELINE COMPANY, a Delaware corporation, its successors and assigns, hereinafter referred to as Grantee, a right of way and easement for the purpose of constructing, maintaining, inspecting, operating, protecting, repairing, replacing, changing the size of or removing a pipeline or pipelines, for the transportation of oil, gas, and the products or derivatives thereof, upon and along a route to be selected by Grantee across, over, through and under the following described lands, of which Grantors warrant they are the owners in fee simple, situated in Any County, State, to wit:

A strip of land twenty-five feet on each side of a line described as beginning at a point 330 feet north of the southwest corner of NE¼ of NW¼, Section 27, thence North 80° East 5361 feet to the east line of NW¼ of NW¼, Section 26, all in Township 5 North, Range 10 West,

together with the right of ingress and egress to and from said pipeline or pipelines, or any of them, over and across said lands and adjacent lands of Grantors with the further right to maintain the right of way and easement herein granted clear of trees, undergrowth and brush to the extent Grantee deems necessary to exercise the rights granted herein.

Should more than one pipeline be laid under this grant, at any time, an additional consideration, calculated on the basis of $5.00 per lineal rod, shall be paid for each line after the first line. It is agreed that all of said pipelines shall be located within a strip of land fifty (50) feet in width, the center line of which shall be the center line of the first pipeline hereafter installed by Grantee across, over, through and under said lands.

Grantors shall have the right to use and enjoy the above described premises, except as to the rights herein granted; and Grantors agree not to build, create, or construct, nor permit to be built, created, or constructed, any obstruction, building, lake, engineering works, or other structure over said pipeline or pipelines. Grantee hereby agrees to pay any damages which may arise to growing crops, timber, fences or buildings of said Grantors from the exercise of the rights herein granted; provided however that after the first of said pipelines has been laid Grantee shall not be liable for damages caused on the right of way by keeping said right of way and easement clear of trees, undergrowth and brush in the exercise of said rights. Said damages, if not mutually agreed upon, to be ascertained and determined by three disinterested persons, one thereof to be appointed by Grantors, one by Grantee, and the third by the two so appointed, and the written award of such three persons shall be final and conclusive.

It is agreed that any payment due hereunder may be made direct to said Grantors or any one of them.

Any pipeline or pipelines constructed by said Grantee across lands under cultivation shall, at the time of construction thereof, be buried to such depth as will not interfere with such cultivation.

The rights herein granted may be assigned in whole or in part.

The terms, conditions, and provisions of this contract shall extend to and be binding upon the heirs, executors, administrators, personal representatives, successors and assigns of the parties hereto.

TO HAVE AND TO HOLD said rights and right of way, easement, estates, and privileges unto the said MNO Pipeline Company, its successors and assigns, so long as said right of way and easement are used for the purposes granted herein.

IN WITNESS WHEREOF, the Grantors herein have hereunto set their hands and seals this the _____ day of _____ 1987.

He also finds that there are significant omissions, and he prepares the following paragraph to be added:

Should the Grantee fail to begin construction of the said pipeline on the right of way herein granted within one (1) year from the date hereof, or should the Grantee discontinue use of the same at any time for a continuous period of one (1) year, all rights and title herein granted and conveyed shall automatically revert to Grantors, their successors or assigns.

Since damages will be settled in advance, the buyer also submits a release for Bryant to sign. The lawyer approves it after noting that it covers only damages on the ROW strip itself and not damages that might be done elsewhere.

Bryant gives these revisions to the buyer; with some reluctance, the company agrees, a new contract is prepared and executed, and the sale is closed. Bryant notes the action on his status map (Figure 16.2). Salvage of the timber is now the job of MNO, and Bryant instructs the forester to inspect the area after construction is complete to see that no damage is done outside the ROW. His CPA tells him that he will not have to pay taxes on the gain realized if he can invest the proceeds in similar property within 12 months, so Bryant and his forester begin looking for a suitable investment.

## CLEARCUT AND PLANT

At the 1987 review conference, the forester reports that there have been no wild fires since the 1985 grazing lease was granted and suggests a plan for SW¼, Section 26, and that part of Section 35 north of Highway 42. The area contains the pasture relinquished by Rice in 1984 and patches of trees suitable for poles, piling, sawtimber, and pulpwood that are too scattered to utilize all growing space. In spite of the absence of fire, natural reproduction in the timbered area has been unsuccessful, and the old pasture is too large an opening for natural seeding. The forester estimates that 25% of the total area of 200 acres is idle. To solve these problems and to provide timber income, he suggests that the entire area be clearcut, burned, treated with TSI work, and planted. He recommends that planting crews utilize natural reproduction wherever possible and use a 12 ft × 12 ft spacing with close attention to care and spacing of seedlings. He estimates total sale volume at $50,000 and total cost of establishing the plantation at $10,000. Considering all facets as usual, Bryant approves the plan, provided all income and expenses will fall in 1988.

During woods work for the sale, the forester modifies the plan by moving the boundary of the sale area slightly west so that it follows the stream. Using the procedure described on pages 209–212, he

solicits sealed bids in early December 1987. The sale announcement
states that cutting shall begin not earlier than 1 January 1988 and end
not later than 30 November 1988. The deed form to be attached is
much simpler. For the first three paragraphs of the form shown on
pages 210–211, he substitutes the following:

For and in consideration of the sum of One Hundred Dollars ($100.00), cash
in hand paid, and other good and valuable considerations, the receipt
and sufficiency of all of which are hereby acknowledged, Robert Bryant,
hereinafter called "Seller," does hereby convey and warrant unto
_____, hereinafter called "Purchaser," all merchantable timber
on the following described lands: (enter description here). Purchaser shall have
the right of ingress and egress on, across, and over the lands owned by Seller for
the purpose of logging the timber conveyed herein.

Remainder of the deed is the same as shown earlier.

Seven bids are received, and Bryant accepts the highest. The
lawyer prepares the conveyance, and the forester closes the sale on
January 1. Cutting is completed on schedule. The same contractor
used in 1979 performs the TSI work, burning, and planting under
supervision of the forester; the entire job is complete by late December. Bryant plots this work on his status map (Figure 16.2). Although
several different operations have occurred on the same area, the most
important aspect is the final condition, so he used only a symbol for
planting to record it.

## SALE OF LAND

In mid-November 1988, H. E. Jones, the man in the boundary-line
dispute, decides to enlarge and consolidate his farm and offers to buy
150 acres described as E$\frac{1}{2}$ of SE$\frac{1}{4}$, Section 34, SW$\frac{1}{4}$ of SW$\frac{1}{4}$, Section 35,
and NW$\frac{1}{4}$ of NW$\frac{1}{4}$ less West 10 acres, Section 2. Jones offers $400 per
acre, provided Bryant will convey some minerals and allow him to pay
for the land over a period of years. Bryant tells him that the area is now
leased to Rice through December 31, that the trade cannot be
effective until after that date, and that he needs a few days to study the
offer.

The tax consequences of the sale are important. Jones wants some
mineral interest, and Bryant decides that the most he is willing to sell
is one-eighth. His depletion basis is (150 acres of land × $10 = $1500)
+ (19 acres of minerals × $5 = $95) = $1595. Subtracting this from the
price of $60,000 leaves a taxable gain of $58,405, and subtracting

combined taxes of 33% ($19,274) leaves net proceeds of $40,726. He can invest this amount at 8% to produce $3258 annually.

Next he calculates his present income from the 150 acres. Rice pays an annual rental of $900, but his lease denies Bryant use of 70 acres of cultivated fields, 15 acres of pasture in NE¼ of SE¼, Section 34, two houses, and barn. Annual ad valorem taxes on these are $197, so net income from the lease is $703 and gets the same tax treatment as the $3258.

The forester inspects the proposed sale area and reports that it contains merchantable timber worth $12,000. Bryant can cut this now or allow it to grow; the forester estimates that annual growth on it will be worth about $750. Although these figures must be reduced by income taxes and selling expenses, they are an argument for keeping the land. The 65 acres of the sale area used by Bryant to grow timber cause an annual tax burden of $81. Additional expense is caused by boundary-line maintenance of 2 miles. Nevertheless, these two expenses are not large enough to offset estimated growth. His CPA checks the calculations and confirms them.

Bryant decides to make the sale provided Jones will pay $500 per acre, which is enough to compensate him for the merchantable timber on the parcel and its growth value. He tells Jones that he will sell for $75,000, convey one-eighth of the minerals, and accept 25% of the purchase price on 31 December 1988 and 25% on December of each of the next three years, with interest at 8% on the unpaid balance. Jones insists on one-quarter of the minerals. Bryant, knowing that he has excellent title information, says that he will provide an up-to-date title opinion and pay all closing costs if Jones will settle for one-eighth. (This shows the value of preparation; Bryant offers a concession that costs him little and retains an extra eighth of the minerals.) They finally agree and meet in Bryant's lawyer's office the next day.

After describing the agreements they have reached, they settle other details brought up by the lawyer. Bryant is to pay ad valorem taxes for 1988 and buy mineral documentary stamps. At Bryant's expense, the lawyer is to prepare an up-to-date title opinion and all necessary papers, give these to Jones or his lawyer by December 26, serve as closing agent, see that all documents are properly recorded, and transfer the assessment from Bryant to Jones. They select 31 December 1988 as the closing date and agree to meet at the same place. Bryant notifies Rice that his lease is terminated. To avoid misunderstanding, the lawyer prepares, and Jones and Bryant execute, the following purchase and sale contract:

25 November 1988

Mr. H. E. Jones
Box 189
Anytown, State

Dear Mr. Jones:

This letter will serve as a memorandum of the agreement reached between us in the office of Mr. Edward Weems [the lawyer] today.

I agree to convey to you by General Warranty Deed, subject to the exceptions hereafter noted, the land described as E½ of SE¼, Section 34; SW¼ of SW¼, Section 35, all in Township 5 North, Range 10 West and NW¼ of NW¼ less West 10 acres, Section 2, Township 4 North, Range 10 West, for which you agree to pay me $75,000.00, subject to approval of the title by your attorney. I will convey to you only an undivided one-eighth interest in the oil, gas, and other minerals; the thirty acres located in Section 2 are already leased to Gilchrist Oil Company, and the conveyance will be subject to this lease.

One quarter of the purchase price will be paid at closing. The balance will be represented by a promissory note executed by you and secured by a mortgage on the land conveyed. The promissory note shall be payable in three equal annual instalments of principal commencing 31 December 1989 and December 31st of each year thereafter plus interest at the rate of 8% per annum on the unpaid balance until paid in full.

I agree to pay all ad valorem taxes for 1988 as well as the cost of all documentary and mineral stamp taxes, title opinion, and closing cost. You will pay ad valorem taxes for the year 1989.

Mr. Weems will make an examination of the title, prepare title opinion, deed, note, and mortgage, and furnish you with all of this by December 26th. We will meet in his office on 31 December 1988 to close this transaction. Mr. Weems is to record all instruments and furnish the necessary proof of the transaction to Gilchrist Oil Company and the county tax assessor.

If this expresses your understanding of our agreement, please indicate your acceptance below.

Yours truly,
ROBERT BRYANT

ACCEPTED:

_____

H. E. Jones


After completing the title examination, the lawyer incorporates the agreements of the purchase and sale contract into the form required by state law. Jones and his lawyer approve everything, the sale is closed on schedule, the closing attorney performs his functions, and Bryant notes the action on his status map (Figure 16.2).

## BOUNDARY-LINE MAINTENANCE

As soon as the sale to Jones is definite, Bryant must change his boundary lines to exclude this portion; the status map shows that boundary-line maintenance is overdue. The forester reports that the paint applied by the surveyor in 1977 and 1979 is visible but dim and should be renewed. Excluding the portion sold to Jones and that maintained by XYZ Paper Company, there are only 6 miles of boundary line; the forester quotes a price of $350 per mile for this work. Bryant orders this work done, receives the forester's written report when it is complete, and plots the action on his status map.

Bryant has now plotted almost the entire history of his timberland for over 11 years on his map, and although it is becoming cluttered, it is still legible and useful. It appeared on 15 January 1989 as shown in Figure 16.2.

## FINANCIAL RECORDS

Bryant's financial records are simple but effective. Just prior to taking over the management, he opened a special bank account for the property and deposits all income in the account and pays all bills from it. He puts a brief explanation on each check stub and deposit slip and keeps his checkbook as a permanent record.

Each year he opens a special file for receipts and expenditures in connection with the property. Into it he puts deposit slips, bank statements, canceled checks, tax receipts, bills from advisers and others rendering services, memoranda of out-of-pocket expenses and trips he takes to administer the land, and so on. At the end of the year, his checkbook and this file are sufficient to prepare his profit and loss statement and income tax return, and he has evidence to substantiate each item. Each December 31, he seals the file and stores it. Everything in it is of transitory importance and does not need to be kept longer than the statutory period for all financial records. Everything in the main file on the property, that containing the forest-management records and so forth, has a bearing on his title and is of permanent importance. Therefore, some separation is necessary to keep the main file down to manageable size.

As you can see from this history, his transactions are infrequent,

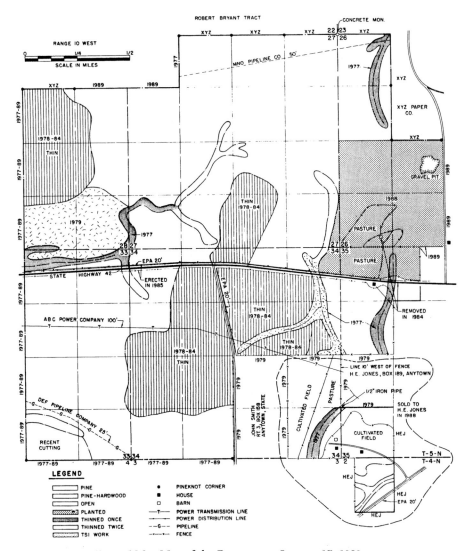

Figure 16.2. Map of the Bryant tract, January 15, 1989.

perhaps two or three receipts and 10 or 12 disbursements a year; therefore, separate books of account are not needed. If he had purchased the tract, even such an important item as depletion basis could be determined from his checkbook alone. The stub of the check for the purchase price should contain the allocation into various components, and the checkbook shows all later transactions in detail.

Twenty-five years after purchase, it is a simple matter to calculate his depletion basis. If your property is larger, you have more frequent transactions and probably need more elaborate records. Your tax adviser can design them.

## CONCLUSION

After three partial cuts and one liquidation, one land sale, one ROW sale, and 12 years' growth, Bryant needs another timber inventory and growth study. He can no longer make accurate financial predictions, and although he does not desire annual incomes, he wants to compare his timberland with other available investments. Fortunately, many important facts gathered in the original inventory are now part of his permanent records. He knows there is no merchantable timber on the area planted in 1988, so there is no need to inventory this. He has a good idea of stand conditions and location of operable volumes. The only missing links are timber volume and growth rate; these may be determined for the tract as a whole by a 5% inventory at modest cost. Therefore, good records have another advantage: they reduce the cost of future inventories.

This has been the story of Robert Bryant's tract for a period of 37 years. His methods are not perfect, and his results leave room for improvement. Nevertheless, through 1989 and beyond, he has found timberland investment a rewarding enterprise. I hope that his example will help you achieve the same results.

# 17

# Long-Term Timberland Investment with Annual Cash Flows

Up to now I have been discussing timberland owners who manage their properties to offset or meld with their incomes from other sources or the fortunes of their investments in other media. This is a highly rational course, for trees will increase in both total volume and unit value until they are cut, and therefore offer many opportunities for sales advantageous to their owner's income stream. Timberland fits in well as a minor part of an owner's assets.

On the other hand, some investors want to specialize in timberland and commit substantial sums to it. They are often experienced in financial matters, understand what real returns are available in various media, and are especially interested in annual cash flows. Such a man is David Wolfe, who has been gradually accumulating timberland for years. For a long time prices rose so steadily that everything he did was right, but several years of double-digit interest rates left him dissatisfied with his performance, so he decided to do something about it. Let us study his actions, for the solutions to his problems have wide application.

## GATHERING BASIC DATA

First, Wolfe must know what he has and make some basic decisions. Most of the information is available in his records or reference books or can be obtained by telephone. He owns 1463 acres of land; roads occupy 23 acres, leaving 1440 acres for growing trees. His land is in the South, and almost all of it supports a natural stand of pines, a mixture of longleaf, slash, shortleaf, and loblolly. The tract is obviously suited to pine; hardwood areas along minor drainages are so negligible that they can be ignored or easily converted to pine.

## SELECTION OF SPECIES

Examination of forestry literature reveals that some pine species grow faster than others and produce more valuable products in a shorter time. Each has its advantages and disadvantages, but Wolfe has a choice because all seem to do well on his land. In practice, he may produce several species, but since research reports on yields of timber stands are made for each species separately, he must select one for the purposes of analysis.

He chooses loblolly pine. It is the leading commercial timber species in southern United States, has been called the second most important timber species in the world, has many desirable biological characteristics, and seems to have been the subject of more research than other pine species.

This decision points to lesson number one: choose a native species, one that is familiar to all. Do not select a species just because remarkable growth rates have been obtained elsewhere. Stick with the species that nature has favored on your land.

## DETERMINATION OF SITE INDEX

What will loblolly pine produce on his land? This depends upon the average site index. He can determine this with great accuracy by a soil inventory; some consultants specialize in this, and he may need one before starting his program. For preliminary calculations, however, he can use information available from the U.S. Soil Conservation Service. The SCS Soil Surveys for his counties have been published, and they contain maps of his soils on aerial photos of a convenient scale. Using these, he determines that his average site index is 80.

## PREDICTION OF VOLUME YIELDS

Many years ago forest managers dealt almost exclusively with natural stands and used yield tables to predict the volumes they could produce at various times in the future. These tables were constructed by measuring many stands of various ages that had developed without disturbance. Consequently, they did not reveal the effects of controlling initial spacing or thinning during the rotation.

After hundreds of thousands of acres were planted during the 1950s and 1960s and the trees reached merchantable size, new yield tables based on these plantings revealed that the older tables underestimated yields, especially in plantations in old fields. Foresters also learned that they could grow bigger trees faster, and thus increase financial returns, by planting the initial seedlings at wider spacings. But they still lacked a good way to predict the effects of various thinnings.

Many of their difficulties have been solved at Virginia Polytechnic Institute and State University by the work of Loblolly Pine Growth and Yield Research Cooperative, a government–industry–university cooperative headed by Dr. Harold E. Burkhart. The cooperative has installed growth plots in loblolly pine plantations across a 12-state area from Virginia south to Georgia and west to east Texas. Remeasured at three-year intervals, these plots provide valuable information on plantation growth and how it is affected by site and stand variables. With these new data added to the work of early researchers and with the help of a powerful computer, Burkhart developed programs that can quickly predict the effects of all important variables. A forest manager can now feed into the computer initial spacing of seedlings, site index, type and timing of thinnings, and rotation age, and in a matter of minutes, out will come the number, size, and volume of all trees at key times in the rotation. Examples of such printouts appear as tables in this chapter. The cooperative is continually making additional measurements and adding them to the data base, thereby improving its predictive ability.

Wolfe decides that, in regenerating stands, he will plant seed or seedlings and not depend entirely on natural reproduction. In this way he can control initial spacing and also utilize genetic improvement whenever possible. He also decides to use the Burkhart computer programs to predict future yields.

## SALE PRICES OF PRODUCTS

His records show that timber prices go up and down over a wide range, and no one can tell what prices might be even two or three months hence. Although any estimate is admittedly a guess, recent actual sales are good guides.

The only sure thing is that he always has the best results when he offers large volumes per acre with volume concentrated in large trees. For instance, he receives top prices when he sells 15 to 20 cords of pulpwood per acre with most of the trees being 9-in. DBH, but has trouble finding a buyer when he sells two cords per acre of 6-ft trees.

He also recognizes the need for making the most accurate estimates possible; trying to be "conservative" may scuttle the enterprise before it is started.

## ESTIMATE OF ANNUAL COSTS

The biggest expenses in operating any timber property are those connected with selling timber. Trees must be marked and measured, sales shown to buyers, deeds prepared, money collected, and logging inspected. After reviewing the work and fee schedules of several consulting foresters, Wolfe decides that he will take timber-selling costs into account by reducing sale prices by an average of 10% for thinnings and 5.6% for harvests.

One annual, custodial expense is ad valorem taxes, which have been about $1.75 per acre. Another is boundary-line maintenance, which has been $0.60 per acre. A third is annual inspection of tracts to detect trespass, adverse possession, or damage from natural causes, which has been $0.30 per acre. Since there will also be small accounting fees and probably small legal fees, he estimates that custodial costs will total $2.75 per acre.

The only other cost is that of regenerating stands. Where hardwood brush is heavy and established pine seedlings are absent, site preparation and planting costs may run $150 to $175 per acre. Where hardwood brush is absent and pine seedlings cover much of the ground, the regeneration job may be done with only a small amount of TSI work at $25 per acre. He therefore estimates that regeneration costs will average $85 per acre.

## CHOICE OF DISCOUNT RATE

Most operations on Wolfe's property involve spending money for investment and expenses now while receiving income only at various times in the future. Therefore, to compare the "then" with the "now," he must choose a discount rate that is commensurate with the advantages and disadvantages of the business. After considering all he has learned from years of timberland operations, he chooses a *real* rate of 7%. (More discussion of real rates and nominal rates appears in

Chapter 8.) This is a high rate, and its effect is to reduce present values of future incomes to a low level. But the rate should fit each investor's unique situation, and 7% is Wolfe's choice, the rate he must have or he will invest his money elsewhere.

## BARE LAND VALUE AS THE MEASURE OF MANAGEMENT PLANS

Wolfe believes that all assumptions and data discussed above are knowns because they came from his records and experience. Therefore, you might say that his only unknown is the value of bare land. This is the value he will calculate, and he will use it as a yardstick to measure the profitability of his alternatives.

Let me define bare land. Bare land is soil and nothing but soil, no minerals, no young growth, no merchantable timber. Its value is what I am talking about when I say "bare land value." Foresters may use other terms in discussing bare land.

How do you calculate bare land value or BLV? First, you predict what crops can be produced during some future period of time, when they can be produced, and how much can be produced in volume and money. Then you estimate how much it will cost to produce them in terms of both initial outlay and carrying charges. Next you put all these present and future returns and costs into a formula and use a discount rate to bring them down to the present (now) so that you can determine their total net effect.

In Wolfe's case, the formula starts out like this:

BLV = yield then discounted to now minus cost now

"Yield then" is made up of several items. Most will come in the harvest, but small amounts will come sooner from thinnings. To bring all yields down to now, Wolfe must increase all thinnings by the discount rate to the date of harvest, add them to the harvest, and then discount the sum to now. The formula should read

BLV = harvest + thinnings raised to harvest date, all discounted to now − cost now

"Cost now" is also made up of several items. The largest is that of establishing the trees in the beginning; this sum will be tied up until the harvest. Others are annual costs for ad valorem taxes, boundary-line maintenance, and so on., some due this year and others not for many years later. He must treat each cost so that it will have its proper effect.

All of the above is more complicated because Wolfe expects that the operation will be permanent; he plans to grow a crop of timber over a certain period and then repeat the process over and over. To account for all this requires a complicated formula which I will not show how to derive. When the time comes, I will just give the formula to you.

## SEARCHING FOR THE CORRECT FOREST-MANAGEMENT PLAN

Before Wolfe sits down at the computer with the Burkhart programs, he knows some of the things he is looking for. First, trees 12 in. DBH are almost perfect for either pulpwood, poles, lumber, or plywood, so competition is keener, demand is steadier, and prices per cubic foot are usually higher than for any other size. Therefore, he wants trees in his harvest to be about 12 in., so his rotation must be about 35 years. Second, to select his crop trees as soon as possible, to keep all trees growing rapidly, and to get cash flow, he wants the first thinning to come early, but he knows that it will not sell readily unless it contains at least five cords per acre. Third, since a second thinning will surely be necessary, he wants it early enough to add more to present value, late enough to contain trees that will sell well, and yet early enough to have a beneficial effect on the main crop trees. Finally, since the regeneration cost will be tied up for many years, he wants to reduce it to a minimum.

The first computer runs reveal that he cannot get optimum satisfaction of all desires simultaneously. For example, planting only 200 seedlings per acre reduces regeneration cost and produces 14-in. trees in 35 years, but reduces the chance for early income from thinnings. On the other hand, planting 1200 per acre produces plenty of trees for thinnings, but raises regeneration cost and reduces the size of the crop trees. Thinning early reduces cash flow from thinning because trees removed are too small to sell well, but it may increase size and value of the harvest; thinning late has the opposite effect. A very heavy, early thinning increases cash flow, but it may eliminate the second thinning and either increase or decrease value at harvest. The best plan will obviously be a compromise.

After many trial-and-error computer runs, he finds that the most promising plan calls for planting 300 seedlings per acre, thinnings at ages 18 and 26, and harvest at age 35.

At age 18, to relieve overcrowding and to produce income, he sells all trees on every fourth row. A printout is in Table 17.1.

At age 26, to groom the main crop trees for harvest, he sells in a thinning the trees as shown in Table 17.2.

The harvest at age 35 contains the trees as shown in Table 17.3.

## FINANCIAL ANALYSIS

Wolfe's next step is to evaluate these cuts. He knows from experience that unit values of trees increase as DBH increases, so he shows the printouts to several timber buyers, asks how much trees of each size are worth, and assigns values according to their opinions. Then he evaluates the cuts as shown in Tables 17.3–17.5.

Before substituting values in the formula, he must allow for one other element. Trees planted in January 1989 will be 35 years old in January 2024. Sufficient time must be allowed to harvest them, however, and also to prepare the ground for planting the next crop. He believes that these activities can be completed in one year; in other words, cutting will begin in January 2024, and the next crop will be planted in January 2025. Although he harvests his crop at age 35, he can do so only at intervals of 36 years because he must allow one extra year for logging and regeneration.

Now he substitutes the figures in the formula that I promised to give you:

$$\text{BLV} = \frac{\$1451.83 + (\$128.39 \times 1.07^{17}) + (\$79.65 \times 1.07^{9}) - (\$85.00 \times 1.07^{35})}{1.07^{36} - 1.000}$$

$$\times\ 1.07 - \frac{\$2.75}{0.07}$$

The $1451.83 is the harvest. The $128.39 term is the thinning at age 18 accumulated 7% compound interest for 17 years. The $79.65 term is the thinning at age 26 accumulated for 9 years. The $85.00 term is the plantation cost accumulated for 35 years. These four expressions bring both income and original investment to the same time 35 years from now. The $(1.07^{36} - 1.000)$ term is an expression to show that this will be repeated at intervals of 36 years forever. The $(\times\ 1.07)$ term shows that, although the incomes will be repeated every 36 years, the first harvest income will be received 35 years from now. The final $2.75/0.07 term shows that the annual custodial expenses will be met forever.

## TABLE 17-1
## Printout at Age 18

| DBH Class | Number Trees | Average Height | Basal Area | Cubic Feet Volume o.b. | Volume Cords to 4 in. | Volume Doyle Board Feet |
|---|---|---|---|---|---|---|
| 5 | 1.7 | 39.3 | 0.2 | 3.7 | 0.0 | 0.0 |
| 6 | 10.0 | 43.5 | 2.0 | 42.2 | 0.4 | 0.0 |
| 7 | 11.7 | 47.4 | 3.2 | 71.0 | 0.7 | 0.0 |
| 8 | 15.0 | 48.3 | 5.2 | 118.2 | 1.2 | 0.0 |
| 9 | 15.0 | 48.8 | 6.7 | 153.4 | 1.6 | 0.0 |
| 10 | 8.3 | 51.4 | 4.7 | 111.4 | 1.2 | 216.7 |
| 11 | 3.3 | 52.8 | 2.0 | 49.5 | 0.5 | 100.0 |
| 12 | 3.3 | 55.9 | 2.5 | 65.7 | 0.7 | 150.3 |
| | 68.3 | | 26.5 | 615.1 | 6.7 | 467.0 |

## TABLE 17-2
## Printout at Age 26

| DBH Class | Number Trees | Average Height | Basal Area | Cubic Feet Volume o.b. | Volume Cords to 4 in. | Volume Doyle Board Feet |
|---|---|---|---|---|---|---|
| 5 | 6.7 | 48.8 | 1.0 | 23.1 | 0.2 | 0.0 |
| 6 | 11.7 | 51.5 | 2.4 | 58.3 | 0.6 | 0.0 |
| 7 | 15.0 | 56.1 | 4.0 | 105.8 | 1.1 | 0.0 |
| 8 | 20.0 | 59.0 | 7.0 | 192.0 | 1.9 | 0.0 |
| 9 | 16.7 | 60.8 | 7.1 | 200.7 | 2.1 | 0.0 |
| Total | 70.0 | | 21.4 | 580.0 | 5.8 | 0.0 |

## TABLE 17-3
## Printout at Age 35

| DBH Class | Number Trees | Average Height | Basal Area | Cubic Feet Volume o.b. | Volume Cords to 4 in. | Volume Doyle Board Feet |
|---|---|---|---|---|---|---|
| 10 | 16.7 | 68.3 | 9.6 | 304.3 | 3.2 | 674.0 |
| 11 | 31.7 | 71.6 | 20.5 | 677.7 | 7.0 | 1616.7 |
| 12 | 31.7 | 74.5 | 24.9 | 855.7 | 8.9 | 2289.3 |
| 13 | 18.3 | 74.6 | 17.0 | 586.3 | 6.1 | 1709.2 |
| 14 | 5.0 | 78.1 | 5.4 | 194.5 | 2.0 | 627.6 |
| 15 | 8.3 | 79.9 | 9.9 | 365.5 | 3.8 | 1260.0 |
| Total | 111.7 | | 87.4 | 2984.0 | 30.9 | 8176.8 |

**TABLE 17-4A**
**Thinning at Age 18**

| DBH Class | Cords or MBF Doyle | Unit Value | Total Value | Less Selling Expenses | Net |
|---|---|---|---|---|---|
| 6 | 0.4 | $ 8 | $ 3.20 | | |
| 7 | 0.7 | 12 | 8.40 | | |
| 8 | 1.2 | 15 | 18.00 | | |
| 9 | 1.6 | 20 | 32.00 | | |
| 10 | 0.217 | 165 | 35.81 | | |
| 11 | 0.100 | 175 | 17.50 | | |
| 12 | 0.150 | 185 | 27.75 | | |
| | | | 142.66 | $14.27 | $128.39 |

**TABLE 17-4B**
**Thinning at Age 26**

| DBH Class | Cords or MBF Doyle | Unit Value | Total Value | Less Selling Expenses | Net |
|---|---|---|---|---|---|
| 6 | 0.6 | $ 8 | $ 4.80 | | |
| 7 | 1.1 | 12 | 13.20 | | |
| 8 | 1.9 | 15 | 28.50 | | |
| 9 | 2.1 | 20 | 42.00 | | |
| | | | 88.50 | $8.85 | $79.65 |

**TABLE 17-5**
**Harvest at Age 35**

| DBH Class | Cords or MBF Doyle | Unit Value | Total Value | Less Selling Expenses | Net |
|---|---|---|---|---|---|
| 10 | 0.674 | $165 | $ 111.21 | | |
| 11 | 1.617 | 175 | 288.98 | | |
| 12 | 2.289 | 185 | 423.47 | | |
| 13 | 1.709 | 195 | 333.26 | | |
| 14 | 0.628 | 205 | 128.74 | | |
| 15 | 1.260 | 205 | 258.30 | | |
| | | | 1537.96 | $86.13 | $1451.83 |

Using values from compound interest tables, he solves the equation as follows:

$$\text{BLV} = \frac{\dfrac{\$1451.83 + (\$128.39 \times 3.159) + (\$79.65 \times 1.839) - (\$85.00 \times 10.677)}{11.424 - 1.000}}{\times 1.07 - \dfrac{\$2.75}{0.07}}$$

$$= \frac{\dfrac{\$1451.83 + \$405.58 + \$146.48 - \$907.55}{10.424}}{} \times 1.07 - \$39.29$$

$$= \frac{\$1096.34}{10.424} \times 1.07 - \$39.29 = \$105.17 \times 1.07 - \$39.29$$

$$= \$112.54 - \$39.29 = \$73.25$$

## CARRYING OUT THE PLAN

If Wolfe owns only 1 acre, he will plant trees now, receive small incomes in 18 and 26 years and a large one in 35 years, and repeat this process over and over. Equal annual incomes will be his, however, if he owns one acre of 35-year-old trees, one of the 34-year-old trees, and so on down the scale, including one acre of bare land, a total of 36 acres. Each year he will thin the 18- and 26-year-old acres, harvest the 35-year-old acre, and plant the bare acre. Annual expenses of $2.75 per acre will be paid on a total of 36 acres.

A diagram of such a tract and its annual operations looks like Figure 17.1.

## FITTING THE TRACT INTO THE PLAN

This is a neat, orderly picture, and Wolfe's operating results will match it as soon as his property matches the picture. Since it is 40 times larger, he must multiply figures by 40.

The main problem is that his tract is like thousands of others. For years he planted trees and performed TSI work because these cultural operations appeared to be wise, were recommended by many foresters, and were partly subsidized by governments. He was sold long ago on the merits of selective cutting and thought that good forestry meant frequent partial cuts, at intervals of four or five years if possible. As a result, he has some timber on every acre but no acres with a heavy stand of big trees. There is too much timber on some and too little on others. He must discover how it differs from the diagram.

# ANNUAL OPERATIONS ON IDEAL 36-ACRE TRACT

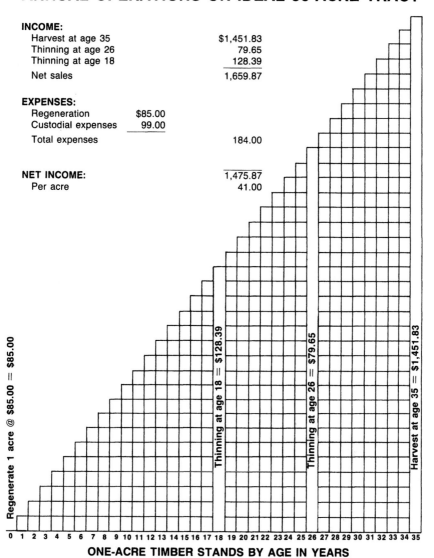

**INCOME:**

| | |
|---|---:|
| Harvest at age 35 | $1,451.83 |
| Thinning at age 26 | 79.65 |
| Thinning at age 18 | 128.39 |
| Net sales | 1,659.87 |

**EXPENSES:**

| | | |
|---|---:|---:|
| Regeneration | $85.00 | |
| Custodial expenses | 99.00 | |
| Total expenses | | 184.00 |

**NET INCOME:**

| | |
|---|---:|
| | 1,475.87 |
| Per acre | 41.00 |

Regenerate 1 acre @ $85.00 = $85.00

Thinning at age 18 = $128.39

Thinning at age 26 = $79.65

Harvest at age 35 = $1,451.83

0 1 2 3 4 5 6 7 8 9 10 11 12 13 14 15 16 17 18 19 20 21 22 23 24 25 26 27 28 29 30 31 32 33 34 35

**ONE-ACRE TIMBER STANDS BY AGE IN YEARS**

Figure 17.1.    Annual operations on ideal 36-acre tract.

The first step is to divide the tract on paper into 36 blocks of about 40 acres each. Although equality of area is not essential, wide departures from the average should be avoided. Physical features, such as roads and large streams, should be used as block boundaries if the features are large enough to be a barrier in logging operations; a large stream passing through the middle of a block would make each cutting operation two logging jobs instead of one, and thereby reduce the price of timber sold each time. Interior lines between blocks need to be established on the ground only temporarily during logging, and extreme accuracy is not necessary. Blocks that correspond with subdivisions of the public land survey will simplify conveyances and reports.

The next step is to number each block to show the age of timber on it, using only the numbers 0 through 35. This is not as hard as it seems, for he is dealing only in approximations, recognizes that maladjustments exist, and is trying merely to fit the blocks into the plan with the minimum of maladjustment. Trial and error will govern the process.

A recent timber inventory giving volumes by DBH for each block would help, but even without one, Wolfe knows a lot about his land from experience and can use aerial photographs to help his memory. As a start, he studies the map and, after selecting the block containing his best timber, numbers it 35. Then he assigns 34 to his next best block, and 33 to the next. Soon his memory becomes hazy, and he cannot remember whether one block is better than another.

Then he starts at the other end of the scale and assigns 0 to the block with the poorest timber, 1 to the next poorest, and so on up the scale until he again has difficulty deciding. At this point, he must make a ground reconnaissance, but he has already numbered perhaps 30% of the blocks and needs to look only at the remainder.

A timber inventory or reconnaissance will not solve all problems; several blocks may be nearly identical because of past management practices. He merely numbers these blocks arbitrarily; if they are identical, this method is as good as any. He soon finds that his timber fits the diagram better than anticipated, so he continues until all blocks are numbered.

Now in his mind's eye, he checks the numbers by considering how the blocks will fit into the first year's operations. Block 35 is to be clearcut; is there enough timber on it to make an attractive sale? Blocks 18 and 26 are to be thinned; are they suitable for this? Block 0 is to be planted; he knows that it is not bare, but it may need some cultural treatment. He may go to the woods again, this time to inspect

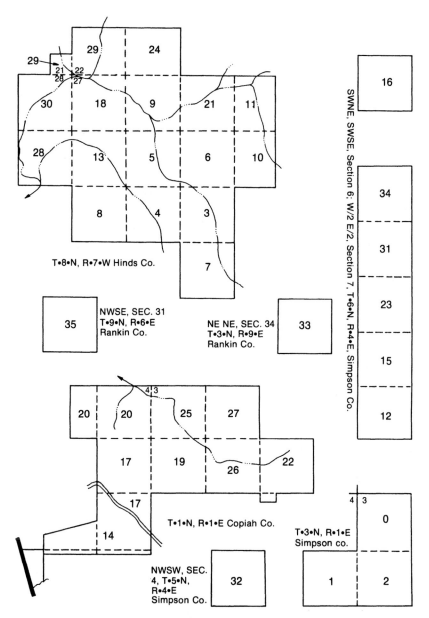

Figure 17.2. Map of Wolfe tract after blocks are numbered.

only four or five blocks. If he discovers that 34 is actually better than 35, all he does is switch numbers. Now he is ready to begin operations. Figure 17.2 is the map of his tract after numbering the blocks.

On other tracts, there might be serious maladjustments. If it is entirely a 10-year-old plantation, there will be no merchantable trees; thinning or harvest will be impossible, and planting unnecessary. Such a tract will produce large incomes at irregular intervals and cannot be made to fit Wolfe's plan without substantial alteration over many years. It will fit only one of the 36 slots. To obtain equal annual incomes, its owner must buy land to fit the other 35 slots.

On the other hand, there might be several surpluses with corresponding deficits, such as four 18-year-old blocks and none aged 19, 20, or 21. Minor adjustments like these reduce efficiency, but will be ironed out gradually as the plan unfolds.

The situation on Wolfe's land is deficits on either end of the scale and surpluses in the middle, particularly in the younger half of the middle. In the past, because he had no outstanding timber, he was forced to offer mediocre sales from time to time. Since he had no plan and was afraid that he might dip into timber capital, he made partial cuts, always leaving some timber, the sight of which reassured him.

This is the kind of situation his new plan will correct. Even in the first year, buyers will be more interested in his timber. Clearcutting block 35 will eliminate any worries about damage to remaining timber (there will be none). By concentrating the major action on one block each year, he postpones it on the other 35, and each year his offerings will be more attractive. He need not fear dipping into capital; the loggers are hardly out of the woods before the block is restocked with trees.

In the beginning, most of the inefficiency will show up in clearcutting the oldest block. For some time these blocks will contain trees of all sizes. The largest may be growing less than 7%; cutting them will improve efficiency. The smallest will be growing more than 7%; cutting them will reduce efficiency. This should not worry Wolfe, however, because there are many dollars in big trees and few dollars in little ones. The planned cut for the first year is enough to meet all expenses and leave a large surplus. Each year his tract will more nearly approach the ideal and will equal it in 36 years. Actually, he should reach the ideal sooner. In the tenth year of operations, he will clearcut a block that was groomed for harvest by a thinning. In the eighteenth year, he will harvest a block that has been thinned twice.

Since all his land is in trees now, he is ahead of schedule on the younger end of the scale. Using as a guide the properties on which I have already installed his system, I estimate that he will reach the ideal in about 18 years. His net cash income from the first year's operations can be estimated by an inventory of block 35, and it should rise each year until it reaches a plateau in the eighteenth year.


## FIRST YEAR'S OPERATIONS

By numbering the blocks, Wolfe has already selected the block for harvest; all that remains is to sell it. While the tract is being reshaped to match the diagram, income is likely to be less than ideal, so getting top dollar is essential. Only one selling method will accomplish this: the sealed-bid, lump-sum, widely advertised method described earlier.

There are good biological reasons for removing everything. Trees adapt themselves to being part of a thick stand; if most of the stand is suddenly removed, the remnants may succumb to windthrow. Stumps and tops from trees cut will be immediately attacked by fungi and insects, which may later attack any live trees standing among the logging refuse. As we shall see later, cultural operations to establish the new stand may kill everything left standing. Finally, if these scattered individuals should survive, they would probably usurp an undue amount of growing space and reduce future yields.

For the first few years, areas scheduled for thinning may be near the borderline for profitable operations. Nevertheless, every effort should be made to carry out the plan. Each dollar of income is important, and these thinnings will also improve future harvest cuts. If, however, maladjustments make commercial thinnings impossible, the areas should be passed over until they come on schedule again.

Since the block scheduled for planting is already in trees, no action is needed on it unless some idle areas need attention.


## SECOND YEAR'S OPERATIONS

In many ways, this year is more interesting than the first. To begin with, Wolfe studies results of the preceding year. Did they meet his expectations? Does the plan still fit conditions expected for the year ahead? If the answer is "no," he can junk the whole setup. This flexibility is highly important; although his plan extends forever into the future, it can be terminated at a moment's notice. No one likes to be locked into a permanent arrangement, and flexibility is as important to timberland managers as to other businessmen. Even if he terminates the plan, he is better off than he was a year ago. He has the money from sales. As soon as he plants block 35, he will have as much timber as before; his timber is more concentrated on the ground because 33 blocks were not touched.

After deciding to continue the plan, he studies the blocks scheduled for cutting. Block 34 is to be clearcut; blocks 17 and 25 are to be thinned. A ground rconnaissance may reveal that it would be better to clearcut block 31 because of a slight change in markets. He solves this problem by merely switching numbers, and he can change thinning areas the same way.

Regenerating block 35 brings up a task that, because of reliance on natural reproduction, he has never faced before. His calculations of BLV emphasize how important it is. At his estimate of $85.00 per acre, regeneration cost is more than land value itself and will be tied up for 35 years; on the other hand, if it is not done properly, all his plans will fail. Skill in regeneration is second in importance only to skill in selling timber.

Each cutover requires a unique regeneration plan, but all of them should reduce costs to a minimum by capitalizing on the natural vigor of loblolly pine. Block 35 presents no unusual problems, so Wolfe decides to use herbicides to establish a competition-free zone 6 ft square on 12-ft centers, to plant a "big" seedling in each zone, and to utilize all well-formed seedlings at least waist high left over from the previous stand. On each acre, therefore, he treats only 300 blocks containing 36 square feet each or 25% of the total area. He thinks that, with this help, the new seedlings will overcome any undesirable competition that develops, and he can eliminate other undesirables later.

The range of regeneration problems that will face him in the future is unlimited. On the cheap end, he will have natural reproduction that is free and free to grow but very thick; nevertheless, a prediction of yields by Burkhart's program and an estimate of regeneration cost, both inserted into the BLV formula, may reveal that it is the most profitable solution. On the costly end, he will have undesirable growth that threatens to capture the site completely and yet is very expensive to eliminate. The only certainty is that spending more than $85.00 plus $73.25 = $158.25 reduces the value of the land to less than nothing. Since loblolly pine has maintained its dominant position for

50,000,000 years without human help, Wolfe thinks that he can solve his regeneration problems.

## APPLICATION OF THE SYSTEM TO SMALLER PROPERTIES

I selected Wolfe's tract as an illustration because it is the minimum size for annual operations. If it were only half as large, 720 acres with blocks of 20 acres, he could probably sell the harvest. Gross sale volume would be $1500 per acre or $30,000, and this is large enough to interest some buyers. Gross sale volumes at ages 18 and 26 would be only $2850 and $1800, however, and such offerings would attract little interest. Therefore, is a 1440-acre tract the minimum size for this management scheme?

No. The solution lies in substituting periodic incomes for annual incomes. On 720 acres, you can schedule cutting operations every two years and still offer blocks of 40 acres each time. If annual incomes are essential, spend half the proceeds when they are received and put the other half in a savings account for use in the off year.

Thirty-six is also divisible by 3, 4, 6, 9, and 12, so 480 acres will permit cuts on a three-year cycle, 360 acres = four-year, 240 acres = six-year, and so on; 18 and 26 are not quite so versatile, but minor adjustments can cure this.

## HOW TO HANDLE PURCHASES OR SALES OF LAND

Few ownerships remain static in area. Over the years, owners often make several land sales or purchases, and other reductions in area may result from ROWs for pipelines, powerlines, and so forth. Reworking the entire plan to maintain blocks of equal area is unnecessary. There will be little change in income or expense until cutting or regeneration is scheduled for the altered block. If a ROW or sale removes all or part of a block, leave this space blank and plan on reduced yields for the year in which cutting is scheduled on it. In the meantime, stay alert for possible purchases to fill the blank.

Follow the reverse procedure with tracts purchased. See which they most nearly resemble among those blocks you already own, and schedule them for treatment at the same time. This will cause abnormal income or regeneration expenses during these years, but this will not be a real problem if the purchase meets the usual requirements of financial analysis. The problem may solve itself if you make so many purchases that total area is gradually increased by purchases of equal blocks in each age class.

## EVEN-AGE VERSUS UNEVEN-AGE MANAGEMENT

Wolfe uses what foresters call even-age management, but some argue for uneven-age management. They say that each tree is unique in its ability to grow and should be treated individually to realize its maximum potential. No doubt each tree is unique, but it is time to discard individual treatment when it seriously reduces profits. Look at the difficulty of applying uneven-age management in actual operations.

First, the uneven-age system calls for holding on each block trees ranging in size from seedlings to largest sawtimber and harvesting them at intervals to remove mature trees and less desirable ones. Many foresters recommend light, frequent cuts to maintain the stand at its best level for growth. Attempting to make such cuts disregards the realities of the marketplace. Logging costs must rise, and stumpage prices must fall, as volume of cut per acre falls. Loggers must also avoid damage to remaining trees, and such care costs money.

Second, in cuts under uneven-age management, trees of all sizes must be harvested, some suitable for sawtimber and others for pulpwood. In spite of increasing efforts at integration, many sawtimber and pulpwood loggers still want to operate independently. Therefore, one cut really becomes two cuts following closely upon each other. Each logger must have enough time to remove his product, and when much volume is involved, each time period will probably be one year. On a five-year cutting cycle, therefore, loggers are working on the same ground two years out of five, and disturbance from felling, skidding, and road building is more or less continuous. Because of the time lapse before pulpwood cutters follow sawtimber cutters, salvage of pulpwood from tops of sawtimber trees is difficult. Furthermore, administrative effort must be spread over a wide area, and this costs money.

Third, because each cut removes only a small fraction of the stand, all trees to be cut must be marked, and logging must be closely inspected to see that no unmarked trees are cut. This costs money. As you can see, Wolfe's selling expenses are 10% on thinnings, but only 5.6% on the biggest part of his annual sales.

Fourth, uneven-age management requires frequent inventories to check on the status of timber capital. Growth predictions are good for

10 years at most, and calculated inventories based on them may contain serious errors after years of operations. Since there is timber on every acre, every acre must be inventoried; under a system like Wolfe's, about one-third of the area need never be inventoried.

Fifth, uneven-age management requires that seedlings develop under larger trees to take their places when larger trees are cut. This appears to eliminate the expense of regeneration, but it may not work out that way in practice. Most desirable timber species are intolerant of shade and do well only in full sunlight. If there is a thick overstory of large trees, the understory soon becomes composed mainly of tolerant and less desirable species; these trees eventually become the main canopy. Under uneven-age management, use of fire to cure this situation cheaply is impossible.

Sixth, and I believe most important of all, most owners cannot comprehend what is taking place in their woods under uneven-age management; the system is so complicated that many foresters do not understand it and few can explain it. Lack of comprehension causes uncertainty, slipshod operations, disappointment with results, and unwillingness to make additional investments. It is almost tragic that these results have strongly influenced the disposition of 170,000,000 acres of southern timberlands. Wolfe's system can correct this situation; it is simple as can be.

## HARDWOOD LANDS

Wolfe's tract contains little hardwood land, but even in the southern pine region, the average tract is often 20% hardwood with variations up to 100%. Is his system applicable to hardwood? Yes.

Many think that uneven-age management is the only system for handling hardwoods. My experience convinces me that *even-age* management may be the best system for hardwoods.

The amount of sunlight necessary for best development varies by species. Intolerant species need unrestricted sunlight; tolerant species will grow under the shade of another tree. The U. S. Forest Service publication, *Management and Inventory of Southern Hardwoods*, Agricultural Handbook No. 181, lists as *intolerant* the following species: ash, birch, cottonwood, all gums, nearly all oaks, sycamore, walnut, and yellow poplar, in other words, most of the valuable species. Listed as *tolerant* are beech, dogwood, elms, hackberry, hickories, maples, mulberry, and pecans, in other words, most of the less desirable species. The few tolerant but valuable species are basswood, cherry, magnolias, and bays, all widely distributed but of lesser importance in the whole picture. Even-age management is ideal for intolerant species.

Absence of knots is the criterion of high-grade hardwood logs, and knots come from limbs. Plenty of light from the side allows limbs to flourish; uneven-age management allows plenty of light from the side. Intense competition from adjoining trees, causing early death of lower limbs, always exists under even-age management. Every logging operation results in reduction of quality in some hardwood trees because heavy machinery bumps into them and knocks off part of the bark, so infrequency of logging is another plus for even-age management.

Tree size and volume per acre are more important in hardwood land because logging is more expensive on lower, wetter sites. This is a strong argument for even-age management where most of the volume is removed in one heavy cut.

Consequently, if your tract contains hardwood sites, I recommend that you treat them the same as pine sites in dividing your tract into blocks; in other words, for the purpose of division, disregard timber type. Unless the premium for large logs is substantial, treat hardwood sites the same as pine sites in cutting operations.

Different treatment, however, is necessary in regeneration. Few nurseries grow hardwood seedlings, and fewer agencies collect and sell hardwood seeds, so planting or direct-seeding is impossible. Fortunately, there are cheaper methods of regeneration. Many hardwood seeds are carried by rodents and flowing water in addition to gravity and wind. Moreover, most hardwoods sprout freely from roots and stumps, a characteristic that assures abundant reproduction in nearly all cases. All of the more desirable hardwoods are vigorous sprouters. Nature does the regeneration work in hardwoods.

This causes some difficulty because it is impossible to control initial spacing, and there is no economical solution to the problem. It appears, however, that unlimited sunlight will allow the more vigorous sprouts or seedlings to crowd out the weaker ones quickly and reach the needed size in time for the first thinning.

What about BLV on hardwood sites? Refer to the 36-year formula again, and assume that hardwood will produce the same volumes as pine in the same time. Although hardwood pulpwood prices are rising, most hardwood prices are about 40% of pine prices for the same size trees. In the formula, reduce the total dollar amounts of the cuts by 60%. Then, since there will be no regeneration costs, eliminate the

($85.00 × 10.677) = $907.55. Solving the equation after these changes gives a BLV of $42.99.

## IMPORTANCE OF RECORDS

Proper records of all forest-management activities become very important under this sytem. You can avoid the expense of periodic inventories only by keeping records. You must have them to know which block to cut when, especially after 15 or 20 years of operations. I cannot overemphasize the importance of keeping adequate records as you go.

## VALUE OF PLANTATIONS BY YEARS

Wolfe can pay $73.25 per acre for bare land and earn 7% compound interest on every dollar invested. Since he estimates cost of regeneration at $85.00, he can pay $158.25 for a plantation just after installation. At the end of one year, his cost will be $158.25 × 1.07 = $169.33 + $2.75 (custodial expenses) = $172.08. At the end of years 18 and 26, he will receive income from thinnings, and his cost must be adjusted for this. Costs for each year's plantations are in Table 17.6.

Although the schedule is developed by compounding costs, it also shows how much each plantation is worth to him. He cannot pay more than the prices shown and earn 7% on invested capital. This is a handy guide for investment decisions.

Suppose the vicinity becomes more thickly settled and a neighbor offers to buy one block for $500.00 per acre. A quick look at the records reveals that the block was planted six years ago; the schedule gives a value of $257.17. Here is a chance to make a profit of over 94%, and if the sale would not impair operations on other blocks, Wolfe should sell it or at least recognize that continued ownership of it cannot be justified for timber-growing alone. On the other hand, he may have a chance to buy a six-year-old plantation at $225.00. If survival in it is adequate, he should make the purchase.

As even-age management becomes more widespread, more plantations may appear on the market, but the usual offerings now are tracts with an uneven-aged stand over the entire area. The system offers one way to appraise such offerings. First, you must have an inventory that shows volume of merchantable timber, amount and distribution of reproduction, and some idea about how many cull trees, if any, are

**TABLE 17-6**
**Costs for Each Year's Plantations**

| Year | Beginning Cost | Add Investment | Add 7% Interest Cost |
|---|---|---|---|
| 1 | $    73.25 | $85.00 | $11.08 |
| 2 | 172.08 | | 12.05 |
| 3 | 186.88 | | 13.08 |
| 4 | 202.71 | | 14.19 |
| 5 | 219.65 | | 15.38 |
| 6 | 237.78 | | 16.64 |
| 7 | 257.17 | | 18.00 |
| 8 | 277.92 | | 19.45 |
| 9 | 300.12 | | 21.01 |
| 10 | 323.88 | | 22.67 |
| 11 | 349.30 | | 24.45 |
| 12 | 376.50 | | 26.36 |
| 13 | 405.61 | | 28.39 |
| 14 | 436.75 | | 30.57 |
| 15 | 470.07 | | 32.90 |
| 16 | 505.72 | | 35.40 |
| 17 | 543.87 | | 38.07 |
| 18 | 584.69 | | 40.93 |
| 19 | 499.98 | | 35.00 |
| 20 | 537.73 | | 37.64 |
| 21 | 578.12 | | 40.47 |
| 22 | 621.34 | | 43.49 |
| 23 | 667.58 | | 46.73 |
| 24 | 717.06 | | 50.19 |
| 25 | 770.00 | | 53.90 |
| 26 | 826.65 | | 57.87 |
| 27 | 807.62 | | 56.53 |
| 28 | 866.90 | | 60.68 |
| 29 | 930.33 | | 65.12 |
| 30 | 988.20 | | 69.87 |
| 31 | 1,070.82 | | 74.96 |
| 32 | 1,148.53 | | 80.40 |
| 33 | 1,231.68 | | 86.22 |
| 34 | 1,320.65 | | 92.45 |
| 35 | 1,415.85 | | 99.11 |
| 0 | 65.88 | | 4.61 |
| | 20,998.87 | | |

| Add Custodial Expenses | Subtract Sales | Year-End Cost |
|---|---|---|
| $2.75 | | $ 172.08 |
| 2.75 | | 186.88 |
| 2.75 | | 202.71 |
| 2.75 | | 219.65 |
| 2.75 | | 237.78 |
| 2.75 | | 257.17 |
| 2.75 | | 277.92 |
| 2.75 | | 300.12 |
| 2.75 | | 323.88 |
| 2.75 | | 349.30 |
| 2.75 | | 376.50 |
| 2.75 | | 405.61 |
| 2.75 | | 436.75 |
| 2.75 | | 470.07 |
| 2.75 | | 505.72 |
| 2.75 | | 543.87 |
| 2.75 | | 584.69 |
| 2.75 | $ 128.39 | 499.98 |
| 2.75 | | 537.73 |
| 2.75 | | 578.12 |
| 2.75 | | 621.34 |
| 2.75 | | 667.58 |
| 2.75 | | 717.06 |
| 2.75 | | 770.00 |
| 2.75 | | 826.65 |
| 2.75 | 79.65 | 807.62 |
| 2.75 | | 866.90 |
| 2.75 | | 930.33 |
| 2.75 | | 988.20 |
| 2.75 | | 1,070.82 |
| 2.75 | | 1,148.53 |
| 2.75 | | 1,231.68 |
| 2.75 | | 1,320.65 |
| 2.75 | | 1,415.85 |
| 2.75 | 1,451.83 | 65.88 |
| 2.75 | | 73.24 |

impeding growth of reproduction. Then you must determine whether sale of all merchantable timber is possible. If not, estimate how much it will cost to remove the culls and to regenerate bare areas, if any. Finally, you must estimate how the tract, after cultural treatment, will compare to a plantation. Will it be the equivalent of a 10- or 15-year-old plantation? If the estimated age is 10, the tract is worth $349.30 per acre less whatever the cultural treatment will cost. If the merchantable timber can be sold, its net value should be added.

This method is admittedly an approximation, but I believe that it is as accurate as any and simpler and faster than most. Estimating what the remaining stand of reproduction is equivalent to is a tricky job, but computer runs with the Burkhart programs will show the details of stands at any age.

## EFFECT OF SITE INDEX

Experienced forest managers know that some acres will grow more timber than others, and our formula gives us a way to evaluate differences in site index (SI). By using the computer to predict yields for SI 70 and SI 90 and then inserting appropriate values in the formula, we obtain the following BLVs at a 7% discount rate:

| SI 70 | $ −4.89 or essentially zero |
| 80 | 73.25 |
| 90 | 147.49 |

A similar calculation reveals that SI 60 land has a minus BLV; in other words, it will not return 7% on capital invested in an attempt to grow timber. If any of Wolfe's land falls in this category, he should postpone efforts to develop it and do what he can to sell it.

These figures emphasize how important it is to determine site index in the first place. The typical way is to measure heights and ages of trees on the tract and then refer to curves in site-index tables. When I asked T. T. Koslowski whether this was accurate, he replied:

Such a procedure usually produces good results and is often the only method available, but it can underestimate the growth potential of a given site. For example, a severe insect infestation while trees are very young or an unusual ice storm that reduced growth for a year or so could reduce height growth enough to reduce the calculated site index below the actual site index. You must be aware of this possibility when making the measurements.

I repeat his warning.

## EFFECT OF COST REDUCTIONS

Wolfe estimates regeneration costs at $85.00. If he can cut this cost by $40.00 by direct seeding or other methods, he will raise BLV by $43.85; on the other hand, if regeneration costs rise by $40.00, BLV falls by $43.85. This is enough to raise or lower the BLV of SI 80 land by 60%. A precommercial thinning soon after planting would have the same effect. Certainly the soundest advice and most careful planning are needed at this point.

## EFFECT OF DISCOUNT RATE

Wolfe chose 7% as the return he required on his investment. Some big timber companies may choose lower rates because timberlands serve primarily as insurance of continued supplies of raw material for their mills. Others with less capital may insist on higher rates. How does the discount rate affect BLV?

Changing the discount rate and nothing else in the formula on page 239, we arrive at the following solutions

| Discount Rate % | BLV per Acre |
|---|---|
| 6 | $143.83 |
| 7 | 73.25 |
| 8 | 25.46 |

This explains why some big timber companies often pay high prices for land. Although they may not use Wolfe's formula, they do use the same principle in evaluating purchases. If he develops his tract so that it will earn 7% and then finds a buyer who uses a 6% rate, he will reap a windfall profit of $143.83 − $73.25 = $70.58 per acre.

## USE OF SUPER SEEDLINGS

Estimates of increased yields from using genetically improved seedlings vary widely, but a common guess is that seedlings from first-generation orchards will increase yields by 15%. Since a given acre makes available only so much sunlight, water, and nutrients, it is hard to see how more wood can be produced in the same amount of time; at any rate, the Burkhart programs will tell the tale once their data base includes enough super-seedling plantations. But by producing it faster or in larger or better-quality trees, super seedlings may increase BLV by this 15% or by the 35% or more that is supposed to be possible from second- and third-generation orchards. Super seedlings cost only a little more than others and have such exciting possibilities that you should use them whenever possible.

## HOW TO HANDLE INFLATION

The occurrence of inflation makes our formula useless for calculating BLV, because it assumes that incomes and expenses will repeat themselves over and over, whereas inflation means that incomes and expenses will change constantly. If you want to factor inflation into the situation, the only way to calculate BLV is to predict what dollar incomes and expenses will be for five rotations (180 years) and then discount them to the present by the *nominal* discount rate. And this brings on more explanation and some huge numbers.

If we assume a steady inflation rate of 4% per year (a modest one compared to some recent years), *per-acre* harvest income in rotation 1 will be $1,537.96 \times 1.04^{35} = \$6,068.79$. With the same inflation rate, it will be $23,947 in rotation 2, $94,497 in rotation 3, $372,884 in rotation 4, and over $1,471,000 in rotation 5. Regeneration costs will similarly go from $85 to $335 to $1324 to $5223 to $20,609.

Assuming that there would be *no* inflation, Wolfe chose a 7% discount rate because he thought that the nature of the business required a *real* return of 7%. If there is inflation, however, he can maintain his position only by raising his 7% rate by a premium equal to the inflation rate and using this new figure, called the *nominal* rate, as a discount rate. The nominal rate is the product (not the sum) of the real rate and the inflation rate, and the formula and calculation in our case is as follows:

$1$ + nominal rate = $(1$ + real rate$) \times (1$ + inflation rate$)$
$1$ + nominal rate = $(1.00 + 0.07) \times (1.00 + 0.04)$
$\qquad\qquad\quad = 1.07 \times 1.04 = 1.1128$
$\quad$ nominal rate = $11.28\%$

I will not take the space to show all the calculations for the next 180 years. Just take my word for it: when you do the work, the BLV you arrive at is $73.25, exactly the same as we found earlier. And what this means is that timberland is a good hedge against inflation.

Furthermore, using nominal rates produces unsatisfactory answers because it is hard to determine what the *current* inflation rate is. The best economists disagree to some extent, and even when they agree, the rate is changing all the time. But our biggest problem is that we need to know the *future* rate, not the current one, and no one can predict a second of the future. Many investors solve the problem as Wolfe did: by choosing the essential real rate and then figuring that timberland, by its nature, will protect them against inflation.

## IS TIMBERLAND REALLY A LONG-TERM INVESTMENT?

Many commentators stress that timberland is a long-term investment, pointing out that trees planted today require 18 years to produce the first income and 35 years to produce the big payoff. (I have often characterized it as a long-term investment to emphasize the point that every action by the investor has an effect for many years to come.) Embarking on such a lengthy project makes many investors nervous. Others rightly think that trying to predict prices, costs, and inflation rates for the next 35 years is ridiculous. But the same situation faces investors considering 30-year bonds; although few timberland investors will live to harvest as sawtimber the seedlings they plant today, how many buyers of long-term bonds will live to collect the principal?

Wolfe does not look upon his tract as a long-term investment at all. A complete cycle of his plan will require 36 years, but his ownership may last only a short time. So far as he is concerned, the tract is just a beautiful biological system that produces a real net income of $41.00 per acre per year. Each $85 of his annual planting costs is the price he pays to insure that each 36-acre portion will produce about $1476 annually forever. If his minimum 7% real return is close to that demanded by other investors in income-producing properties, the portion should sell readily at about $21,000. Consequently, Wolfe looks critically at his asset at least once a year, reviews results of the immediate past, guesses only about the immediate future, and thus undertakes his project no more than one year at a time.

For most investors, neither timberland nor long-term bonds are long-term investments in the sense that they maintain their ownerships for many, many years. The real differences between them are that bonds are liquid but do not protect against inflation, whereas timberland is not liquid but does protect against inflation. And when they are priced on a yield basis, southern timberlands are becoming more liquid yearly.

## ALLOCATION OF PURCHASE PRICE FOR DEPLETION PURPOSES

The formula is useful in dealing with the Internal Revenue Service. When you acquire timberland by any means, you are required by tax laws to allocate part of the purchase price to timber and part to land. The part allocated to land cannot be depleted until the land is disposed of, and owners are usually anxious to set this as low as possible to increase depletion and minimize tax liability in timber sales.

Although the IRS will agree to any allocation that seems reasonable, its agents may not know what "reasonable" means, and they have no objection to a high land value because this eventually raises the government's share of all timber-sale proceeds. Each IRS agent is overloaded with tax returns from every conceivable type of business and can not be an expert on all. If many forest owners are less than experts about their business, they should expect some lack of knowledge among IRS agents. This being true, IRS agents may set land values on the basis of remarks they hear in their daily work. When someone says that "timberland is selling for about $250.00 per acre," they may not understand that part of this amount is BLV and that other parts are reproduction and merchantable timber. Therefore, they become suspicious when an owner allocates $75.00 to land and the rest to timber.

The formula can help in dealing with them. Wolfe has good land and sells timber at good prices, so his BLV is closer to the gossip than others. Under the same conditions SI 70 land is worth less than half as much, and SI 60 land has a negative value. Poor markets for all products, high costs of regeneration and management, or poor suitability for better timber species might also wipe out BLV or reduce it to nearly zero. It is hard for the IRS to dispute facts when you know how to explain to them how you arrived at the facts.

## CONCLUSION

I have used the system outlined in this chapter successfully for 25 years on tracts ranging in size from 720 to over 20,000 acres. It is easy to understand, and the biology of timberland investment is complicated enough without adding an intricate and esoteric scheme of management.

The system nearly always increases profits. This is true because it offers timber buyers the kind of timber they want in the way they want it and does not try to force them to take whatever the grower wants to sell. With this system, the dog wags the tail and not vice versa.

The system increases the comfort level of the owner. He sees that his timber capital is not being depleted because every acre clearcut is promptly regenerated. He rejoices that logging damage to remaining trees has been reduced to insignificant levels. He realizes that he is continually raising the productivity of his whole tract by planting at better spacings and introducing super seedlings whenever possible. Finally, he understands that the biological conditions created by his management are close to ideal for the development of loblolly pine: starting in the full sunlight of open spaces and growing in pure stands with overcrowding relieved by thinning.

Wolfe's system came from an actual tract that my company manages in southern Mississippi. The owner uses the 35-year plan because he thinks that, over the long haul, it will produce trees most in demand in his market. As further illustration of how to find the highest BLV and of how stands of trees develop, I have set forth in Appendix I the steps we went through for another actual property in southern Georgia. Although the most profitable spacing there is also 300 per acre, nothing is sacred about this number. The correct spacing for each tract is a unique number and depends on growth rate, market values for units of volume by DBH classes, and discount rate used by the owner.

In a few minutes with a pocket calculator, you can learn whether you can capture additional profit and comfort. Wolfe's 35-year rotation with thinnings at ages 18 and 26 may be the most profitable plan for many tracts, and by solving our equation using timber prices in your locality, you can estimate how much improvement is possible. Your first calculations may also reveal that your methods of selling timber do not produce maximum prices, that certain expenses are too high, or that site index is too low. If the exercise indicates that exciting gains are likely, you can go on to an accurate determination of site index and much more computer work to test different forest-management plans.

Your hard work and analytical judgment may have an unexpected payoff if your tract, for one reason or another, is revealed as a *poor* producer. Very few timberland investors make such a thorough investigation, and the timberland market, inefficient to begin with, is washed by periodic waves of euphoria. If you know you have a low-grade tract, you will not spend money trying to develop it, and you will seize the chance to unload it on the next wave.

It pays to know how to make money growing trees.

# Analysis of S. Georgia Tract

Following Wolfe's procedure of determining the most profitable forest-management plan by finding the highest BLV, I made an analysis of another actual tract, this one in southern Georgia. As you can see from the worksheets reproduced below, prices are considerably different, sawtimber is measured by Scribner rule, and regeneration costs are increased by $10 per acre for each increase of 100 seedlings planted.

Here is a summary of results of the calculations:

| Forest-Management Plan | BLV/Acre for Various Initial Spacings | | |
| --- | --- | --- | --- |
| | 300/Acre | 400/Acre | 500/Acre |
| No thinnings, harvest at 20 | $216.82 | $184.05 | $156.75 |
| No thinnings, harvest at 25 | 220.16 | 197.41 | 182.70 |
| No thinnings, harvest at 30 | 188.05 | 163.23 | 150.54 |
| Fourth-row thinning at 20, harvest at 30 | 203.96 | 170.32 | 161.43 |

The key finding from these calculations is that, for all plans tested, the most profitable spacing is 300 per acre, so the owner now plants at this rate with confidence that he will be OK even if conditions change quite a bit in the future. I think that I tested enough plans to explore all feasible options, and because the 25-year BLV was highest, the owner divided his tract into 26 blocks. He is not locked into this plan, however, but can change it quickly to match very big changes in markets. The worksheets follow.

## PLANT 300/ACRE, NO THINNINGS, HARVEST AT 20

### COMPUTER PRINTOUT

| DBH class | Number trees | Average height | Basal area | Cubic Feet Volume o. b. | Volume Cords to 4 in. | Volume Scribner Board Feet |
|---|---|---|---|---|---|---|
| 4 | 1.3 | 38.8 | 0.1 | 2.6 | 0.0 | 0.0 |
| 5 | 16.0 | 42.1 | 2.1 | 43.4 | 0.3 | 0.0 |
| 6 | 20.0 | 46.9 | 4.1 | 91.6 | 0.9 | 0.0 |
| 7 | 32.0 | 49.9 | 8.7 | 205.3 | 2.1 | 0.0 |
| 8 | 41.3 | 50.9 | 14.5 | 346.8 | 3.5 | 0.0 |
| 9 | 57.3 | 53.4 | 25.0 | 622.9 | 6.4 | 0.0 |
| 10 | 49.3 | 54.3 | 26.3 | 663.7 | 6.9 | 1809.7 |
| 11 | 24.0 | 55.8 | 15.7 | 407.1 | 4.2 | 1279.3 |
| 12 | 10.7 | 58.0 | 8.3 | 223.6 | 2.3 | 768.9 |
| 13 | 2.7 | 62.4 | 2.4 | 69.3 | 0.7 | 254.3 |
| Total | 254.7 | | 107.3 ' | 2676.2 | 27.3 | 4112.2 |

### EVALUATION OF CUT

| DBH Class | Cords or MBF Scribner | Unit Value | Total Value | Less Selling Expenses | Net |
|---|---|---|---|---|---|
| 6 | 0.9 | $ 15 | $13.50 | | |
| 7 | 2.1 | 19 | 39.90 | | |
| 8 | 3.5 | 24 | 84.00 | | |
| 9 | 6.4 | 40 | 256.00 | | |
| 10 | 1.810 | 170 | 307.70 | | |
| 11 | 1.279 | 185 | 236.62 | | |
| 12 | 0.769 | 200 | 153.80 | | |
| 13 | 0.254 | 210 | 53.34 | | |
| | | | 1,144.86 | $64.11 | $1,080.75 |

### CALCULATION OF BLV

$$\text{BLV} = \frac{\$1080.75 - (\$85.00 \times 1.07^{20})}{1.07^{21} - 1.000} \times 1.07 - \frac{\$2.75}{0.07}$$

$$= \frac{\$1080.75 - (\$85.00 \times 3.870)}{4.141 - 1.000} \times 1.07 - \$39.29$$

$$= \frac{\$1080.75 - \$328.95}{3.141} \times 1.07 - \$39.29 = \$216.82$$

## PLANT 300/ACRE, NO THINNINGS, HARVEST AT 25

### COMPUTER PRINTOUT

| DBH Class | Number Trees | Average Height | Basal Area | Cubic Feet Volume o. b. | Volume Cords to 4 in. | Volume Scribner Board Feet |
|---|---|---|---|---|---|---|
| 5 | 9.3 | 46.7 | 1.3 | 29.8 | 0.2 | 0.0 |
| 6 | 10.7 | 51.5 | 2.2 | 53.2 | 0.5 | 0.0 |
| 7 | 25.3 | 55.5 | 7.1 | 184.7 | 1.9 | 0.0 |
| 8 | 29.3 | 57.9 | 10.3 | 279.2 | 2.8 | 0.0 |
| 9 | 46.7 | 58.8 | 21.1 | 577.4 | 6.0 | 0.0 |
| 10 | 46.7 | 60.3 | 25.2 | 707.5 | 7.3 | 2090.4 |
| 11 | 37.3 | 62.1 | 24.2 | 695.7 | 7.2 | 2284.3 |
| 12 | 17.3 | 64.1 | 13.5 | 399.9 | 4.1 | 1419.3 |
| 13 | 10.7 | 65.8 | 9.8 | 297.3 | 3.1 | 1110.5 |
| 14 | 2.7 | 70.5 | 2.8 | 90.7 | .9 | 352.6 |
| Total | 236.0 | | 117.4 | 3315.6 | 34.1 | 7257.1 |

### EVALUATION OF CUT

| DBH Class | Cords or MBM Scribner | Unit Value | Total Value | Less Selling Expenses | Net |
|---|---|---|---|---|---|
| 6 | 0.5 | $ 15 | $ 7.50 | | |
| 7 | 1.9 | 19 | 36.10 | | |
| 8 | 2.8 | 24 | 67.20 | | |
| 9 | 6.0 | 40 | 240.00 | | |
| 10 | 2.090 | 170 | 355.30 | | |
| 11 | 2.284 | 185 | 422.54 | | |
| 12 | 1.419 | 200 | 283.80 | | |
| 13 | 1.111 | 210 | 233.31 | | |
| 14 | 0.353 | 220 | 77.66 | | |
| | | | 1,723.41 | $96.51 | $1,626.90 |

### CALCULATION OF BLV

$$BLV = \frac{\$1626.90 - (\$85.00 \times 1.07^{25})}{1.07^{26} - 1.000} \times 1.07 - \frac{\$2.75}{0.07}$$

$$\frac{\$1626.90 - (\$85.00 \times 5.427)}{5.807 - 1.000} \times 1.07 - \$39.29$$

$$= \frac{\$1626.90 - \$461.30}{4.807} \times 1.07 - \$39.29 = \$220.16$$

. . . .

## PLANT 300/ACRE, NO THINNINGS, HARVEST AT 30

### Computer Printout

| DBH Class | Number Trees | Average Height | Basal Area | Cubic Feet Volume o. b. | Volume Cords to 4 in. | Volume Scribner Board Feet |
|---|---|---|---|---|---|---|
| 5 | 4.0 | 51.1 | 0.6 | 14.9 | 0.1 | 0.0 |
| 6 | 5.3 | 55.5 | 1.0 | 27.5 | 0.3 | 0.0 |
| 7 | 13.3 | 58.4 | 3.6 | 100.1 | 1.0 | 0.0 |
| 8 | 26.7 | 62.5 | 9.5 | 276.5 | 2.8 | 0.0 |
| 9 | 26.7 | 63.6 | 11.8 | 348.8 | 3.6 | 0.0 |
| 10 | 49.3 | 65.5 | 26.8 | 814.6 | 8.5 | 2525.2 |
| 11 | 38.7 | 67.6 | 25.0 | 783.9 | 8.1 | 2661.8 |
| 12 | 30.7 | 68.6 | 23.8 | 753.9 | 7.8 | 2725.7 |
| 13 | 14.7 | 70.3 | 13.5 | 438.3 | 4.5 | 1662.0 |
| 14 | 8.0 | 73.0 | 8.4 | 282.3 | 2.9 | 1104.0 |
| Total | 217.3 | | 124.1 | 3840.5 | 39.7 | 10678.7 |

### Evaluation of Cut

| DBH Class | Cords or MBF Scribner | Unit Value | Total Value | Less Selling Expenses | Net |
|---|---|---|---|---|---|
| 6 | 0.3 | $ 15 | $ 4.50 | | |
| 7 | 1.0 | 19 | 19.00 | | |
| 8 | 2.8 | 24 | 67.20 | | |
| 9 | 3.6 | 40 | 144.00 | | |
| 10 | 2.525 | 170 | 429.25 | | |
| 11 | 2.662 | 185 | 492.47 | | |
| 12 | 2.726 | 200 | 545.20 | | |
| 13 | 1.662 | 210 | 349.02 | | |
| 14 | 1.104 | 220 | 242.88 | | |
| | | | 2293.52 | $128.44 | $2,165.08 |

### Calculation of BLV

$$\text{BLV} = \frac{\$2165.08 - (\$85.00 \times 1.07^{30})}{1.07^{31} - 1.000} \times 1.07 - \frac{\$2.75}{0.07}$$

$$= \frac{\$2165.08 - (\$85.00 \times 7.612)}{8.145 - 1.000} \times 1.07 - \$39.29$$

$$= \frac{\$2165.08 - \$647.02}{7.145} \times 1.07 - \$39.29 = \$188.05$$

. . . .

## PLANT 300/ACRE, FOURTH-ROW THINNING AT 20, HARVEST AT 30

### COMPUTER PRINTOUT OF THINNING AT 20

| DBH Class | Number Trees | Average Height | Basal Area | Cubic Feet Volume o. b. | Volume Cords to 4 in. | Volume Scribner Board Feet |
|---|---|---|---|---|---|---|
| 5 | 5.3 | 42.9 | 0.7 | 14.5 | 0.1 | 0.0 |
| 6 | 8.0 | 45.9 | 1.6 | 35.0 | 0.3 | 0.0 |
| 7 | 5.3 | 51.2 | 1.5 | 36.1 | 0.4 | 0.0 |
| 8 | 16.0 | 50.8 | 5.6 | 132.9 | 1.3 | 0.0 |
| 9 | 10.7 | 54.1 | 4.7 | 117.9 | 1.2 | 0.0 |
| 10 | 17.3 | 53.2 | 9.3 | 230.9 | 2.4 | 624.7 |
| 11 | 8.0 | 56.5 | 5.2 | 135.7 | 1.4 | 426.5 |
| 12 | 8.0 | 59.0 | 6.3 | 170.4 | 1.8 | 589.4 |
| 13 | 1.3 | 60.1 | 1.1 | 31.6 | .3 | 113.2 |
| Total | 79.9 | | 35.9 | 905.0 | 9.3 | 1753.8 |

### EVALUATION OF CUT

| DBH Class | Cords or MBF Scribner | Unit Value | Total Value | Less Selling Expenses | Net |
|---|---|---|---|---|---|
| 6 | 0.3 | $ 15 | $ 4.50 | | |
| 7 | 0.4 | 19 | 7.60 | | |
| 8 | 1.8 | 24 | 31.20 | | |
| 9 | 1.2 | 40 | 48.00 | | |
| 10 | 0.625 | 170 | 106.25 | | |
| 11 | 0.427 | 185 | 79.00 | | |
| 12 | 0.589 | 200 | 117.80 | | |
| 13 | 0.113 | 210 | 23.73 | | |
| | | | 418.08 | $41.81 | $376.27 |

COMPUTER PRINTOUT OF HARVEST AT 30

| DBH Class | Number Trees | Average Height | Basal Area | Cubic Feet Volume o. b. | Volume Cords to 4 in. | Volume Scribner Board Feet |
|---|---|---|---|---|---|---|
| 5 | 4.0 | 50.1 | 0.6 | 14.2 | 0.1 | 0.0 |
| 6 | 4.0 | 53.6 | 0.8 | 20.0 | 0.2 | 0.0 |
| 7 | 8.0 | 57.4 | 2.1 | 57.2 | 0.6 | 0.0 |
| 8 | 17.3 | 62.1 | 6.0 | 175.0 | 1.8 | 0.0 |
| 9 | 24.0 | 63.6 | 10.6 | 312.9 | 3.2 | 0.0 |
| 10 | 29.3 | 66.4 | 16.3 | 500.9 | 5.2 | 1579.5 |
| 11 | 26.7 | 68.1 | 17.5 | 554.2 | 5.8 | 1899.1 |
| 12 | 18.7 | 69.1 | 14.3 | 455.6 | 4.7 | 1644.2 |
| 13 | 9.3 | 70.6 | 8.4 | 273.2 | 2.8 | 1031.7 |
| 14 | 4.0 | 74.3 | 4.4 | 149.3 | 1.5 | 589.3 |
| 15 | 1.3 | 77.8 | 1.6 | 57.1 | .6 | 229.8 |
| Total | 146.7 | | 82.5 | 2569.8 | 26.5 | 6973.6 |

EVALUATION OF CUT

| DBH Class | Cords or MBF Scribner | Unit Value | Total Value | Less Selling Expenses | Net |
|---|---|---|---|---|---|
| 6 | 0.2 | $ 15 | $ 3.00 | | |
| 7 | 0.6 | 19 | 11.40 | | |
| 8 | 1.8 | 24 | 43.20 | | |
| 9 | 3.2 | 40 | 128.00 | | |
| 10 | 1.580 | 170 | 268.60 | | |
| 11 | 1.899 | 185 | 351.32 | | |
| 12 | 1.644 | 200 | 328.80 | | |
| 13 | 1.032 | 210 | 216.72 | | |
| 14 | 0.589 | 220 | 129.58 | | |
| 15 | 0.230 | 220 | 50.60 | | |
| | | | 1531.22 | $85.75 | $1,445.47 |

CALCULATION OF BLV

$$\text{BLV} = \frac{\$1531.22 + (\$376.27 \times 1.07^{10}) - (\$85.00 \times 1.07^{30})}{1.07^{31} - 1.000}$$
$$\times \, 1.07 - \frac{\$2.75}{0.07}$$

$$= \frac{\$1531.22 + (\$376.27 \times 1.967) - (\$85.00 \times 7.612)}{8.145 - 1.000}$$

$$\times 1.07 - \$39.29$$

$$= \frac{\$1531.22 + \$740.12 - \$647.02}{7.145} \times 1.07 - \$39.29 = \$203.96$$

· · · ·

## PLANT 400/ACRE, NO THINNINGS, HARVEST AT 20

### Computer Printout

| DBH Class | Number Trees | Average Height | Basal Area | Cubic Feet Volume o. b. | Volume Cords to 4 in. | Volume Scribner Board Feet |
|-----------|--------------|----------------|------------|-------------------------|-----------------------|----------------------------|
| 2 | 1.8 | 29.9 | 0.1 | 1.1 | 0.0 | 0.0 |
| 3 | 1.8 | 36.2 | 0.1 | 2.2 | 0.0 | 0.0 |
| 4 | 7.1 | 40.9 | 0.7 | 14.4 | 0.0 | 0.0 |
| 5 | 21.3 | 43.6 | 2.8 | 60.4 | 0.4 | 0.0 |
| 6 | 39.1 | 47.9 | 7.8 | 179.1 | 1.7 | 0.0 |
| 7 | 53.3 | 50.0 | 14.1 | 333.5 | 3.3 | 0.0 |
| 8 | 69.3 | 51.6 | 24.4 | 590.3 | 6.0 | 0.0 |
| 9 | 71.1 | 53.2 | 31.1 | 770.7 | 7.9 | 0.0 |
| 10 | 37.3 | 54.1 | 19.8 | 500.8 | 5.2 | 1362.5 |
| 11 | 24.9 | 57.2 | 16.1 | 425.5 | 4.4 | 1342.6 |
| 12 | 3.6 | 61.3 | 2.8 | 79.2 | 0.8 | 278.2 |
| Total | 330.7 | | 119.8 | 2957.3 | 29.8 | 2983.3 |

### Evaluation of Cut

| DBH Class | Cords or MBF Scribner | Unit Value | Total Value | Less Selling Expenses | Net |
|-----------|-----------------------|------------|-------------|-----------------------|-----|
| 6 | 1.7 | $ 15 | $25.50 | | |
| 7 | 3.3 | 19 | 62.70 | | |
| 8 | 6.0 | 24 | 144.00 | | |
| 9 | 7.9 | 40 | 316.00 | | |
| 10 | 1.363 | 170 | 231.71 | | |
| 11 | 1.343 | 185 | 242.46 | | |
| 12 | 0.278 | 200 | 55.60 | | |
| | | | 1083.97 | $60.70 | $1023.27 |

CALCULATION OF BLV

$$\text{BLV} = \frac{\$1023.27 - (\$95.00 \times 1.07^{20})}{1.07^{21} - 1.000} \times 1.07 - \frac{\$2.75}{0.07}$$

$$= \frac{\$1023.27 - (\$95.00 \times 3.870)}{4.141 - 1.000} \times 1.07 - \$39.29$$

$$= \frac{\$1023.27 - \$367.65}{3.141} \times 1.07 - \$39.29 = \$184.05$$

. . . .

## PLANT 400/ACRE, NO THINNINGS, HARVEST AT 25

COMPUTER PRINTOUT

| DBH Class | Number Trees | Average Height | Basal Area | Cubic Feet Volume o. b. | Volume Cords to 4 in. | Volume Scribner Board Feet |
|---|---|---|---|---|---|---|
| 3 | 1.8 | 37.0 | 0.1 | 1.7 | 0.0 | 0.0 |
| 4 | 3.6 | 41.4 | 0.3 | 6.5 | 0.0 | 0.0 |
| 5 | 14.2 | 49.2 | 2.0 | 48.0 | 0.4 | 0.0 |
| 6 | 17.8 | 53.2 | 3.7 | 93.5 | 0.9 | 0.0 |
| 7 | 49.8 | 55.4 | 13.6 | 353.9 | 3.6 | 0.0 |
| 8 | 39.1 | 58.5 | 13.8 | 377.7 | 3.8 | 0.0 |
| 9 | 69.3 | 58.7 | 30.6 | 838.1 | 8.7 | 0.0 |
| 10 | 55.1 | 60.9 | 30.0 | 849.1 | 8.8 | 2532.9 |
| 11 | 37.3 | 63.1 | 24.3 | 710.7 | 7.4 | 2354.6 |
| 12 | 14.2 | 64.6 | 11.3 | 338.6 | 3.5 | 1213.4 |
| 13 | 1.8 | 68.9 | 1.7 | 53.5 | 0.6 | 203.2 |
| Total | 304.0 | | 131.4 | 3671.4 | 37.6 | 6304.1 |

EVALUATION OF CUT

| DBH Class | Cords or MBF Scribner | Unit Value | Total Value | Less Selling Expenses | Net |
|---|---|---|---|---|---|
| 6 | 0.9 | $ 15 | $13.50 | | |
| 7 | 3.6 | 19 | 68.40 | | |
| 8 | 3.8 | 24 | 91.20 | | |
| 9 | 8.7 | 40 | 348.00 | | |
| 10 | 2.533 | 170 | 430.61 | | |

EVALUATION OF CUT (*Continued*)

| DBH Class | Cords or MBF Scribner | Unit Value | Total Value | Less Selling Expenses | Net |
|---|---|---|---|---|---|
| 11 | 2.355 | 185 | 435.68 | | |
| 12 | 1.213 | 200 | 242.60 | | |
| 13 | 0.203 | 210 | 42.63 | | |
| | | | 1672.62 | $93.67 | $1578.95 |

CALCULATION OF BLV

$$BLV = \frac{\$1578.95 - (\$95.00 \times 1.07^{25})}{1.07^{26} - 1.000} \times 1.07 - \frac{\$2.75}{0.07}$$
$$= \frac{\$1578.95 - (\$95.00 \times 5.427)}{5.807 - 1.000} \times 1.07 - \$39.29$$
$$= \frac{\$1578.95 - \$515.57}{4.807} \times 1.07 - \$39.29 = \$197.41$$

. . . .

## PLANT 400/ACRE, NO THINNINGS, HARVEST AT 30

COMPUTER PRINTOUT

| DBH Class | Number Trees | Average Height | Basal Area | Cubic Feet Volume o. b. | Volume Cords to 4 in. | Volume Scribner Board Feet |
|---|---|---|---|---|---|---|
| 3 | 1.8 | 40.0 | 0.1 | 2.0 | 0.0 | 0.0 |
| 4 | 1.8 | 43.2 | 0.2 | 3.9 | 0.0 | 0.0 |
| 5 | 8.9 | 53.2 | 1.4 | 35.4 | 0.3 | 0.0 |
| 6 | 7.1 | 55.4 | 1.4 | 37.6 | 0.4 | 0.0 |
| 7 | 32.0 | 60.1 | 8.8 | 248.6 | 2.5 | 0.0 |
| 8 | 37.3 | 63.1 | 13.2 | 388.4 | 3.9 | 0.0 |
| 9 | 44.4 | 63.6 | 20.1 | 594.0 | 6.1 | 0.0 |
| 10 | 55.1 | 66.3 | 29.6 | 910.9 | 9.5 | 2824.9 |
| 11 | 44.4 | 67.0 | 29.0 | 898.2 | 9.3 | 3046.8 |
| 12 | 24.9 | 70.0 | 19.3 | 626.4 | 6.5 | 2279.7 |
| 13 | 10.7 | 70.8 | 9.8 | 318.9 | 3.3 | 1209.5 |
| 14 | 1.8 | 73.6 | 1.8 | 62.1 | .6 | 242.7 |
| Total | 270.2 | | 134.7 | 4126.5 | 42.5 | 9603.6 |

EVALUATION OF CUT

| DBH Class | Cords or MBF Scribner | Unit Value | Total Value | Less Selling Expenses | Net |
|-----------|----------------------|------------|-------------|----------------------|-----|
| 6 | 0.4 | $ 15 | $ 6.00 | | |
| 7 | 2.5 | 19 | 47.50 | | |
| 8 | 3.9 | 24 | 93.60 | | |
| 9 | 6.1 | 40 | 244.00 | | |
| 10 | 2.825 | 170 | 480.25 | | |
| 11 | 3.047 | 185 | 563.70 | | |
| 12 | 2.280 | 200 | 456.00 | | |
| 13 | 1.210 | 210 | 254.10 | | |
| 14 | 0.243 | 220 | 53.46 | | |
| | | | 2198.61 | $123.12 | $2075.49 |

CALCULATION OF BLV

$$\begin{aligned} \text{BLV} &= \frac{\$2075.49 - (\$95.00 \times 1.07^{30})}{1.07^{31} - 1.000} \times 1.07 - \frac{\$2.75}{0.07} \\ &= \frac{\$2075.49 - (\$95.00 \times 7.612)}{8.145 - 1.000} \times 1.07 - \$39.29 \\ &= \frac{\$2075.49 - \$723.14}{7.145} \times 1.07 - \$39.29 = \$163.23 \end{aligned}$$

$\cdot \quad \cdot \quad \cdot \quad \cdot$

## PLANT 400/ACRE, FOURTH-ROW THINNING AT 20, HARVEST AT 30

COMPUTER PRINTOUT OF THINNING AT 20

| DBH Class | Number Trees | Average Height | Basal Area | Cubic Feet Volume o. b. | Volume Cords to 4 in. | Volume Scribner Board Feet |
|-----------|--------------|----------------|------------|-------------------------|----------------------|---------------------------|
| 2 | 1.8 | 29.9 | 0.1 | 1.1 | 0.0 | 0.0 |
| 3 | 1.8 | 36.2 | 0.1 | 2.2 | 0.0 | 0.0 |
| 4 | 0.0 | 0.0 | 0.0 | 0.0 | 0.0 | 0.0 |
| 5 | 3.6 | 46.1 | 0.6 | 12.7 | 0.1 | 0.0 |
| 6 | 7.1 | 46.5 | 1.3 | 28.4 | 0.3 | 0.0 |
| 7 | 17.8 | 50.7 | 4.6 | 110.2 | 1.1 | 0.0 |
| 8 | 23.1 | 52.1 | 8.2 | 199.1 | 2.0 | 0.0 |

Computer Printout of Thinning at 20 (*Continued*)

| DBH Class | Number Trees | Average Height | Basal Area | Cubic Feet Volume o. b. | Volume Cords to 4 in. | Volume Scribner Board Feet |
|---|---|---|---|---|---|---|
| 9 | 8.9 | 51.3 | 4.0 | 95.2 | 1.0 | 0.0 |
| 10 | 21.3 | 53.6 | 11.4 | 285.0 | 3.0 | 773.0 |
| 11 | 12.4 | 56.3 | 8.0 | 210.1 | 2.2 | 658.7 |
| 12 | 3.6 | 61.3 | 2.8 | 79.2 | 0.8 | 278.2 |
| Total | 101.2 | | 41.0 | 1023.3 | 10.4 | 1709.9 |

Evaluation of Cut

| DBH Class | Cords or MBF Scribner | Unit Value | Total Value | Less Selling Expenses | Net |
|---|---|---|---|---|---|
| 6 | 0.3 | $ 15 | $ 4.50 | | |
| 7 | 1.1 | 19 | 20.90 | | |
| 8 | 2.0 | 24 | 48.00 | | |
| 9 | 1.0 | 40 | 40.00 | | |
| 10 | 0.773 | 170 | 131.41 | | |
| 11 | 0.659 | 185 | 121.92 | | |
| 12 | 0.278 | 200 | 55.60 | | |
| | | | 422.33 | $42.23 | $380.10 |

Computer Printout of Harvest at 30

| DBH Class | Number Trees | Average Height | Basal Area | Cubic Feet Volume o. b. | Volume Cords to 4 in. | Volume Scribner Board Feet |
|---|---|---|---|---|---|---|
| 5 | 10.7 | 51.3 | 1.6 | 38.8 | 0.3 | 0.0 |
| 6 | 8.9 | 56.9 | 1.8 | 49.5 | 0.5 | 0.0 |
| 7 | 19.6 | 59.8 | 5.5 | 155.2 | 1.6 | 0.0 |
| 8 | 26.7 | 62.2 | 9.4 | 273.4 | 2.8 | 0.0 |
| 9 | 28.4 | 63.2 | 12.4 | 365.0 | 3.8 | 0.0 |
| 10 | 51.6 | 67.0 | 28.3 | 878.7 | 9.1 | 2768.3 |
| 11 | 26.7 | 69.3 | 17.2 | 551.3 | 5.7 | 1886.1 |
| 12 | 16.0 | 71.1 | 12.4 | 406.1 | 4.2 | 1481.4 |
| 13 | 3.6 | 72.0 | 3.2 | 105.6 | 1.1 | 400.1 |
| Total | 192.0 | | 91.8 | 2823.6 | 29.1 | 6535.9 |

EVALUATION OF CUT

| DBH Class | Cords or MBF Scribner | Unit Value | Total Value | Less Selling Expenses | Net |
|---|---|---|---|---|---|
| 6 | 0.5 | $ 15 | $ 7.50 | | |
| 7 | 1.6 | 19 | 30.40 | | |
| 8 | 2.8 | 24 | 67.20 | | |
| 9 | 3.8 | 40 | 152.00 | | |
| 10 | 2.768 | 170 | 470.56 | | |
| 11 | 1.886 | 185 | 345.91 | | |
| 12 | 1.481 | 200 | 296.20 | | |
| 13 | 0.400 | 210 | 84.00 | | |
| | | | 1456.77 | $81.58 | $1375.19 |

CALCULATION OF BLV

$$BLV = \frac{\$1375.19 + (\$380.10 \times 1.07^{10}) - (\$95.00 \times 1.07^{30})}{1.07^{31} - 1.000}$$

$$\times 1.07 - \frac{\$2.75}{0.07}$$

$$= \frac{\$1375.19 + (\$380.10 \times 1.967) - (\$95.00 \times 7.612)}{8.145 - 1.000}$$

$$\times 1.07 - \$39.29$$

$$= \frac{\$1375.19 + \$747.66 - \$723.14}{7.145} \times 1.07 - \$39.29 = \$170.32$$

·   ·   ·   ·

## PLANT 500/ACRE, NO THINNINGS, HARVEST AT 20

COMPUTER PRINTOUT

| DBH Class | Number Trees | Average Height | Basal Area | Cubic Feet Volume o. b. | Volume Cords to 4 in. | Volume Scribner Board Feet |
|---|---|---|---|---|---|---|
| 3 | 8.9 | 33.5 | 0.4 | 8.6 | 0.0 | 0.0 |
| 4 | 22.2 | 40.4 | 2.0 | 42.3 | 0.0 | 0.0 |
| 5 | 26.7 | 45.2 | 3.8 | 83.1 | 0.7 | 0.0 |
| 6 | 60.0 | 47.2 | 11.6 | 261.4 | 2.4 | 0.0 |
| 7 | 73.3 | 49.7 | 19.9 | 467.0 | 4.7 | 0.0 |
| 8 | 91.1 | 52.4 | 32.3 | 792.9 | 8.1 | 0.0 |

### Computer Printout (*Continued*)

| DBH Class | Number Trees | Average Height | Basal Area | Cubic Feet Volume o. b. | Volume Cords to 4 in. | Volume Scribner Board Feet |
|---|---|---|---|---|---|---|
| 9 | 57.8 | 54.2 | 25.6 | 647.8 | 6.7 | 0.0 |
| 10 | 53.3 | 56.0 | 28.7 | 748.9 | 7.8 | 2105.8 |
| 11 | 8.9 | 57.4 | 6.0 | 158.5 | 1.6 | 510.3 |
| Total | 402.2 | | 130.3 | 3210.5 | 31.9 | 2616.1 |

### Evaluation of Cut

| DBH Class | Cords or MBF Scribner | Unit Value | Total Value | Less Selling Expenses | Net |
|---|---|---|---|---|---|
| 6 | 2.4 | $ 15 | $36.00 | | |
| 7 | 4.7 | 19 | 89.30 | | |
| 8 | 8.1 | 24 | 194.40 | | |
| 9 | 6.7 | 40 | 268.00 | | |
| 10 | 2.106 | 170 | 358.02 | | |
| 11 | 0.510 | 185 | 94.35 | | |
| | | | 1040.07 | $58.24 | $981.83 |

### Calculation of BLV

$$\text{BLV} = \frac{\$981.83 - (\$105.00 \times 1.07^{20})}{1.07^{21} - 1.000} \times 1.07 - \frac{\$2.75}{0.07}$$

$$= \frac{\$981.83 - (\$105.00 \times 3.870)}{4.141 - 1.000} \times 1.07 - \$39.29$$

$$= \frac{\$981.83 - \$406.35}{3.141} \times 1.07 - \$39.29 = \$156.75$$

. . . . .

## PLANT 500/ACRE, NO THINNINGS, HARVEST AT 25

### Computer Printout

| DBH Class | Number Trees | Average Height | Basal Area | Cubic Feet Volume o. b. | Volume Cords to 4 in. | Volume Scribner Board Feet |
|---|---|---|---|---|---|---|
| 3 | 6.7 | 35.5 | 0.3 | 6.8 | 0.0 | 0.0 |
| 4 | 8.9 | 43.9 | 0.8 | 18.2 | 0.0 | 0.0 |

COMPUTER PRINTOUT (*Continued*)

| DBH Class | Number Trees | Average Height | Basal Area | Cubic Feet Volume o. b. | Volume Cords to 4 in. | Volume Scribner Board Feet |
|---|---|---|---|---|---|---|
| 5 | 20.0 | 48.1 | 2.6 | 62.0 | 0.5 | 0.0 |
| 6 | 37.8 | 53.4 | 7.6 | 193.9 | 1.8 | 0.0 |
| 7 | 57.8 | 55.1 | 15.5 | 402.4 | 4.0 | 0.0 |
| 8 | 71.1 | 57.4 | 25.0 | 671.1 | 6.8 | 0.0 |
| 9 | 75.6 | 60.2 | 32.9 | 924.3 | 9.5 | 0.0 |
| 10 | 46.7 | 61.8 | 25.7 | 737.7 | 7.7 | 2233.3 |
| 11 | 42.2 | 64.2 | 26.8 | 797.7 | 8.3 | 2634.5 |
| 12 | 8.9 | 64.8 | 6.9 | 206.4 | 2.1 | 733.7 |
| Total | 375.6 | | 144.2 | 4020.6 | 40.7 | 5601.5 |

EVALUATION OF CUT

| DBH Class | Cords or MBF Scribner | Unit Value | Total Value | Less Selling Expenses | Net |
|---|---|---|---|---|---|
| 6 | 1.8 | $ 15 | $27.00 | | |
| 7 | 4.0 | 19 | 76.00 | | |
| 8 | 6.8 | 24 | 163.20 | | |
| 9 | 9.5 | 40 | 380.00 | | |
| 10 | 2.233 | 170 | 379.61 | | |
| 11 | 2.635 | 185 | 487.48 | | |
| 12 | 0.734 | 200 | 146.80 | | |
| | | | 1660.09 | $92.97 | $1567.12 |

CALCULATION OF BLV

$$\text{BLV} = \frac{\$1567.12 - (\$105.00 \times 1.07^{25})}{1.07^{26} - 1.000} \times 1.07 - \frac{\$2.75}{0.07}$$

$$= \frac{\$1567.12 - (\$105.00 \times 5.427)}{5.807 - 1.000} \times 1.07 - \$39.29$$

$$= \frac{\$1567.12 - \$569.84}{4.807} \times 1.07 - \$39.29 = \$182.70$$

## PLANT 500/ACRE, NO THINNINGS, HARVEST AT 30

### Computer Printout

| DBH Class | Number Trees | Average Height | Basal Area | Cubic Feet Volume o. b. | Volume Cords to 4 in. | Volume Scribner Board Feet |
|---|---|---|---|---|---|---|
| 3 | 4.4 | 36.1 | 0.2 | 4.6 | 0.0 | 0.0 |
| 4 | 4.4 | 45.4 | 0.4 | 9.2 | 0.0 | 0.0 |
| 5 | 8.9 | 53.5 | 1.3 | 33.2 | 0.3 | 0.0 |
| 6 | 20.0 | 55.7 | 3.8 | 101.0 | 0.9 | 0.0 |
| 7 | 48.9 | 60.7 | 13.3 | 379.9 | 3.8 | 0.0 |
| 8 | 57.8 | 60.9 | 20.3 | 578.5 | 5.9 | 0.0 |
| 9 | 62.2 | 64.1 | 27.4 | 818.2 | 8.4 | 0.0 |
| 10 | 57.8 | 66.6 | 31.6 | 976.6 | 10.2 | 3064.2 |
| 11 | 42.2 | 69.4 | 28.1 | 902.2 | 9.4 | 3122.5 |
| 12 | 17.8 | 72.3 | 13.3 | 445.3 | 4.6 | 1618.9 |
| 13 | 8.9 | 71.8 | 7.8 | 257.4 | 2.7 | 969.8 |
| Total | 333.3 | | 147.6 | 4506.1 | 46.1 | 8775.4 |

### Evaluation of Cut

| DBH Class | Cords or MBF Scribner | Unit Value | Total Value | Less Selling Expenses | Net |
|---|---|---|---|---|---|
| 6 | 0.9 | $ 15 | $13.50 | | |
| 7 | 3.8 | 19 | 72.20 | | |
| 8 | 5.9 | 24 | 141.60 | | |
| 9 | 8.4 | 40 | 336.00 | | |
| 10 | 3.064 | 170 | 520.88 | | |
| 11 | 3.123 | 185 | 577.76 | | |
| 12 | 1.619 | 200 | 323.80 | | |
| 13 | 0.970 | 210 | 203.70 | | |
| | | | 2189.44 | $122.61 | $2066.83 |

### Calculation of BLV

$$\text{BLV} = \frac{\$2066.83 - (\$105.00 - 1.07^{30})}{1.07^{31} - 1.000} \times 1.07 - \frac{\$2.75}{0.07}$$

$$= \frac{\$2066.83 - (\$105.00 \times 7.612)}{8.145 - 1.000} \times 1.07 - \$39.29$$

$$= \frac{\$2066.83 - \$799.26}{7.145} \times 1.07 - \$39.29 = \$150.54$$

. . . .

## PLANT 500/ACRE, FOURTH-ROW THINNING AT 20, HARVEST AT 30

COMPUTER PRINTOUT OF THINNING AT 20

| DBH Class | Number Trees | Average Height | Basal Area | Cubic Feet Volume o. b. | Volume Cords to 4 in. | Volume Scribner Board Feet |
|---|---|---|---|---|---|---|
| 4 | 6.7 | 39.0 | 0.6 | 12.1 | 0.0 | 0.0 |
| 5 | 8.9 | 44.0 | 1.3 | 27.3 | 0.2 | 0.0 |
| 6 | 24.4 | 47.0 | 4.6 | 104.7 | 1.0 | 0.0 |
| 7 | 15.6 | 48.8 | 4.4 | 101.0 | 1.0 | 0.0 |
| 8 | 24.4 | 52.2 | 8.6 | 211.6 | 2.2 | 0.0 |
| 9 | 20.0 | 53.3 | 9.1 | 226.3 | 2.3 | 0.0 |
| 10 | 17.8 | 56.4 | 9.7 | 254.9 | 2.6 | 726.9 |
| 11 | 6.7 | 57.8 | 4.5 | 119.8 | 1.2 | 386.9 |
| Total | 124.4 | | 42.8 | 1057.7 | 10.4 | 1113.9 |

EVALUATION OF CUT

| DBH Class | Cords of MBF Scribner | Unit Value | Total Value | Less Selling Expenses | Net |
|---|---|---|---|---|---|
| 6 | 1.0 | $ 15 | $15.00 | | |
| 7 | 1.0 | 19 | 19.00 | | |
| 8 | 2.2 | 24 | 52.80 | | |
| 9 | 2.3 | 40 | 92.00 | | |
| 10 | 0.727 | 170 | 123.59 | | |
| 11 | 0.387 | 185 | 71.60 | | |
| | | | 373.99 | $37.40 | $336.59 |

COMPUTER PRINTOUT OF HARVEST AT 30

| DBH Class | Number Trees | Average Height | Basal Area | Cubic Feet Volume o. b. | Volume Cords to 4 in. | Volume Scribner Board Feet |
|---|---|---|---|---|---|---|
| 3 | 2.2 | 36.1 | 0.1 | 2.2 | 0.0 | 0.0 |
| 4 | 6.7 | 46.2 | 0.6 | 13.9 | 0.0 | 0.0 |
| 5 | 11.1 | 54.6 | 1.6 | 43.1 | 0.3 | 0.0 |
| 6 | 13.3 | 56.0 | 2.7 | 70.8 | 0.7 | 0.0 |
| 7 | 22.2 | 58.7 | 5.7 | 157.4 | 1.6 | 0.0 |
| 8 | 46.7 | 63.1 | 16.6 | 489.6 | 5.0 | 0.0 |
| 9 | 42.2 | 64.8 | 18.8 | 568.4 | 5.9 | 0.0 |
| 10 | 40.0 | 68.3 | 21.3 | 673.4 | 7.0 | 2108.5 |
| 11 | 40.0 | 69.2 | 26.7 | 855.1 | 8.9 | 2960.0 |
| 12 | 11.1 | 73.3 | 8.6 | 290.5 | 3.0 | 1068.3 |
| 13 | 2.2 | 69.3 | 1.9 | 61.8 | 0.6 | 230.9 |
| Total | 237.8 | | 104.6 | 3226.3 | 33.0 | 6367.6 |

EVALUATION OF CUT

| DBH Class | Cords or MBF Scribner | Unit Value | Total Value | Less Selling Expenses | Net |
|---|---|---|---|---|---|
| 6 | 0.7 | $ 15 | $10.50 | | |
| 7 | 1.6 | 19 | 30.40 | | |
| 8 | 5.0 | 24 | 120.00 | | |
| 9 | 5.9 | 40 | 236.00 | | |
| 10 | 2.109 | 170 | 358.53 | | |
| 11 | 2.960 | 185 | 547.60 | | |
| 12 | 1.068 | 200 | 213.60 | | |
| 13 | 0.231 | 210 | 48.51 | | |
| | | | 1565.14 | $87.65 | $1477.49 |

CALCULATION OF BLV

$$BLV = \frac{\$1477.49 + (\$336.59 \times 1.07^{10}) - (\$105.00 \times 1.07^{30})}{1.07^{31} - 1.000}$$

$$\times 1.07 - \frac{\$2.75}{0.07}$$

$$= \frac{\$1477.49 + (\$336.59 \times 1.967) - (\$105.00 \times 7.612)}{8.145 - 1.000}$$

$$\times 1.07 - \$39.29$$

$$= \frac{\$1477.49 + \$662.07 - \$799.26}{7.145} \times 1.07 - \$39.29 = \$161.43$$

# Table of Compound Interest Rates

| Year | 4% | 5% | 6% | 7% | 8% | 9% | 10% |
|------|------|------|------|------|------|------|------|
| 1 | 1.040 | 1.050 | 1.060 | 1.070 | 1.080 | 1.090 | 1.110 |
| 2 | 1.082 | 1.103 | 1.124 | 1.145 | 1.166 | 1.188 | 1.210 |
| 3 | 1.125 | 1.158 | 1.191 | 1.225 | 1.260 | 1.295 | 1.331 |
| 4 | 1.170 | 1.216 | 1.262 | 1.311 | 1.360 | 1.412 | 1.464 |
| 5 | 1.217 | 1.276 | 1.338 | 1.403 | 1.469 | 1.539 | 1.611 |
| 6 | 1.265 | 1.340 | 1.419 | 1.501 | 1.587 | 1.677 | 1.772 |
| 7 | 1.317 | 1.407 | 1.504 | 1.606 | 1.714 | 1.828 | 1.949 |
| 8 | 1.369 | 1.477 | 1.594 | 1.718 | 1.851 | 1.993 | 2.144 |
| 9 | 1.423 | 1.551 | 1.689 | 1.828 | 1.999 | 2.172 | 2.358 |
| 10 | 1.480 | 1.629 | 1.791 | 1.967 | 2.159 | 2.367 | 2.594 |
| 11 | 1.539 | 1.710 | 1.898 | 2.105 | 2.332 | 2.580 | 2.853 |
| 12 | 1.601 | 1.796 | 2.012 | 2.252 | 2.518 | 2.813 | 3.138 |
| 13 | 1.665 | 1.886 | 2.133 | 2.410 | 2.720 | 3.066 | 3.452 |
| 14 | 1.732 | 1.980 | 2.261 | 2.579 | 2.937 | 3.342 | 3.798 |
| 15 | 1.801 | 2.079 | 2.397 | 2.759 | 3.172 | 3.642 | 4.177 |
| 16 | 1.873 | 2.183 | 2.540 | 2.952 | 3.426 | 3.970 | 4.595 |
| 17 | 1.948 | 2.292 | 2.693 | 3.159 | 3.700 | 4.328 | 5.054 |
| 18 | 2.026 | 2.407 | 2.854 | 3.380 | 3.996 | 4.717 | 5.560 |
| 19 | 2.107 | 2.527 | 3.026 | 3.617 | 4.316 | 5.142 | 6.116 |
| 20 | 2.191 | 2.653 | 3.207 | 3.870 | 4.661 | 5.604 | 6.728 |
| 21 | 2.279 | 2.786 | 3.400 | 4.141 | 5.034 | 6.109 | 7.400 |
| 22 | 2.370 | 2.925 | 3.604 | 4.430 | 5.437 | 6.659 | 8.140 |
| 23 | 2.465 | 3.072 | 3.820 | 4.741 | 5.871 | 7.258 | 8.954 |
| 24 | 2.563 | 3.225 | 4.049 | 5.072 | 6.341 | 7.911 | 9.850 |
| 25 | 2.666 | 3.386 | 4.292 | 5.427 | 6.848 | 8.623 | 10.835 |
| 26 | 2.772 | 3.556 | 4.549 | 5.807 | 7.396 | 9.399 | 11.918 |
| 27 | 2.883 | 3.733 | 4.822 | 6.214 | 7.988 | 10.245 | 13.110 |

| Year | 4% | 5% | 6% | 7% | 8% | 9% | 10% |
|------|-------|-------|--------|--------|--------|--------|--------|
| 28 | 2.999 | 3.920 | 5.112 | 6.649 | 8.627 | 11.167 | 14.421 |
| 29 | 3.119 | 4.116 | 5.418 | 7.114 | 9.317 | 12.172 | 15.863 |
| 30 | 3.243 | 4.322 | 5.743 | 7.612 | 10.063 | 13.268 | 17.449 |
| 31 | 3.373 | 4.538 | 6.088 | 8.145 | 10.868 | 14.462 | 19.194 |
| 32 | 3.508 | 4.765 | 6.453 | 8.715 | 11.737 | 15.763 | 21.114 |
| 33 | 3.648 | 5.003 | 6.841 | 9.325 | 12.676 | 17.182 | 23.225 |
| 34 | 3.794 | 5.253 | 7.251 | 9.978 | 13.690 | 18.728 | 25.548 |
| 35 | 3.946 | 5.516 | 7.686 | 10.677 | 14.785 | 20.414 | 28.102 |
| 36 | 4.104 | 5.792 | 8.147 | 11.424 | 15.968 | 22.251 | 30.913 |
| 37 | 4.268 | 6.081 | 8.636 | 12.224 | 17.246 | 24.254 | 34.004 |
| 38 | 4.439 | 6.385 | 9.154 | 13.079 | 18.625 | 26.437 | 37.404 |
| 39 | 4.616 | 6.705 | 9.704 | 13.995 | 20.115 | 28.816 | 41.145 |
| 40 | 4.801 | 7.040 | 10.286 | 14.974 | 21.725 | 31.409 | 45.259 |

APPENDIX **III**

# Interview with Leon Hood and Ben Stevens*

Success in selling timber depends strongly on knowing how the timber market works, and nothing exemplifies this market better than the independent timber buyer. These buyers, usually individuals or small companies, buy from and sell to everybody everyday, and they back their judgments with their own money, sometimes large amounts of it. (Many expert buyers work for big companies, but they use company money, which makes a difference.) We recently interviewed two of the best, Leon Hood of Adel, Georgia, and Ben Stevens of Hattiesburg, Mississippi, in their home territories on different days, and we have presented below each one's answers to the same questions.

JMV: Tell us about your operations.

HOOD: We operate in a nine-county area in south Georgia centered on Adel. Although we have bought timber from time to time for years, we didn't get into it full-time until 1983. We use one logging contractor (my uncle), who loads about 15 trucks a day. In 1986 our total purchases were $1,600,000, and we carry about $400,000 of purchased timber in inventory at all times.

STEVENS: We operate in about 25 counties in the southeastern quadrant of Mississippi and have about 20 pulpwood yards. Starting with my father, we have been buying pulpwood in this territory for more

* From *Tree Topics*, April 15, 1987, copyright James M. Vardaman & Co., Inc., Jackson, Mississippi.

than 60 years. In a normal year, we buy 200,000 cords of pulpwood, a large volume of sawtimber, and some poles.

JMV:  How do you learn about timber tracts for sale?

HOOD:  We get 85% of them from consultants and 15% from personal contacts with and referrals from landowners. We are in a very competitive market. We regularly receive about five sale announcements a week from one or more of 22 consultants (there are six in Moultrie alone). In addition to the big companies, there are four other buyers just like us and usually five to seven bids on each sale.

STEVENS:  Since we have been in the market for more than six decades, we have developed many contacts with landowners (some of whom have sold us timber several times), loggers, and pulpwood producers, and they produce many leads. But our territory is quite varied. Competition is fierce south of U.S. Highway 84, moderate between 84 and Interstate 20, and because the demand for pulpwood there is small, modest north of I-20. The 17 pulp mills drawing wood from our area are all south of I-20. Eight to ten consultants produce 50% to 60% of the tracts south of 84, 25% or less between 84 and I-20, and very few north of I-20. The other tracts come from our contacts.

JMV:  How much information is usually furnished by the sellers?

HOOD:  Some consultants furnish a 100% tally of sawtimber; others provide a 20% line-plot cruise. I'd rather have the 100% tally; if you go out there and tape every tree, you know you've got the volume right. All of them usually furnish a good map and a right of way (ROW). Landowners rarely furnish anything except the land lot numbers and a general description of how they want you to cut the tract.

Sometimes consultants, especially those using 20% cruises, overestimate a tract, but we and other buyers, because we can't afford to cut out short, will bid on what our check-cruises show the volume to be. Then it looks like no one is willing to pay a fair price, whereas the real problem is the consultant's overestimate. Poor estimates don't fool anybody.

STEVENS:  The consultants furnish detailed data, and most provide 100% tallies of sawtimber. We check-cruise these and bid on our own figures. Most landowners don't give us anything but the legal description.

JMV:  How do you outbid larger companies and then later sell part of the timber to them?

HOOD: We concentrate on mixed tracts. When the tracts contain straight pine sawtimber, it's hard for us to compete. But if there are also some poles and hardwood and maybe 50% pulpwood, we can sort them out, deliver each product to a mill specializing in it, and earn a small premium by doing so. That's how we compete.

STEVENS: The objective of most big companies is to get timber to operate their mills, and I learned a long time ago that, when a tract contains exactly what they want, we can't outbid them. Since we don't operate a mill, our objective is to get the most out of a tract. We are better sorters of trees for different markets; when there is a mixture of sizes and species, we are very competitive. When a tract is very large, we aren't strong bidders because we don't want to tie up a huge sum in one place; it's better for us to buy several tracts scattered over our operating area. On the other hand, there are times when the big mills have bought all the timber they want to carry in inventory, so they back off, and we become the major market.

JMV: What steps do you follow in making a bid, and how much does it cost?

HOOD: If a tract looks promising, we use an independent forester to check-cruise it, and his charges usually run $2.00 an acre. Then we go behind him to look at wood quality and ground conditions so as to estimate sale prices and logging costs. Some plantations here have a lot of *Cronartium* cankers, and since this part of the tree is suitable only for pulp chips, all the mills we sell to will cull it. When they are paying the price for wood to make lumber, plywood, or poles, they won't stand for too many chips. Someone has to be sure about the boundary lines too, so by the time we are ready to bid, our average cost in time and money is over $500.

STEVENS: We check-cruise every tract, and one of our experienced people investigates quality of the timber and logging conditions, so preparing each bid costs us between $500 and $1,000. We look at 800 to 1,000 tracts a year and manage to buy 20% to 30% of them.

JMV: What do you do if there is no access to a public road?

HOOD: Access to a public road is essential, and we require landowners to furnish it. If there is no access, we don't bid.

STEVENS: We require landowners to furnish access. Our position is that, if a landowner can't get a ROW from his neighbors, we can't either. There are enough problems involved in handling a tract of timber without getting into a fuss about a ROW.

JMV: How carefully do you check the seller's title?

HOOD: We use a lawyer to do a complete check on all titles, for we buy lump-sum 95% of the time and can't afford to take any chances on this. In addition, the mills we sell to don't buy from just anybody; they want to know where every load is coming from and that we have good title to the wood.

STEVENS: We check every title. Several recent court decisions have held that it's the buyer's responsibility to know where each load of wood comes from. If it later turns out to have been stolen, we are out the money paid to the person who hauled it to us, and we may also have to pay the same amount to the rightful owner, not just the stumpage but the delivered price.

JMV: How do you log the timber?

HOOD: All our logging is tree-length; we cut no short wood. We use nothing but independent contractors, some for logging and others for hauling. About 80% of our purchases are clearcuts. My uncle operates the loader and sorts the material into the most valuable products. To get any volume production, we have to log tree-length; when you start blocking up the trees, it takes much longer to get anything done and costs a lot more too. The shears we use for felling, the skidders, and the loaders are big enough to handle any tree in the woods.

STEVENS: We use nothing but independent contractors, but the methods they employ vary with conditions in our area. South of 84 we have to use tree-length logging. The extra handling and other costs of running timber through a pulpwood yard can reduce the amount available for stumpage by 60% and render us noncompetitive. Also the mills can't handle the traffic problem caused by the great number of shortwood trucks needed to bring in the necessary volume. So south of 84 60% of all logging is tree-length, and the proportion is growing.

Along I-20 rail transportation is a big factor because the mills are far away. Tree-length logging is not feasible because you must cut wood into short lengths that can be loaded on a railroad car. The Stone Container mill at Hodge, Louisiana, is more than 200 miles from our yards in central Mississippi, a feasible haul on one railroad but much too far for a truck. This situation is one cause of the difference in stumpage prices up there.

JMV: Do you have many chances to buy timber from tracts in the landowner-assistance programs run by many companies?

HOOD: No. As near as we can tell, the companies running the programs sell the timber to themselves.

STEVENS: No. Most of what we get are pulpwood thinnings, and all of it is north of 84.

JMV: Once a logging contractor leaves the woods with a load, do you worry that he will take it to an unauthorized mill and sell it for his own account?

HOOD: I've had only one logger try to steal from me, and I caught him in the act and got my money back. Now I use one contractor for logging and another for hauling, so they check against each other. Most other companies do the same. Finally, since every buyer is responsible for getting clear title to all his purchases, "hot" wood is very hard to sell.

STEVENS: No, because we have so many men in the field checking on our operations and because we deal with contractors whom we have known for years. Another reason is the responsibility I described that buyers must know where the wood comes from; everyone is scared to buy wood that may be stolen.

JMV: How important is tree size to you?

HOOD: Very. The tree shear has to get in position to grasp each tree, clip it, and then pile it for the skidder. The grapple on the skidder can grab and hold enough trees to contain two cords, so in five or six trips the skidder can drag the normal truckload of ten cords. We usually haul wood 80 to 90 miles and, in an unusual situation last week, hauled pulpwood 158 miles; therefore, each truck must carry a full load of ten cords.

With chipping saw wood and ordinary sawtimber, we can load a truck with 35 to 40 trees. It would take 100 8-inch pulpwood trees to make a load. It would take 222 6-inch pulpwood trees, more than there is room for, and many of them wouldn't be long enough to a 3-inch top to reach between the bunkers of the 40-foot trailer; the shear and the skidder would have to work hard all day to get two or three loads. Consequently, 6-inch trees are worthless to us.

STEVENS: Very, where we log tree-length, and not very, where we log short wood. The difference is in the amount available for stumpage, so landowners get a big price for big trees and a little price for little trees even when the trees are processed into the same product.

# APPENDIX IV

# Glossary

Timberland investment has its own terminology, and we need to define some terms to make sure we know what we are discussing. Sometimes a bare definition is not sufficient. I suggest that you read these definitions and then refer to them from time to time as necessary.

BILTMORE STICK—a graduated stick about 3 ft long used mostly to make rough measurements of tree diameters quickly. The user holds it against the tree and a specific distance from his eye, lines up one end with one side of the tree, and reads diameter from the graduation where other side intersects the stick. Improper use can cause large errors in volume estimates.

CUTTING CYCLE—the frequency of logging operations on the same area, expressed in years. Let us assume that you own a tract that contains trees of all sizes and ages. If you have decided to cut this tract every 10 years to thin the small trees and harvest the large ones, you have chosen a 10-year cutting cycle.

DBH AND DBH CLASSES—the abbreviation DBH means diameter breast high (4.5 ft above ground level) outside the bark and is expressed in inches. Careless speakers often use the term to mean DBH class, but it is necessary to know the difference. Trees are divided into 1-in. and 2-in. DBH classes for convenience. With a 1-in. class, a 10-in. DBH tree is more than 9.5 in. DBH and less than 10.5 DBH. With a 2-in. class, a 10-in. DBH tree is more than 9.0 in. DBH and less than 11.0 in. DBH. Keep this in mind; you will avoid many arguments.

DELIVERED PRICE—the sum paid for the tree at mill or railroad.

EASEMENT—the right or privilege of making limited use of another's property.

EMINENT DOMAIN—the power to take private property for public use. National or state legislatures may pass this power to agencies that serve the public, such as pipeline companies, highway departments, and power companies.

HARDWOOD—a loose term generally including all species of trees that lose their leaves in winter. Some hardwoods such as magnolia retain leaves throughout the year; other species such as larch and bald cypress lose their leaves but are not hardwoods. Hardwoods do not bear cones, softwoods do. Any forester can explain what the term includes in your area.

INCREMENT BORER—a small tool used by foresters to determine growth of a tree. It is a hollow tube with a handle on one end and a spiral cutting bit on the other. When pressed against the bark and turned by hand, it moves into the tree toward the heart and cuts a section slightly smaller than a pencil. This section, called an increment core, can be removed from the hollow tube with an extractor, which is also part of the tool. With most species, the increment core shows each annual ring clearly and allows you to determine how fast the tree is growing. Damage to the tree is insignificant compared with the value of the information obtained.

LOGGING COST—the sum necessary to move the tree from the woods to a mill or railroad.

MBF—a convenient way to write "thousand board feet."

MERCHANTABLE TIMBER—any timber that can be sold. Merchantable trees usually have a minimum DBH of 5 in., but certain products such as fence posts may come from smaller trees.

POLES AND PILING—particularly straight trees that meet exacting requirements so far as diameter and taper are concerned can be manufactured into poles and piling. In general, piling comes from sawtimber trees and poles from both sawtimber and pulpwood trees. Trees processed into poles and piling often bring 50% more stumpage than when used for other purposes. The danger in special cuts for poles and piling is that you may not find a buyer for the remaining timber.

POSSESSION, ADVERSE AND OTHERWISE—see discussion beginning on page 75.

PULPWOOD TREES—trees over 5 in. DBH that are unsuitable for sawtimber because of size, crook, or other defect. Trees cannot be classified as pulpwood on the basis of size alone.

PULPWOOD VOLUME MEASURES—see discussion starting on p. 92.

REPRODUCTION—well-established seedlings from about knee height up to pulpwood size. Occasionally they are separated into DBH or age classes.

ROTATION—the period of years required to reproduce, grow, and harvest stands of timber in order best to accomplish definite objectives of management. The final crop of a pulpwood rotation is pulpwood; the final crop of a sawtimber rotation is sawtimber; and the second type of rotation is about twice as long as the first in time. There are other technical forestry aspects to defining this term, but they are not necessary for your purposes.

SAWTIMBER TREES—usually trees 11 in. DBH and up, but definition of the term varies with species and geography. They must be reasonably straight and free of defects caused by fungi, insects, fire, or the way in which the tree developed. Sawtimber trees may be manufactured into lumber, veneer logs, poles, or piling; the term is only a general one that primarily designates a major division by size. Definition of the term may also vary with changes in economics. You can saw a two-by-four from a small tree, but logging of small trees is expensive and is usually practical only during strong lumber markets. As prices decline, lumber companies often raise the minimum diameter of the trees they will buy.

SAWTIMBER VOLUME MEASURES—see discussion starting on p. 93.

SEED-TREE CUT—removal of all merchantable timber except those trees necessary to produce seed for the next crop.

SLASH—tops and limbs left in the woods after cutting operations.

SOFTWOOD—all species that are not hardwoods.

STAGNATION—as the term is commonly used in forest management, *stagnation* occurs when too many trees are growing on the same area. In the fierce fight for water, light, and food, these trees are barely able to stay alive. Since the productive capacity of the soil must be divided among so many individuals, growth appears to stop, but it is only hard to see because it is so widely distributed. You can understand what this does to your annual imcome. The good manager tries to prevent stagnation by proper planning, or to relieve it by thinning as soon as possible.

STATUTE OF LIMITATIONS—see discussion on page 136.

STUMP DIAMETER—usually, the average diameter outside the bark measured 12 in. above ground level on the high side of the tree. A rule of thumb says that the diameter inside the bark at this point equals DBH; remember that this is only a rule of thumb. Stump diameter is often used in timber sales, and you do not encounter diameter classes in this case. A conveyance should specify the height above the ground, whether inside or outside the bark, and how to determine average diameter.

STUMPAGE PRICE—the sum paid the owner for the tree as it stands on its stump.

SUPPRESSED TREES—those that have nearly lost the battle for survival. Overtopped by their neighbors and reduced to a pole with only a skimpy crown, they may die within a short time and have usually lost the ability to resume normal growth if released.

THINNING—partial cutting where the material removed is sold and produces some return. It is done to prevent or relieve stagnation and to concentrate growth on better trees in the stand. *Precommercial* thinning is done before the trees that are cut are large enough to be sold, and it may be included under TSI work. Although it is nearly always a deductible expense, the cost is apt to be prohibitive even when you use machines designed for the purpose. An ounce of prevention is worth several pounds of cure.

TIMBER CRUISE—means the same as *timber inventory*. The term probably arose because the man performing the work navigates a path through the property much as a ship's captain follows his path on a cruise.

TRESPASS—as a management problem in timberland management, trespass generally means theft or unauthorized cutting of timber.

TSI—stands for timber stand improvement and means almost anything done to improve the condition of a timber stand without producing revenue at the same time. Pruning and removal of worthless trees that impede the growth of desirable trees are examples.

# Index

Accounting, 3, 5, 104, 119–131, 198–199, 204, 230–232. *See also* Certified public accountant (CPA)

Adverse possession, *see* Possession, adverse

Aerial Photographs, *see* Photographs, aerial

Agricultural Stabilization and Conservation Service (ASCS), 9, 10, 19, 21, 96, 98

Appraisal, timberland values, 16, 53, 105–109

Area Redevelopment Administration, 54

Association of Consulting Foresters, 14

Attorney, *see* Lawyer

Auction sale, 32, 40, 148

Bare land value (BLV), 117, 237–244, 250, 254, 258, 259–260, 262, 263, 264–281

Big timber companies, 2, 19, 37, 73, 101, 103, 104, 110, 144, 154, 160–169, 286, 288

Bonus, mineral lease, 60–62, 222

Boorstin, Daniel, 28

Boundary lines, 16, 18, 19, 21, 22, 60, 73–77, 80, 81, 82, 103, 122, 123, 129, 135, 139, 140, 144, 188, 189, 199, 204, 208—209, 211, 215–216, 221, 228, 230, 236, 237

Brown, R. Baxter, 4

Bureau of Land Management, 137

Burkhart, Harold E., 72, 94, 115, 116, 162, 235, 250, 258, 260

Case history, successful timberland investor, 183–232

Casualty loss, 86–88, 89, 125

Certified public accountant (CPA), 14, 130, 189, 204, 213, 215, 216, 220, 226

Chain of title, *see* Title

Christman trees, 57

Clutter, Jerry, 98

Comptroller of Currency, 155

Consulting forester, *see* Forester, consulting

Continuous forest inventory (CFI), 103

Contract:
    purchase and sale of land, 132–134, 146, 229
    real estate agency, 147–148
    timber-sale, 40, 42–43, 138, 210–211, 214–215

Contractor:
    forestry services, 19, 21, 22, 86, 139–140, 217, 227
    logging, 42, 44, 287, 288

Cooperatives, landowner, 22

Costs, 17–18, 22, 69–90, 107, 112, 113–114, 122–124, 133–134, 141, 148–149, 154, 157, 168, 184, 199, 209, 216, 226, 230, 236, 237–238, 239–244, 245, 252, 256–257, 259, 264–281, 286

Cubbage, Frederick W., 164

Damage:
    appraisal, 16, 18, 45
    caused by fire, 16, 45, 136, 140
    caused by mineral operations, 16, 45, 55–56, 62–63, 65, 66, 223
    caused by timber operations, 57, 72–73, 263
    connected with rights of way, 16, 45, 48–51
    tax treatment, 45, 121

Danger trees, 50, 188, 200, 202, 204

Deeds:
    quitclaim, 136–137
    timber, 40, 42–43, 138, 210–211, 214–215

**293**